Educational Requirements for the 1970's

Educational Requirements for the 1970's

An Interdisciplinary Approach

EDITED BY
STANLEY ELAM
AND
WILLIAM P. McLURE

Published for Phi Delta Kappa

FREDERICK A. PRAEGER, *Publishers*
New York • Washington • London

FREDERICK A. PRAEGER, PUBLISHERS
111 Fourth Avenue, New York, N.Y. 10003, U.S.A.
77-79 Charlotte Street, London W.1, England

Published in the United States of America in 1967
by Frederick A. Praeger, Inc., *Publishers*

Introduction © 1967 by Frederick A. Praeger, Inc.

Library of Congress Catalog Card Number: 67-20476

Printed in the United States of America

Foreword

In the early 1950's the American educational system came under sharp public scrutiny as a consequence of dramatic Soviet scientific achievements. Real improvement in teaching, particularly in languages, mathematics, and sciences, was one result of this examination. Another consequence was the realization that the educational system *could* be changed and improved. Only when a system can be caused to change does a dialogue about the future of that system generate widespread interest.

There are many forces impinging on education that will affect its direction and development in the years to come. The schools are under much pressure to accept a significant role as instruments of social change. There are new media and technology, which result in increased learning efficiency. There are a growing number of agencies and groups who feel that education cannot remain the exclusive domain of the professional educator. There is a call for excellence for all involved in the learning process. Without attempting to evaluate the goodness of these and other forces, it can be said they are real and will have impact.

The dialogue included in this book is essential in that it places these forces in perspective. They are examined in terms of the role the schools will need to play in our developing socio-economic system. It seems clear that, in the future, more and different demands will be made upon the educational system. It will not be enough that it is a possibility for each person to develop to his capability; this must become a high probability as well.

R. Louis Bright
Associate Commissioner for Research
U.S. Office of Education

Contents

Educational Requirements for the 1970's

Editors' Introduction

Education today is entering one of its most critical periods in the life of this nation.

Such statements sound hollow to those who would point out that education as an institution has reached a pinnacle in public esteem.

It is true that we have come to expect education to provide all things for all people: the preservation of enduring social values, the maintenance of a stable society, the creation of a better way of life. It is the means to increase man's productivity, the basis for scientific and technological advance, and the hope for humanistic rationality. For some, it has become the elixir to fulfill all human needs—physical, social, economic, and political. For others, it has taken on the character of a mere tool. For still others, it has a magic or mystical quality.

Herein lies the danger. Education has become too fully accepted too quickly and too lightly. Expectation in some quarters has outrun knowledge and understanding.

Many changes in education itself—in government, in commerce, and in other facets of society—are based more on propositions than on understanding. There is need today to raise some caution signs against the intrusion of a certain kind of irrationality in the name of education. There should be a redoubling of effort to develop and use the processes of research and logical analysis as a means to speed up the advancement of knowledge and understanding, thereby reducing the chances of serious error.

Phi Delta Kappa stands for research, service, and leadership. These goals can easily be translated as research, development, and dissemination, which are the sequential phases in the extension of knowledge and understanding.

The need to organize a Commission of Education, Manpower, and Economic Growth to round out Phi Delta Kappa's program emphasis became obvious only a few years ago. After the commission was created, in 1963, the broad challenge to it was clear: to promote the rational processes of research, development, and dissemination in education, and to analyze the contributions of education to society.

Soon the idea of examining educational requirements of the next decade in the light of economic, political, technological, and social developments took shape. The stage for this examination became the symposium. The players in the first act were scholars in anthropology, economics, education, government, and sociology. Colleagues in these fields were the audience.

The dialogue presented in these pages was planned as an initial step to generate ideas for research and practice through the interaction of scholars from different fields. The authors of the major papers and the other participants have exemplified two fundamental requirements for such an interchange. One is to present and interpret knowledge gained from different sets of intellectual processes of inquiry as represented in various disciplines. The other is to point out the limits of knowledge.

Solon Kimball presents an anthropological approach to some of the philosophical, pedagogical, and structural areas of change in education. His propositions are provocative, but constructive, and are supported by evidence that is related to anthropological patterns.

Fred Strodtbeck concentrates on subcultural groups in dealing with certain aspects of learning and adaptation. His investigations reveal the influence or conditioning of environment (education) on the individual. This is a contrast, perhaps supplementary and not contradictory, to Kimball's explanation of some phenomena that have inherited (anthropological) effects.

Arthur M. Ross presents a pragmatic approach to problems of unemployment through full utilization of education and other agencies of society.

Leonard Lecht introduces procedures for estimating manpower demands in the economy. The other side of this problem, namely, estimating school needs to educate individuals with the requisite capabilities, is implicit in his paper.

Hector Correa defends the assumption on which he has constructed a theoretical analysis of the contribution of education to economic development. In the discussion which follows his paper, he is challenged to admit the existence of alternative assumptions.

Gerhard Colm hails the trend in planning as an essential, rational process in establishing priorities among functions of government. This process may be called "goals research." It is not a substitute for judgment, but a supplement. While Colm's emphasis is on the economics of national goals, he is also concerned with manpower. And manpower consists of human beings, for whom economic considerations are only one important value. This age of change is accompanied by an increased goals-consciousness of the American. Colm thinks long-range planning will become more sophisticated and more widely accepted than at present. Implications for educational planning are only mentioned. These will have to wait for treatment in depth elsewhere.

John K. Folger has summarized the discussions to point up some of the implications and hypotheses for research that come out of these papers and interactions. He has captured some of the thought that may provide an essential link for those who wish to draw upon this material.

If these discussions provoke members of the academic community and leaders in other fields to consider new strategies of inquiry into many complex and unanswered questions in education, efforts of the symposium group will be more than repaid. Members of the Phi Delta Kappa Commission on Education, Manpower, and Economic Growth have already been richly rewarded.

WILLIAM P. McLURE, *Chairman*
Phi Delta Kappa Commission on
Education, Manpower, and
Economic Growth

STANLEY ELAM, *Editor*
Phi Delta Kappa Publications

1

Culture, Class, and Educational Congruency

SOLON T. KIMBALL

Despite the great variety of their cultural forms, the communities of mankind have, throughout time, possessed in common the need to transmit their cultural heritage to each oncoming generation. It is thus that societies ensure their continuity and establish the conditions necessary for further cultural growth.

Although the methods, procedures, and organizations that are used to educate the young may vary greatly from one society or epoch to another, there is one aspect common to all: The young must pass through an extended stage of dependency during which physical maturity is reached and the skills and knowledge necessary for adulthood are acquired. It is during this period of dependency that basic learning occurs, but it should be noted that there is no causal link between dependency and learning. The period and nature of dependency vary according to the culture, as does the substance of the learning.

There are, of course, significant differences among various cultures in the methods used to instruct the young. Among some nonliterate peoples, the process is, at times, so informal that untrained observers have reported that education of the young is lacking. Such comments reflect on the competency of the observers and not upon the effectiveness with which each new generation learns from, and is instructed by, its elders. The Western tradition, which links significant learning with formal classroom instruction, constitutes a much too narrow formulation

6

of what education encompasses. Only recently have we begun to recognize that success or failure in school learning is related to the pattern of learning acquired by the child in the cultural setting of his home.

The differences in methods of teaching and learning become particularly significant when examined in the context of the culture in which they appear. We are immediately struck by the correspondence between educational activities and those found in the familial, economic, political, and religious aspects of the society being studied. In traditional societies, the educational process reflects, and is in harmony with, the values, practices, and human groupings in other parts of the society. Such congruencies should not be surprising, but, since professional educators do not seem to have understood the importance of this observation, it is necessary to emphasize the point.

Examples of such lack of understanding abound. The history of the introduction of schools into colonial possessions by the British, French, and Dutch is one in which the practices that obtained in the mother countries were transferred almost unaltered, with no consideration given to native practices or needs.* In the schooling provided the American Indians, the Puerto Ricans, or the people of the Philippines, the policy of the U.S. Government was no different. The same insensitivity may be currently observed in some of the practices recommended by education specialists who advise on educational development in other countries.

The principle of educational congruency applies with equal cogency to modern nations. Among these, change is accepted as normal, although its pace varies from one sector to another. Unless educational modernization is seen as deserving continuous attention, there is a great danger that innate conservative tendencies will prevail. Obviously, such a disjunctive condition would necessitate corrective measures.

The very fact of rapid change in the modern nation underscores our need to scrutinize the extent to which education is congruent with other aspects of the society. In the relatively

---

* See, for example, John Wilson, *Education and Changing West African Culture* (New York: Columbia University Teachers College Press, 1963).

stable traditional cultures, the very processes associated with the transmission of culture perpetuated the cultural heritage from one generation to the next under conditions of minimal change. The tempo of our times is vastly different. We accept change as a fact of life, and there are some who see current changes as revolutionary.*

Under conditions of rapid change, we can no longer assume that the knowledge or practices that served us adequately in the past are sufficient for either the present or the future. Hence, we must rethink what we mean when we speak of education as the transmission of the cultural heritage. The sense in which we use this concept when we specify the Navaho Indians, the tribes of New Guinea, or even an early agrarian period in American history is not applicable to the present. In such examples, the past and present are expected to be replicated in the future. Today, we cannot operate under such an assumption. Instead, we must consciously construct an educational system to serve a society that is in a state of continuous emergence.

If we had the opportunity to construct such an educational system, how should we go about it? As the first order of business, we must decide what segments of our cultural heritage will be included in the curriculum. This is necessary, not only because the cornucopia of knowledge from our intellectual and technical worlds is already overflowing and new knowledge is added daily, but also because differential utilities necessitate the setting of priorities. In recent decades, we have made such selective discriminations largely as a response to new demands rather than through rational assessment. Now we must build selective process into educational procedure.

Two additional problems confront us. We need a new philosophy of curriculum practice and, concurrently, a reorganization of elementary and secondary school administration that will provide a favorable environment for the learning process. The first of these two problems has already been examined in *Education and the New America*.† In that study, James McClellan and

---

* Robert Theobald, *Free Men and Free Markets* (New York: Clarkson N. Potter, 1963).

† Solon T. Kimball and James E. McClellan, *Education and the New America* (New York: Random House, 1963).

I argued that full participation in the modern world requires the acquisition of intellectual skills in the areas of mathematics and logic, esthetics, experimentation, and the methodology of natural history. I shall not attempt to summarize our line of reasoning. I will repeat our belief that a modern educational system must emphasize the acquisition of cognitive skills of a different order than those traditionally stressed. We believe that our proposals represent a step in the direction of a new philosophy of pedagogy.

The need for reordering the administrative structure may be less obvious. Let us ask, however, if an urban school system that derives its structure and procedures from the pattern of a municipal bureau or from a factory system dating from the early part of the century, or from both, can provide the organizational framework within which the needed curricular changes can be realized. It seems probable that any comparative study of organizational systems would easily establish that the structure and practices of urban school administrations are more archaic than those of any other major institution. This inflexibility has been demonstrated by their reluctance or failure to meet new conditions or to incorporate new programs. Until the learning function actually becomes the paramount goal, and until custodial, house-keeping, and managerial functions are relegated to their proper service roles, we can expect little change in the present situation. I shall give further consideration to the current relevance of educational philosophy and practice, curriculum, and administration later in this paper. These questions will then be examined within the context of the congruency between the present corporate and scientifically oriented society and human aspirations on the one hand, and the educational process on the other. It is to the study of these dimensions that I now turn.

THE ROOTS OF AMERICAN CULTURE

It is fashionable these days to derive the origins of American culture from the Judaeo-Christian and Graeco-Roman traditions of the Mediterranean. Only in the most general sense should this postulate be accepted. While it is true that the Mediterranean influence spread with the extension of the Roman Empire into Celtic and Germanic Europe, it must be remembered that this cultural intrusion was eventually assimilated and transformed.

Our civilization shows evidences of Judaeo-Christian and Graeco-Roman influences from the Mediterranean, but our cultural roots are based in the Anglo-Saxon and Celtic traditions of northern Europe.

The more obvious aspect of this mixed inheritance is found in our political system with its delicate balance of powers, its elected legislature, its provision for judicial review and interpretation, and its political and human ideals as expressed in the Declaration of Independence and the Bill of Rights. Human liberties are defended, new perspectives asserted, and economic and social tensions adjudicated through the ritual of law and the courts.

But a broad range of American values and organizational methods have their origin in the religious tradition. The Protestant denominations encompassed the equalitarianism of the Baptists and New England Congregationalists as well as the hierarchy of the Methodists and Episcopalians and the strict, but human, posture of the Presbyterian elders. Through all of them ran the theme of the need for man to shape the world in the service of his and God's purposes. The individual was the instrument through which this transformation was to be achieved as each utilized his capabilities in work and sought the advance of the whole through the struggle for self-improvement.

These generalities of organization and thought are relatively easy to identify and give us a sense of similarity in cultural origin that closer scrutiny does not support. Our historians have called attention to the differences that distinguished Puritan, Quaker, or Cavalier, but only recently have we begun to assess these various groups as bearers of distinct cultural traditions. From this perspective, we now look for distinguishing features in settlement patterns, groupings, behavior, and values. This approach permits us to identify each group against a background of community and culture, to search for European origins, and to understand their transformations in the new environment.* These traditions became associated with geographical regions and provided the basis for sectional conflict. Only with the ascendance of urban

* See Conrad M. Arensberg, "American Communities," *American Anthropologist,* LVII (1955); and Jackson Turner Main, *The Social Structure of Revolutionary America* (Princeton, N.J.: Princeton University Press, 1965).

industrialism, in the early part of the twentieth century, did we acquire a type of community that subordinated regional tensions to a more inclusive cultural and organizational framework. My purpose, now, in briefly examining each of the cultural traditions is not only to further substantiate congruency but also to show the diversity in our origins. From England into the Northeast came peoples carrying the tradition of the argicultural village. They built their habitations around a central commons, or green, at one end of which they usually erected the meeting house that served the religious and civic functions of the commonalty. Only the addition of a miller, blacksmith, and other artisans broke the occupational uniformity of agrarian life. These village New Englanders were deeply committed to communal equalitarianism, preparation for which required a minimum level of literacy for all. As need arose, the older settlements hived off colonies. These claimed unoccupied territory and perpetuated the pattern of life of the mothering group. The New England pattern of agrarian subsistence has long since been abandoned, but other of its qualities have been woven into the fabric of national life.

The plantation tradition of the tidewater, black belt, and delta areas of the South offers a vivid contrast in almost every particular. Production for a world market required large acreages and a plentiful supply of organized field labor. The need both for capital and for managerial skills contributed to development of a clearly defined upper class. The lower classes included those in servitude and the dispossessed or marginal whites. Extensive kinship linkages, the code of the gentleman, and governance by an elite gave the upper class a cohesive life style based on family, manners, and politics. The vital thrust of this tradition as a force in national affairs was shattered by the Civil War.

Three other traditions deserve brief mention. The hills and mountains of what we now call Appalachia attracted another breed of people. They were primarily of the Celtic tradition, which brought with it a sense of territory (but no love for the soil) and a subsistence pattern of agriculture based upon patch farming and unfenced pastures for grazing. Their strongest loyalty was to an extended kin group, and their code demanded direct physical retribution for personal offense. They were deeply equalitarian, even to the extent of rejecting education as fostering inequalities among men. Since the middle of the nineteenth century, Appalachia has been outside the main stream of American development. Only recently has its plight become a matter of national concern.

The fourth and last of the principal agrarian traditions was that which I designate as "town and country." Here we encounter the farm homestead situated on its own tract of cultivated land. Each farm was occupied by a family whose ties to nearby and comparable families were contained within a web of reciprocal obligations. They called these activities "neighboring." Their early agricultural practices produced small surpluses, which they marketed in nearby towns. From the towns they received those goods and services that their homogeneous localities did not provide.

Townsmen and countrymen, although different from one another, created an economic and social symbiosis. It was this cultural tradition that was concentrated in the southern Piedmont, in the Middle Colonies, and in upper New York State. From these areas came the settlers who poured into the great Mississippi heartland and, once there, built a society of Main Street towns and rural neighborhoods that gave the predominant cultural tone to American civilization until superseded by the forces of industrialism. Later, with the appearance of the new agricultural and transportation technology, this tradition rapidly evolved into the pattern of commercial production and soon lost the older social cohesiveness of the locality.

The urban and commercial tradition that flowed from London and other European cities represents the fifth major cultural stream. Research by Bridenbaugh* has given us a clear picture of the organization and ways of life in the chief port cities—Boston, Newport, New York, Philadelphia, and Charles Town—at the time of the Revolution. All were significant as points of transshipment of goods to and from the hinterland. Three of them were also important centers of political power. Their cultural heterogeneity was expressed in institutional arrangements for

---

* Carl Bridenbaugh, *Cities in the Wilderness: Urban Life in America, 1625–1742* (New York: G. P. Putnam, 1964).

commerce, government, and religion and in distinct social classes based on wealth and prestige. They were religious and educational centers where literature, the arts, and theater were cultivated. Merchants, bankers, and professional men could follow an upper middle-class way of life, which allowed for refinement of taste and freed their wives from onerous domestic or home industry tasks. The environment favored intellectual stimulation, and some scientific societies were established even at this early time. The cultural richness was much greater than anything that provincial towns or the agrarian countryside could provide.

EDUCATION AND COMMUNITY

It is when we examine the formal educational arrangements for each type of community that we can observe the broad congruency between education and the social and cultural aspects of a society. The communal equalitarianism of New England required a level of civic and religious participation possible only with a literate citizenry. Hence, both family and community were held responsible for educating the young. The contrast with the two-class system of the plantation South further illuminates the principle of congruency. There, formal education was primarily a privilege of the elite and was provided by tutors or private schools. Other groups were not excluded from access to formal learning, except under later restrictive laws that governed the treatment of slaves. But, where facilities existed they were oftentimes the result of philanthropic (upper-class) benevolence. Moreover, there was neither a public nor a private responsibility that required literacy of field hands. In the context of such limits to early schooling, it is clear that it was no cultural anachronism that Virginia and North Carolina established the first free, public universities. Through educating their own children for the professions, especially law, a governing elite could assure the perpetuation of a political and social system; the risk of the lower class availing itself of the public universities was minimal.

The other cultural traditions of early America also exemplify the principle of congruency. The equalitarianism of the Appalachian uplands was rooted both in a system of family obligations, which prescribed the behavior of an extended kindred, and in a

religion based on the belief in other-worldliness, which emphasized the spirit rather than the intellect. Such a cultural posture
denied the relevance of formal education; in fact, the development of the intellect was correctly seen as creating inequalities
among men and contributing nothing to spiritual insight, which
came as a gift from God. Only through a countervailing thrust
of vigorous individualism could the force of education gain a
foothold. Those who were thus caught up faced both exclusion
and isolation and were usually lost to another cultural tradition.
Abraham Lincoln was born in this tradition and he carried many
of its mannerisms and values into the Presidency.

The system of formal education in the "town and country" pattern yields yet another variant and further substantiation of congruency. Each rural neighborhood was served by its own school
—the romanticized one-room school—presided over by a school-
marm drawn from the same cultural milieu as her pupils. The
school was basically an extension of the family, and the teacher's
role was little different from that of an older sister or a spinster
aunt. The schools of the town reflected the greater heterogeneity
of its environment. The town's elementary schools were an extension of the community, but the advanced schooling provided in
the private academies, which were later replaced by public high
schools, was for children drawn from the town's higher social
classes and for ambitious and talented children from the countryside. Here, again, we observe the symbolic relationship of town
and country in operation.

The relatively complex pattern of the urban schools mirrored
the divisions based on social class, religion, and ethnic background. There were schools for rich and poor, for those of varying religious faiths, and for other groups. Entrance into many
occupations, however, came only after one had served an apprenticeship in shop, office, or profession.

Certain aspects of this description may still be encountered in
the educational situation today. But it would be misleading to
assume that today's school system or its practices represent an
evolutionary development from the past—although we cannot
deny certain connections. Changes in the human environment
have produced innovations and contributed to the loss of some
aspects. The one-room school has almost disappeared. Private

academies evolved into public high schools. Teacher-training institutions, technical institutes, land-grant colleges, and the graduate school have appeared and spread in response to new conditions.

THE NEW AMERICA

American civilization has moved on a course that takes us ever further from our agrarian past. The mill town appeared in the first half of the nineteenth century as the new industrial processes and the factory system spread from England. Then came the growth of the industrial cities associated with new industries and mass production. Now we are in the new age of science, and metropolis is the shape of the new human community. It possesses many features that distinguish it from the past.

The cultural outlines of this new America are readily discernible. Its physical manifestation is metropolis, where the spatial grouping reveals the social and cultural directions of an emerging civilization. The new monumental civic centers attest to the growth of public service and of a rising interest in the arts. In the great new office buildings, one finds the centers of control and planning for commercial and industrial enterprises whose operations may be purely local or may reach to the far corners of the earth. Within the central city, one may find clusterings of facilities and people that give expression to other functions, such as education or health. Moving outward, one encounters suburb, shopping center, and industrial park.

Among some of our older cities, such as New York, Philadelphia, or Chicago, a double transformation is occurring in the core or inner city. Immense wealth is being expended for the reconstruction of the central business and financial districts in an attempt to revitalize these areas. In contrast, the nearby residential areas have received tens of thousands of Negroes and Puerto Ricans dispossessed from areas once based on the older agrarian tradition, but now in the process of transformation to modern agriculture. In many respects, these people are the casualties of the transition. Metropolis becomes their refuge, but the skills they bring with them are inadequate for anything but menial employment; hence, they must either remain marginal in their participation in the new America or, even more debasing, become parasitic. The attention we now give to programs of rehabilitation is a measure both of the problem and of our need to help the newcomers make adjustments.

The main thrust of American civilization, however, is elsewhere; in order to understand its significance we need to examine the characteristic social groupings of corporate organization, nuclear family, and voluntary organization. We must also keep in mind the division of life between the public and the private aspect; formal schooling is the channel that links the two and prepares the child for his participation in the public world.

The corporate form of organization provides the framework within which the majority of Americans now work. In structure and operation, it bears little resemblance to the town meeting of New England, the threshing ring of the rural neighborhood, the labor gang of the plantation, or the workshop of the city artisan. These were forms of human organization of another age. Furthermore, we must distinguish the corporate form from the classical bureaucracy described by Max Weber (although it may contain bureaucratic elements) and from the system of ranked positions found in a traditional army (although the principle of hierarchy may be present). The corporate form is able to assemble quantities of energy and diversities of skill for the purpose of solving specific problems. Its variety of internal distinctions should be viewed less as an arrangement to express status and more as the basis for achieving its multiple goals. The postwar American university typifies the emergent corporate structure more clearly than does either government or industry, although both of these are undergoing a massive reformation in this new direction. Unfortunately, the structure of the urban American public school system has shown little modification since the days, in the early part of this century, when it was set in the mold of municipal and industrial bureaucracy. An extensive restructuring is long overdue.

Within the private world of the individual, the significant group is the nuclear family.* It is the unit of reproduction and

---

* For an exploration of this theme, see Solon T. Kimball, "Cultural Influences Shaping the Role of the Child," *The National Elementary Principal, Those First School Years*, XL (1960), 18–32.

nurturance, and it provides a sanctuary of intimacy for all its members. From the relationships of its members comes the psychic pattern that prepares and commits its young to participate in the public world. The modern American family differs from other family types in several respects. Neither parents nor young expect that the children, as adults, will necessarily remain associated with the household of their birth, the locale in which they came to maturity, or occupational choices of the preceding generation. The discontinuity is not significant, however, because the basic posture of poised mobility, in both the geographical and social sense, is firmly preserved. But mobility cannot be achieved through the family alone; it depends upon the learnings that the child receives from formal schooling.* If the school does not, or cannot, provide the young with necessary skills and knowledge, or if it provides these in inadequate measure, then the individual is excluded from full participation in our type of civilization.

We must also accept, however, that the failure may be attributed in part to the cultural milieu from which the child comes. Gans† has shown, for example, the restrictive impress of Italian families, which prevented their children from partaking, or wishing to partake, of the full possibilities of education as a device for advancement. The Italian parents clearly understood the threat to group cohesion that education posed. The principle we derive from this illustration has broad applicability. We can state it as follows: Those who hold a prior commitment to the cultural particularism of family, community, race, ethnic group, or social class are in greater or lesser measure barred from full participation in our society. To the extent that they impose these restrictions upon their children, the children are also disadvantaged. The magnitude of discrimination may not be quantitatively large or limited primarily to those who are descendants of a defunct agrarianism, but even the exclusion of a few represents a defect in our society. That the changes in American society have en-

* A study that throws light on this subject is John R. Seeley, R. Alexander Sim, and Elizabeth W. Loosley, *Crestwood Heights: A Study of the Culture of Suburban Life* (New York: Basic Books, 1956).

† Herbert J. Gans, *The Urban Villagers: Group and Class in the Life of Italian Americans* (Chicago: The Free Press of Glencoe, 1962).

gaged the great majority of our people is a testimonial of strength. In fact, Americans have been the architects of their own transformation.

The last of the major types of social groupings that are characteristically American is the volunteer association. This is the technical term that encompasses the vast number of clubs, associations, organizations, societies, councils, fraternities, lodges, and other groups that surround every aspect of American life. There is no activity, category, or interest that lacks some organized kind of espousal. From stamp collecting to investing, from barbering to surgery, from young to old, or rich to poor, Americans join with their similars to investigate, protest, compare, or celebrate.

The American's capacity to create and utilize organization is a trait that reaches to our very beginnings. In the now famous Mayflower Compact of 1620, the Pilgrims set down the rules that were to govern their relationships. Two hundred years later, de Tocqueville marveled at the ease with which Americans joined together to solve their problems. He also observed that, once the particular issue had been resolved, they would disband, but could reconstitute themselves readily if the necessity arose. During the Civil War, most of the military companies that marched from the towns of the North, and many from the South, were formed on the associational pattern. Today, in our schools and colleges, students and professors alike are confronted by a vast array of activities and interests calling for the coordinate efforts of like-minded peers.

It is in and through these associations that the young learn the skills they later will carry into adult roles. Only among the poor do we find a deficiency in this organizational capacity, a fact that those who are now attempting to organize representational councils among them are discovering anew. And, if we look closely, we learn that the schools which serve the children of the slums are the most deficient in providing extracurricular programs. Educators might well contemplate the significance of such a fact.

In these three forms of social groupings, then, we encounter the significant structures of American society. The corporate form provides the instrumentality through which much of the work of the world is accomplished. The family nurtures the young, offers a haven from stress, and perpetuates flexibility for adaptation by means of the posture of mobility. The voluntary association provides the interstitial fibers that connect the parts into a vast interrelated whole. There is more, however, which requires attention, and this analysis leads, next, to the inner life.

THE PSYCHIC PATTERN

Earlier, I called attention to the psychic pattern that the child acquires within the family, but which holds such great importance for his participation in the public world. Our task now is to establish the relevance of psychic patterns to the individual's behavior in the social order. In examining the connections between psychic, cultural, and social spheres, we come to understand both the extent to which there is mutual reinforcement among them and the kind of tensions they generate in the individual. For example, there is no aspect of human need or aspiration for which our society fails to offer the possibility of unlimited realization. We find one expression of this in the widely prevalent belief that money, although the root of all evil, can buy anything—that is, almost anything—but it cannot buy happiness, which must be pursued.

The more sophisticated know that there are many routes, other than the monetary one, by which to move toward goals. None escapes, however, making the payment that pursuit of the dream exacts, although the fairy tale fantasies of childhood would lead us to believe otherwise. The fact is, before an individual can hope to reach any of the promised rewards, he must prepare himself, and the magnitude of his effort is believed to be roughly commensurate with the magnitude of his achievement. Each forward step, however, engenders new efforts for reaching succeeding goals; thus, preparation becomes a never-ending requirement. Those whose original preparation was inadequate, or those who have withdrawn or been defeated, may be counted as the casualties. That they are not now involved does not invalidate the manner in which the system works. Their failure may be due to an inadequate internalization of the psychic base necessary for commitment. It is to that aspect that I now turn.

If the child-rearing practices of the American family are successful, the child learns that full achievement of adult status is accomplished outside the home. He also expects that, during a portion of his preparatory period (the years of advanced schooling), he may be absent from his family. The preparation for separation from family has been called "independence training." Although the physical displacement is obvious and necessary, the achievement of full independence is largely illusory. Quite apart from the difficulty of shedding deeply embedded habituation to parental direction, the individual has been bound by psychic ties that he can seldom, if ever, escape. These are particularly evident in the areas of anxiety, shame, and guilt.

The obvious expression of anxiety appears as prudence—the need to be careful. The child has been carefully schooled to avoid the dangers that threaten his own well-being and that of others; he has also been taught that, if "things" work, it is because of the care and attention bestowed upon them. Both humans and machines need checkups and tune-ups, and extraneous items must be removed. The consequence of such training is to develop a sense of the orderliness of time and space and of the placement and movement of objects in them. Orderliness becomes a *sine qua non* for accomplishment and finds no better expression than the insistence of teachers that, in the classroom, the orderly behavior of pupils is a necessary condition for learning. How else may we interpret the distress teachers show when they encounter children who have not been thus socialized.

The less obvious expression of anxiety manifests itself in a pervasive insecurity. Although we continually make demands upon the individual, as a child or adult, we have few ways of giving reassurance concerning successful performance. The individual remains uncertain of his own capabilities and of his performance in relation to these. He must continually seek assurances, and failure or rejection can be devastating. Whatever the response to his efforts, he has also learned that the resolution of his difficulties resides within himself and, hence, he must continue to struggle. For those who remain with the struggle, even the accolade of others furnishes a doubtful proof of success, since each achievement is a transitory phase toward the next step. Those who attempt to escape the tensions of struggle by withdrawing from the competitive situation experience relief only temporarily, since competition is primarily an internal state.

Giving up, however, is far more difficult than might be imagined, since anxiety is coupled with shame and guilt. Through the formative years, each individual acquires an enormous and unpayable debt to his parents. He is in debt to them for the opportunities they have given him—for life itself. It is his duty, as a child, to utilize the benefits accorded him; as an adult, he validates the trust that has been placed in him. He does this by fulfilling his sense of their aspirations, an assignment that cannot be forgotten, even after his parents' death. It is an obligation he also transmits to his children and, hence, its perpetuation is transgenerational. The pangs of conscience that erupt following the violation of some moral rule are superficial pains compared to those that one suffers consequent upon the violation of obligations to oneself and to one's family. Thus, anxieties about one's capabilities and the wise use of opportunities are linked to a fear of shaming oneself and others and to the guilt that ensues if one is unable to meet one's moral obligations.

Intimately associated with the pattern of anxiety, shame, and guilt is the need to act upon the world. Many foreigners have marveled at American vitality and have explained our behavior as youthful exuberance. We can hardly accept such an interpretation. As we grow into mature nationhood, there is no sign of a slackening of the energy with which we attack problems. In politics, in sports, in courtship, in business, in the invasion of outer space, even in the muted infighting of a university campus, we are playing orderly but violent games. Even those who proclaim their desire for peace use violent measures to attract attention to their cause. If this aggression erupts into uncontrolled violence, orderliness is destroyed, and feelings of anxiety and guilt are intensified. Therefore, the destructive aspects of aggressiveness must be contained, and this we do by turning our activities into games, the rules of which must be strictly observed and their observance impartially enforced if we are to avoid chaos.

Thus far I have been describing and tracing the interconnections of the characteristic American social groupings and of the psychic qualities of those who are fully participant in our society.

As the analysis proceeds, remarkable congruencies, which contribute to our great cohesion as a people, become evident. Our social framework contains and directs the lively tensions that arise among and within groups and, in most instances, channels aggressive energies into productive purposes. There still remains, however, one major area for exploration. It is essential that the aspects of world view that are distinctly American be made explicit. We need to know about these in order to understand ourselves as individuals and as social beings. Once this question has been explored, we will be ready for the final task—to seek the relevancies between the educational enterprise and contemporary society and, if necessary, to offer some advice.

World View—Interdependency and System

Each of the cultural traditions that rooted in American soil in the colonial period reflected somewhat different views about the nature of man, his relation to the world, and his destiny. Nevertheless, the similarities among them were probably greater than the differences. The Old World rigidity, encompassed in a pattern of thought that accepted absolutes, a fixity of the universe, and sharp polarities, was particularly evident in the religious tradition. But there was also a strong current of empirical pragmatism, which granted to the individual the capacity for intervention. In addition, the literary legacy left by the cultivated minds of this early period shows much more than a concern with theology and the supernatural; it also reveals a strong bias toward rational explanation and experimentation.

Periods of crisis provided fertile ground for the transformation of older views and the introduction of new ones. The rapid development of the North and West after the Civil War provided a favorable environment for the doctrine of progress that Herbert Spencer espoused in a series of popular lectures in Eastern cities. Until the advent of the Depression of the 1930's, Americans held no doubts about the superiority of their way of life, about a future filled with unending rewards. We are all aware of the great changes that followed in the wake of the two world wars and of the intervening trauma of boom and crash. Their detailing has no particular relevance at the moment. What I should like to do, however, is attempt to describe an emerging pattern of thought that flows out of these changes and constitutes the conceptual basis for a world view only now being formulated.

The cornerstone of this pattern is the concept of interdependence. Although most of us are accustomed to thinking in terms of identities and particulars, we are gradually learning that this atomistic point of view cannot give us a comprehension of the whole. We are only now beginning to understand that the sum of the parts does not constitute a whole. We likewise recognize that the whole is not an addition, but a process. In the nature of the relationships that lead to cooperation or strife between the nations of the world, in the connections between industrial processes and pollution, in the effect of human environment upon normal and pathological behavior, and in many other ways, we are beginning to understand *interdependencies*. We are beginning to view the events of the world as expressions of systems—what Darwin called the web-of-life.

This new view is of immense significance because it brings with it, and is built upon, correlative changes in other habits of conceptualization. For example, when we think in systemic terms, we study change rather than statics. Because we know that modification of a system's environment, or of its components and their relationships, will have repercussions on either environment or system, or both, we seek to discover what these changes are and the processes associated with them. Under such circumstances, we can no longer accept the fixity we have attributed to absolutes; we must accept variability as an aspect of the natural world. Variability must not be confused with either relativity or uncertainty. The latter term has been applied to certain problems connected with measuring the behavior of subatomic particles, and the former pertains to the perspective from which a phenomenon is viewed. In contrast, variability refers to the capacity for modification.

When we accept the viewpoint of variable interdependencies, we no longer concentrate upon determining the fixed qualities or essences of things. In fact, we can no longer assume that things stand as isolated particulars that can be examined in and of themselves. Instead, we must now seek for the relationships among things. We discover that, as these relationships change—such as those between digestive and neural processes, or those between the members of a family—the quality of the particulars also changes. In this approach, we see items as variables, and our search centers on the relationships between them, since from discoveries of regularities among them comes the power of prediction.

Inevitably, this method of thought brings changes in the kinds of questions we ask when we attempt to understand the nature of the world. Definition and identification become subordinate to the search for principles that explain *process*. This difference can be illustrated by comparing the collector, who seeks to classify and arrange the specimens he has gathered under some *a priori* scheme of classification, with the ecologist, who attempts to observe and explain the succession of plant or animal types under conditions of an unstable environment. The latter is concerned with process; he asks questions about the nature of change under certain conditions. The classical taxonomist is a collector and classifier, concerned exclusively with the nature of things. His approach can lead us no further than static formulations.

This new mode of thought necessitates imparting a new meaning to the concept of knowledge. The quiz-kid is knowledgeable in that he has a great store of facts ready for instant recall. An encyclopaedia and an almanac are inert repositories of facts. No one can deny that facts may prove to be useful bits of information. They may also turn out to be utterly worthless. The point is that information acquires significance only when it becomes relevant to a problem. Under such circumstances, the important intellectual quality is the capacity to recognize and solve problems, and this is what the thrust of deliberate education ought to be about.

Those who contend that this is what the schools now do had better look again. In particular, they should look at examinations if they are to discover what knowledge is being sought. They will find that "acquaintance with facts," one of the definitions Webster gives for knowledge, is the basis upon which we judge student competence in most areas of study. This standard of judgment is of a piece with the pattern of thought that deals in particulars, absolutes, statics, and essences. It views learning as a causal consequence of the rewarded response to stimuli, a theory that requires of the learner no greater cerebral capacity than that of a dog learning tricks. This simplistic view of learning is far from adequate. Humans resemble other animals in their need for motor skills, but mankind, with its use of symbols and its capacity for abstract thought, possesses mental processes that are immensely more complex. Man is capable of making explicit those very processes that differentiate him from other forms of animal life. The cognitive skills he must have, before he can think in terms of systems, variability, relationships, and processes, are not inherent in the information he accumulates; they are a derivative of the capability to define and solve problems. Within this formulation, the concept of knowledge is extended to include the processes as well as the results of our cognitive activities.

Educational Congruencies

The problem with which we must now deal is that of deciding what kind of educational enterprise is needed; once again, the basic issue is that of congruency. On several occasions in this paper, allusions were made to the existing situation in education. The evidence from these illustrations leads to the conclusion that the present situation is disorderly and disjunctive. It may well be that the legacy inherited from our past, during which education was primarily a conservator rather than an innovator, explains this condition. Certainly, the long insulation of the schools and of professional educators from the main streams of development in technology, thought, and organization would seem an equally plausible reason. Whatever the explanation, the fact remains that those who run our schools do not evidence an awareness of the crucial position and role they now hold, and schools are woefully deficient in meeting the educational needs of society.

This is not the place to offer specific prescriptions for the modernization of the educational system. I assert, however, that it cannot be accomplished by reshuffling the bits and pieces of a curriculum, adding a little of this or subtracting a little of that. The transformation that is required is much more fundamental. It means bringing the organizational structure of the schools into accord with those corporate forms that now serve other functions so well. It means modifying the curriculum so as to emphasize the teaching of basic disciplines of thought and to put subject matter particularism in a subordinate position. And it means testing for problem-solving cognitive skills, for the ability to demonstrate an understanding of the variabilities and interdependencies of systems. Finally, it means building into our teaching practices the self-testing and self-correcting measures that are essential for the functioning of any viable system. These goals imply a very different philosophy of pedagogical practice and of learning.

DISCUSSION

McLure [presiding]: In these sessions we hope to provide the authors with an opportunity for further elaboration, clarification, and, if need be, defense. We hope, too, that the discussions will concentrate on implications of all kinds, dealing with matters such as the nature of contributions from various disciplines, questions for further research, and difficulties associated with the application of knowledge to the solution of problems.

Klein: Mr. Kimball, it seems to me that you actually have described an emerging societal structure, and perhaps some form of tabular presentation of the data would have been helpful. I would add, too, that you tended to apologize for the suggestions you made, and I see no reason why you should have to. The conclusions are logical, from my point of view, and should be stated in the affirmative.

Kimball: Do you have an illustration of the kind of conclusion you would like to see more affirmatively stated?

Klein: In your concluding statement you conveyed a feeling that you did not wish to be presumptuous; yet you did offer constructive criticism and you suggested ways by which the educational family might look at itself. I am saying only that there was, perhaps, a professional reserve, which was not really necessary.

Kimball: There is, in this regard, a question of strategy. If educational change is going to come, it will come, in very large measure, through professional educators. There are going to be pressures from the outside, it is true. There will be new conditions that necessitate change. But it is also true that educators have to lead in making changes, because they represent the educational enterprise in America. They have a deep investment in it. Although, at least at one point, the criticism I offered may have been very harsh, I have acknowledged that the educational enterprise in America has done a remarkably good job.

But the educational enterprise must do a better job, and the better job has to take place under conditions that are different from those of the past. Hence, there is the need for a conscious and continuous re-evaluation, not with a view to adding a little of this or taking away a little of that, but toward making a radical reconstruction.

KLEIN: Could I take you one step further in your concept of corporate structure as the model on which the administration of public schools should be organized? Would you care to elaborate on how the structure should be modified to implement the changes you alluded to?

KIMBALL: I think one way to discuss it is to start with an analogy. The traditional army is one in which the front-line soldier needs to learn only the proper responses to commands from above. Only a simple stimulus-response kind of learning is needed. Hence, in the training of the traditional army, the great amount of time given to "Squads right," "Squads left," "Forward march," and "Halt" is all part of the habituation by which individuals learn to respond to their superiors irrespective of the situation.

The traditional factory system presents essentially the same kind of learning situation. So does the hospital or the prison. And, unfortunately, so does the school, in large measure.

What happens is that, as the organizational system becomes more complex (by "organizational system" I mean the society), this stimulus-response kind of learning becomes inadequate. It is inadequate because the problems confronting those who operate these traditional institutions today are vastly different and more complex than the problems of the past. Hence the much larger numbers of people that have to be brought into the process, both at the higher (professional) level and at the custodial level, if the tasks of these institutions are to be accomplished.

Today, the student is completely subjected to an organized administrative, supervisory, and instructional pattern in which he has no opportunity to participate except as passive recipient. This situation may train people to be "Whiz-Kids," to pass the Regents' Examination of New York State, or to do well on the Educational Testing Service's examinations, but it does not develop diverse skills for solving problems. Currently, instruction is geared to the demands of these tests. As such, it may fill students with information, but it doesn't give them any sense of the significance of this information or of its relevance to the problems they are going to meet.

Increasingly, the problems that we face have no single answer. The answers we evolve are always contingent answers. The contingency is based upon the nature of our analysis of the variables, and these variables can change. Thus, we find no single solution, but multiple solutions. The way we have trained our teachers and the way that some of us, ourselves, teach is to oversimplify the instructional process by assuming that the type of problem we present has a single answer.

To comment further on organizational structure, we find considerable differences among the states. Although New York City is notorious for the rigidity of its school system, another large urban system, that of Kansas City, Missouri, has great flexibility, which demonstrates that rigidity is not an unavoidable consequence of urban systems.

If ever a school system needed to be flexible, it is the urban school system of today. Four or five years ago in New York, administrative officials announced a great reform: They were going to ask for only 600 reports annually from each principal. Because this represented a reduction of 400, it was counted a great advance. Also in New York, the stated policy, until very recently, was that parents were to be excluded from school participation. This parallels the old factory system's practice of putting big steel fences around plants in order to keep everything out; the internal hierarchy can then function without external interference. In the schools, this kind of organization needs to be restructured, but not in the direction of further supervision or specialization. It should be restructured so that learning becomes the real focus. Learning is not the focus now, although it is claimed to be. The real focus is the organizational structure and the services of the organizational structure.

DAVID: You dealt primarily with the formal educational system, that is, with our system for instructing the young. It seems to me there are some extensions of your general thesis, and it is quite important that the formal educational system recognize them. Many occupations are developing in professional and technical fields that require continuous relearning, or problem-solving ability. It would appear that one of our big tasks in these years of change is to provide education in relearning, education that allows the adult to develop new techniques of problem-solving. The question is: How do we create an institution that will adequately do that job?

In many corporations, various formal educational channels for training on the job already exist. They may have a very high problem-solving component. For example, there is the training that is given to IBM technicians and to people who service computers.

How do we establish an institutional link between the organizations that are doing educational training outside our formal educational system and the formal educational system that deals with our youth? I think that is one of our problems. And the other is: How do we modify the formal educational system so that it can deal with the problem of adult education?

KIMBALL: I think you have given part of the reply to your own question when you refer to what IBM and other corporations are doing for the whole area of in-service training.

For instance, Clark and Sloan* made a survey of the development of formal education beyond that provided by traditional schools. They discovered that the sums of money spent by corporations, by churches, by community adult-education programs, and by the armed services far exceed the amounts spent by the formal system of elementary and secondary schools and colleges and universities. Clark and Sloan concluded that, unlike the past, the nature of the modern world is such that we may now expect that retraining or lifelong formal education of some type will be mandatory for a very large segment of our population—probably an increasing segment.

---

* Harold F. Clark and Harold S. Sloan (eds.), *Classrooms in the Factories* (New York: New York University Press for the Institute of Research, Fairleigh Dickinson University, 1958); with the assistance of Charles A. Hebers, *Classrooms in the Stores* (New York: Columbia University Teachers College Press for the Institute for Instructional Improvement, Inc., 1962); and *Classrooms in the Military* (New York: Columbia University Teachers College Press, 1964).

Some changes going on within the formal system are most interesting. Two such changes are the development of what is called the community college and of the post-high school two-year technical school. The explanation given to me for this latter development is that the graduate of our engineering institutions some thirty or forty years ago had the kind of subprofessional skills needed for practical engineering work. Recent changes in the curriculum of engineering schools have been of such magnitude that graduates are now highly qualified in mathematics, mechanics, and the theoretical aspects of engineering, but not in the practical engineering skills that formerly were part of the curriculum. Hence, the two-year technical school turns out a cadre of trained people to take the subprofessional jobs that are now so prevalent.

As one measure of this, it is estimated that there are 5 million unfilled jobs in the United States, but these are not positions that those who are now unemployed can fill. They are positions requiring a high degree of technical capability. Interestingly enough, this development of the technical school seems to be proceeding at the most rapid rate in the American South and in the American West.

BUSHNELL: First, I would like to comment on your support for the training activities of industry and the military. You seem to assume that because the military is proficient in developing the skills required to handle new weapons systematically, they are also proficient teachers. True, they are very good at providing the trained manpower to operate these new weapons—even five years in advance of their actual use. They are very effective in devising step-by-step instructional methods. Unfortunately, when you examine their methods closely, and this is equally applicable to industry, you could call it "by the numbers" teaching. It is very similar to what you described as stimulus-response learning; very little problem-solving takes place.

Additionally, I would like to point out that problem-solving through the use of computers is now being tried in some of the newer occupational fields and these should be examined.

Finally, there are other types of programs at the adult level, such as the Great Books course and the various management development programs, that utilize case studies. Some of these might provide interesting models for updating educational programs for adults.

KIMBALL: Yes, I think so. Presumably there was a time when an adequately educated person had at his command a considerable amount of the world's available knowledge. Now it is almost impossible for an individual to keep abreast of what is going on in a single discipline. If the requirement for functioning in an organization is knowledge—and, to some extent, it is always knowledge—then we are facing a very difficult problem; the quantity of knowledge a person would have to master is overpowering. But, if the requirement is ability to define a problem and then determine the kind of knowledge needed to get solutions, a different emphasis, or a new addition to the type of education we now have, is needed.

BUSHNELL: In that regard, your paper mentions a principle, or really a hypothesis, that states, "Those who hold a prior commitment to the cultural particularism of family, community, race, ethnic group, or social class are in greater or lesser measure barred from full participation in our society." It occurred to me that some cultures emphasize adaptation to the processes of change and give considerable emphasis to education.

KIMBALL: One needs to make a distinction between the private life of the individual and his public life. American society permits, probably to a greater extent than ever before, a pluralistic cultural life at the level of the individual's private life. On the other hand, if the individual is going to be a full participant, a general capability is demanded, which includes both knowledge and problem-solving capacity at the public level. In the case of religious or ethnic groups, it may still be possible for them to preserve the essences of their traditional past within the larger framework I referred to. What will probably happen, though, is that this will not occur, so that the private life of an individual will also begin to resemble the private lives of other people. Increasingly, as represented by recent decisions of the Supreme Court, distinctions are being made between the fulfillment of your public function and the freedom you have in your private world.

LECHT: I was quite interested in your mention of the post-high school technical institutions. I wonder if this isn't quite significant as an indicator of a major shift in vocational training. Much of vocational training is likely to be moved out of the high schools—that is, out of nontheoretical skill training—into post-high school institutions, which emphasize more basic scientific principles and their relationship to technology. So, this is one of the big areas where our school systems are likely to change radically in the next decade.

KIMBALL: I am well aware that there is a heightened tension between the old vocational people and the new technical people. This is an argument I know I should stay out of, so I can accept your statement as being a fact and anybody here who has a different position can talk with you about it. I can tell you I am on your side.

LECHT: I haven't really followed the academics of this. You mentioned, for example, that engineers currently being trained aren't getting many of the basic techniques the engineer had a generation ago. Therefore, there is a grade or position created for a junior professional or subprofessional who has these techniques. But I think something else is happening. A large number of occupations that require a new type of technical training are being created.

KIMBALL: Correct. Atomic physicists and computer repairmen are examples.

BEASLEY: I have been concerned about the ability of schools to develop adaptability. If one of the schools' purposes is to meet manpower needs of the future, maybe training in adaptability is something on which we must concentrate. You proposed that schools do more to teach cognitive skills for problem-solving. Do you feel that the teaching of problem-solving skills will increase adaptability in students?

KIMBALL: I think this is in the realm of both speculation and discussion and is still outside the realm of proof. But, as an example, some schools now teach geography not by having students memorize the names and locations of lakes, rivers, cities, or such things, but by actually presenting the characteristics of a territory. Students are provided with facts and with criteria for evaluating their relevance; they are then posed some problems, such as: "These are the conditions under which cities appear. On the basis of the facts that you have, where would cities appear upon this particular map with this particular distribution of features?" The students are not faced with information to be memorized, but with seeing how you put something together. They may not agree, but reaching agreement isn't the objective. The solutions are based on variables and, hence, represent contingent answers. The goal is to develop the capacity to see facts in relation to criteria and processes. I would think that its realization would create a more adaptable mind.

BEASLEY: You feel that instead of looking at it as a closed-end type of answer, it is all a contingency?

KIMBALL: Yes. As illustration, the pattern of thought characteristic of peoples in traditional societies does not encourage the search for alternative solutions to a problem. Instead, it is assumed that there is a right answer, which can be found in historical or supernatural precedent. In contrast, we are beginning to accept the value of multiple answers based on contingencies.

BEASLEY: Let's say we are structuring a school system and one of our goals is to teach the students to look at process rather than memorize static facts. Do you think that the development of these problem-solving skills would be the best method of reaching this goal and of preparing students for the rapidly changing social and economic world they face?

KIMBALL: I think it is essential.

FOLGER: Let me press you a little further on this question of organization for flexibility. If I understand one of your points, it was that what we need is a more corporate, problem-oriented type of organization in contrast to a more traditional, bureaucratic type of organization. The example you gave of the corporate type was the university and the example of the traditional bureaucratic type was the public school system. I find it difficult, myself, to see that the corporate form of the university has promoted the goals of problem-solving any more effectively than the bureaucratic structure of the public school system.

KIMBALL: I would argue that the American university represents the most flexible of all the institutional arrangements we now have. I would argue it on the basis that, from the relatively simple structure of the 1900's, it has evolved into a type of institutional arrangement that can absorb almost any kind of activity and provide it with an organizational form—such as institutes and curriculum centers. The university structure is tremendously complex by virtue of the greater diversity in types of functions it now attempts to fulfill.

FOLGER: I accept this. But it doesn't necessarily follow, it seems to me, that this organizational flexibility has directed attention toward the need to get students to be more effective problem-solvers and to be more adaptable, which were the goals you were looking for.

KIMBALL: Whether this is so or not would be an interesting proposition to investigate. I can say only that the nature of the university is to focus inquiry on problems rather than on the accumulation of certain types of critical or other skills, and this by itself indicates movement in the desired direction.

BUSHNELL: Profit-making firms offer a capability for making practical applications of basic research findings resulting from university research programs. By linking university capabilities with those of the private sector, we might be able to bring about widespread changes in education, which, if left to the more traditional dissemination processes, would take years to accomplish. Industry has proved itself, in other fields of activity—such as nuclear power and weapon development—capable of translating complex research data into useful applications for public consumption. Therefore, we might look to the universities for leadership in devising a reliable approach to teaching sixth-graders logic. We could then enlist the help of private industry in implementing these curriculum improvements on a massive basis. I might even go so far as to say that industry could do the job of developing curriculum, training teachers, and supplying the needed instructional materials more efficiently than universities. What's happening in atomic physics helps to substantiate my argument. Many satellite engineering firms have sprung up around universities where the basic discoveries in nuclear physics were generated. These profit-making firms succeeded in applying these discoveries to a variety of consumer needs; I might add that not all of them were consumer needs.

KIMBALL: I would like to propose an alternative, and suggest that what you propose is dangerous.

In 1916, Ellwood P. Cubberley published a work entitled *Public School Administration** in which he advocated that schools be organized and function on the basis of the factory system. He also reported on the application of tests, developed by educational psychologists, that made it possible to group students on the basis of intelligence measurements. In the second decade of the century, school systems in a dozen or more cities in the United States employed what were called efficiency experts, a term that probably reflected the influence of Frederick W. Taylor, who was then writing about efficiency in industry. These efficiency experts, curiously enough, were not organizational experts; rather, they measured intellectual capabilities of children, and these measurements were then used as the basis for placing children in classrooms.

Cubberley explicitly argued that the school should model itself upon the factory system. He drew several parallels, such as that between the board of directors and the school board. He even went so far as to view students as raw products that needed to be shaped by an assembly-line arrangement in which the terminal product was varied or, as we phrase it these days, the manpower needs of the nation were being met.

I cannot agree with this philosophy. Why was it at this time, when the urban schools really found themselves in the position of seeking new organizational forms and modifications of curriculum, that the factory system or, more probably, the municipal bureau became the model of organization? Why was it that Cubberley's generation didn't turn to the university as the model for the secondary school and even for the primary school? The university represents the highest form of human organization we know. It merits this distinction because of its greater complexity, its immense capacity to attract people of great skills, and its organization simplicity, in the sense of its being able to bring to-

* New York: Houghton Mifflin.

gether people of different skills for the solution of problems. Why isn't this a more desirable model than that of industry?

BUSHNELL: I don't think I was suggesting that we model the public schools after industry, and I would certainly endorse your position that this would be an unfortunate move. I am suggesting that industry has some organizational capability for bringing about massive innovation in educaton, once given direction on how to move or where to move. It can apply the kind of critical mass of talent necessary to implement these changes.

KIMBALL: This may be true. I understand that IBM is now willing to try, on an experimental basis, to teach reading through computers. Maybe they will be successful. If they are successful, perhaps reading should be taught through contract with IBM. I don't know, but it seems to me that there are several alternatives. The decision we make must be judged on the basis of its consequences for the larger purposes of American society.

McLURE: Most of the learning theory that we have has been acquired from the study of animals under laboratory conditions. I don't know whether the monkey is developing a cognitive skill when he solves the problem of getting from one part of a maze to another. Could you give a little more interpretation of what you mean by problem-solving, at a given level, that might be produced efficiently by IBM or perhaps more efficiently by some other kind of organizational structure? I would like to have a more distinct idea of this problem-solving function that is a part of the child's development.

STRODTBECK: I think that one of the things that Mr. Kimball has done in proposing these concrete instances is to activate our thinking about the pitfalls and the shortcomings of the emphasis on problem-solving. I just wonder how those children in that geography class he mentioned are ever going to find Indianapolis, which seems to be so incongruously related to most water-land-transportation perspectives. And I'm sure whenever we see a classroom teacher at work we have the intuitive feeling that a very complicated computer is working in each of her transactions with children. When she talks about what she is doing we get such an impoverished conception of what has really taken place. So one of our problems, when we find the bright young engineers from IBM giving us suggestions as to ways of helping the teacher, is to get the colloquy going, to get the bright young engineer to understand something more of the hidden wisdom that a teacher develops after exposure to a situation for long periods.

BURNETT: At the elementary school level, the issue is not whether you are going to teach information or whether you are going to operate in one way or another. The point is, you can't teach information from all of the disciplines.

Let me use one particular example from a curriculum project in which I worked. Take an important concept from biology, if you will. It's big; it holds lots of possibilities for organizing lots of particular data. The problem is, how do you talk to third- or fourth-grade children about such a major concept?

One of the ways is to create a problem situation—in this case, an ant colony. The ant colony simulated the kinds of processes that the ants went through in the wild. We brought it into a classroom and just left it there for children to look at. They were interested for a while. But they soon dropped this interest and we then had to develop some kind of conceptual interest based on problem-solving.

We taught them to ask questions in order to manufacture problems. In trying to find answers to the problems, they invented ways to experiment. But to set up experiments they needed equipment and there they ran into the problem of the organization of the school. We didn't have the personnel available to make it possible for the children to go to a shop in the school and build the kind of equipment they needed if they were to set up a situation that would enable them to answer their questions by observing what happened to the ants.

The second problem we ran into was the orientation of the teacher. The teacher is a very complex machine in operation and a great deal more than a machine. But, commonly, *she* is solving the problems, not the children. So we were trying to get both the teacher and the children, in association, to solve the problems. It was a complex kind of thing. The children weren't responding just in terms of particular information to the question of the teacher. They really had to find out things about the ants.

The additional problem, however, was that teachers felt shy about not having the answers ready. Many of these teachers had never bothered to fool around with ants. And, of course, they didn't know any answers, and that upset them.

We ran into another difficulty. When you have a situation in operation and you try to set up a problem like this, you can't do it in forty minutes. You must have some kind of time-space flexibility if you are going to get people to operate in this way in respect to problems and systems. You have to change so many things in structure.

KIMBALL: This is a very good illustration, and thank you so much for bringing it out, because it does give emphasis to the points of congruence and conceptual development. It seems, from our data in anthropology, that children in primitive societies learn through developing patterned thought, rather than linear thought like the monkey. In patterned thought, a sort of rough sketching of a system is done first and then additional experience adds detail that fills out the pattern, or perhaps even modifies the pattern, but not extensively. Human beings learn in total situations, presented initially by family experience in very early childhood.

DAVID: This interchange suggests another objective of our school system. We are training people to gratify themselves as consumers, to make use of this tremendous national product that we are capable of producing and which we will produce more efficiently if we can solve problems better. The main agents that I see in training this sort of gratification are the family, our news media, television, and the formal channels of education. Can a formal educational system, making better use of these media outside the classroom, train people to make more effective use of their leisure time so that they understand the difference between short-run gratification and long-run gratification?

KLEIN: As a people, we represent a wide diversity. The question really, as suggested by Mr. Kimball, is how to increase the capacity for cohesiveness among these diversified groups and then, as required, form other structures. In other words, you are really suggesting that we are an institution with no boundaries, or that boundaries are flexible.

Then we have the matter of becoming aware of how to teach and of how people acquire skills. I would suggest that perhaps technology can be viewed in terms of tools. Then the energies of the university can be conceived in terms of the expansion of the tools. Would you care to comment on the new technology and the appropriate role of the teacher in relation to it?

KIMBALL: On this matter of boundaries, perhaps we can start by adding two more dimensions to the corporate system. One is that the corporate system is transgenerational; the university is not bound by a set time span. Second, the corporation, the corporate form, has become transcommunity; it isn't located in just one community. It can operate throughout the world. When you add these two characteristics to the corporate form, in contrast to the community as a form or to the family as a form, you come up with a much greater flexibility. And I think that your suggestion is correct, then; your problems, or your organizational system, are no longer boundaried problems or systems. So, increasingly, we are breaking out of the limitations that locality imposes upon us.

I am not quite sure what you meant by your last sentence and the question you posed.

KLEIN: The teacher has been perceived as both a transmitter of knowledge and an agent of change. It now seems that technology may release the teacher for the second, and perhaps more significant, function—that of innovator or catalyst in the creation of change.

KIMBALL: That is what those who are optimistic about this kind of innovation would hold to be the outcome. It seems to me that we ought to see if it isn't our goal.

I have often wondered how we can justify keeping, on the faculties of American universities, teachers whose only job is to assign themes to students and to correct these themes. This seems to me to be an immense waste of good human energy; it so constricts a person who has been assigned the task that to be creative is difficult. There isn't the time or energy left for creativity. If we can assign such tasks to some kind of programed, or machine, learning, then we can get this burden off the back of the teacher.

LLOYD: May I speak about that last point: the redundant

teacher. I think we all appreciate that we have many types of universities in the United States—the well-established private and public ones and the very new ones, which a few short years ago were small teachers' colleges and have now gone through tremendous expansion. As the process of incorporation goes on in response to incentives of various kinds to market demands, we have emphasized the more specialized studies. This emphasis has its very important points, but I am sure it has been at the expense of general education in many of these new institutions. I am making this point because it seems to me that what you are arguing for, in relation to the development of cognitive skills, is an education that develops a spirit or sense of community as well as diverse capabilities.

In recent years, new developments have frequently been at the expense of this broader education, out of which—getting away from just theme writing and this sort of thing—ought to come the kinds of learning that encourage adaptability and growth in perception, regardless of whether individuals are going to be engineers or college presidents.

If I am right, the corporate form of the university may encounter other problems. You may be speaking from the experience of Harvard and Columbia. I don't think we can speak the same way in regard to the less developed universities. In a Harvard or a Columbia, there is an atmosphere that encourages great staff participation in determining educational policy and avenues of experimentation. In the less developed institutions, we have much of the kind of system that I think you inveigh against in your comment about the structure at the elementary and secondary levels.

KIMBALL: Does your university have any kind of contact of an ongoing nature with lesser institutions of higher education in the vicinity?

LLOYD: No, not yet. We probably will as the junior colleges develop.

KIMBALL: This is one of the developments that come with the growth of central institutions having great resources and skills. They need not be bounded, but can extend their influence in a variety of ways to the less well-endowed, less well-equipped institutions. They serve as focal points for diffusion and thus enrich others, so that these other institutions are no longer as isolated as they once were. There are a very large number of universities in America—thirty or forty, maybe more—that are exerting influences on a broad educational front.

LLOYD: I don't think it's a problem of isolation. It's a problem of attitude, of perception of the function of education. This is what I am getting at. To use one quick illustration: Committee T of the American Association of University Professors has been working for some years to draft a statement on faculty participation in decision-making processes within the corporate structure. I don't think this is a matter of real concern to Chicago or Northwestern or Harvard. It is a very great matter of concern elsewhere, especially if "the corporate structure" means that what you really want to get is a quality of expertise at the top level—sensitive to the demands and needs of society as these affect what goes on in the university, what goes on in the curriculum—at the expense of any participation on the part of the faculty.

KIMBALL: Maybe I haven't made my own position clear. I see the faculty, not the administrative staff, as the heart of the system. The administrative staff should serve as a facilitating agency, so that the faculty group can perform its functions in terms of the nature of the problems of our types of society.

STRODTBECK: Let me ask this question, then: Isn't it true that 50 per cent of the students who enter as freshmen very quickly drift out of the system? And isn't there something to be said for a form of organization in which one-third of the power is held by a politicized student body, one-third by the alumni, and one-third by the faculty?

KIMBALL: I am not quite sure one can cut the pie that way. But it's a perfectly good proposal. To leave the students out of effective participation means that the heart of the system is impaired.

FLANIGAN: Does the cognitive-skill failure that you identify with current methods of teaching apply to all of the students?

KIMBALL: I can't answer that. I just don't have the information that's needed. All I have at hand, all any of us have at hand, with which to make a judgment are the kinds of textbooks used in high schools, the kinds of laboratory work asked of students in these schools, and the kind of accepted teaching procedure, in which the teacher asks for specific kinds of answers to specific kinds of questions. To me, all this adds up to a failure to develop cognitive skills.

FLANIGAN: Some of the graduates go on to become technicians, scientists, and others who will innovate, and some do not. Is your concern with everyone, or just with those who are failing to make the grade in society?

KIMBALL: This is another real question that American policymakers must decide how to deal with. The only answer I can give is that our system ought to offer opportunities to everyone. Maybe the capabilities of everyone aren't such that they can move to the peaks, but at least the opportunities should be there. I think we would agree that they are not there now.

FLANIGAN: But don't we have to identify those for whom there are presently opportunities and those for whom there are none? What else should be done for the group we are not bringing along?

KIMBALL: We do indeed have to identify each group.

GARFIELD: Haven't we, in terms of legislation and funds, rededicated ourselves to bringing these people into the society?

KIMBALL: Yes. This is what we are doing.

GARFIELD: And isn't this really broadening our philosophic base? We are at least making it more realistic. There is a definite commitment, I hope.

KIMBALL: I think so.

DANIEL: I would like to take up a matter you mentioned early in your presentation—the problem of reordering the structure of administration. I think it is a serious problem. Last summer, I had a chance to be a consultant at several of the institutes operating under federal legislation such as the Civil Rights Act. You talk about change. These teachers will tell you: "We cannot do a thing unless there's a change in administration." This means a change on the part of school boards and principals. It looks to me as though the learning function is not the central problem of our system of education in many parts of the nation. I gather that's what you are saying here.

KIMBALL: May I ask what your experience was? As you were the consultant to these programs, did you discover that the school systems were able to incorporate the new programs, or did you find that these new programs had to be set up apart from the traditional school systems, or was there some combination?

DANIEL: Some combination. In one place it was quite clear that all change would have to come from without. This situation arose in a Southern state. To get funds under the Civil Rights Act for an institute on desegregation and to prepare teachers for service in places where integration is taking place, a Roman Catholic college had to do the training. The public school administrators would take no part in planning. There was even the possibility of threats that participants might lose their jobs. And when the director, a very knowledgeable person, asked, "What do you do next year when you return?," his frequent answer was, "I can do nothing unless there is some directive from above."

Another illustration occurred at an institute for the disadvantaged, operating under the National Defense Education Act [NDEA]. Teachers were asked about their problems. The first answer was: "My problem is my principal in working, with disadvantaged children, in any new thing I want to try to do."

KLEIN: There is another aspect to this. In a corporate structure, you have competition. For the first time on the American educational scene, you are getting a competitive model. I believe part of the philosophy behind the infusion of federal funds has been an indirect attempt, on the part of the Administration, to use this money to bring about change. I am beginning to observe, in my visits to school systems, a new sensitivity and, on the part of the establishment, an attempt to adapt. I feel that, had it not been for this added force, such change would not have occurred. So your statement about change coming from within is accurate only when this stimulus from outside is present.

FOLGER: But you are talking about the principle of competition, aren't you?

KLEIN: Yes.

FOLGER: This can exist in a variety of organizational forms. Various types of organizations can compete.

I would like to come back to the point that there isn't any real evidence that the corporate form, as represented by the university, has addressed itself any more directly than the public school to the preparation of people for the kind of complex world they are going to have to live in. I would argue that the organizational structure is probably not determinate here in the sense that I think you implied in your paper, Mr. Kimball.

KIMBALL: I am not sure I am saying that it is so much determinate as that, in this instance, an organizational structure that has great complexity also has great flexibility for possible change. Some of the tensions, which are now appearing in universities or which have been there for some time, are tensions between the established departmental structure and the new institutes and centers.

FOLGER: And between the university and the students who are complaining about the kind of education they are getting.

McLURE: I would like to return to the question of external influences. The public school system, historically, has been "community bound." It grew up in association with the community concept—big, little, and in-between. It has always responded to the influences in the community as well as to those from outside. Keeping this in mind, I would say there is another phenomenon here that you have not mentioned. I refer to the capacity of the school system to use resources derived from outside the community. In effect, people in the system who have freedom to use these resources as they perceive their needs will be responding to external influences. But the capacity is not always activated. Is there something in the public school system that makes it too rigid to adjust—either because it's too small, serving too few clientele to utilize resources adequately, or because it is politically and sociologically bound to the community?

KIMBALL: I think you have given us another significant dimension here. You and some of the others have said that influences from outside the community may, because of the power that a well-funded program carries, modify the local school system in ways that it would not have tolerated if left to itself. What you are saying, then, is that there is a dynamic relationship between the larger society, represented in this instance by the state or federal government, and the local school system. As changes occur in the larger area, they are reflected in the local system. Consider the money that has been spent by the National Science Foundation on physics, biology, and other studies. The consequences of these expenditures have already begun to percolate into school systems, bringing changes that would never have occurred otherwise. But the impact has been indirect.

McLure: Let's pursue this further. In this state, the Chicago school system was the first to be prepared to put the 1965 federal aid program into operation, and it is the largest system. I wonder if many of the implicit rigidities in the big systems to which you allude do not, mainly, result from a scarcity of resources rather than from structural faults? This may explain why regional—intermediate—administrative districts and centers for various functions come into existence to handle special problems and resources for small districts. The larger system *can* and *does* respond to these problems if it is given adequate resources.

Kimball: I am certain this is so. But, on the other hand, we have Martin Mayer's report, in his book *The Schools,* that there is a little rural school in western Arizona that is doing a magnificent job with a varied group of children as a result of the kind of leadership provided by the teachers in that school. And, in a slum school in Tucson—limited as it is by the background of the children, most of whom are Spanish and American Indian— he finds a remarkable educational job being accomplished, this time by virtue of the leadership of the principal. He finds some classrooms in New York City that, in spite of bureaucratic pressures from above, have teachers who are doing remarkable jobs.

Well, these isolated instances of excellence appear all over the country and seem to have no real connection with the situation —a fact that could lead us in another direction. We might conclude that it is neither a matter of organization nor of money, but a question of the qualifications and the integrity and imagination of those who work in the system. But these qualities still aren't enough to explain the quality of instruction. As you and I know, well-prepared teachers can go into teaching situations in which the environment is so restrictive that they quickly become very discouraged.

STOIKOV: I would like to raise a different issue. In your paper, Mr. Kimball, you suggested that Americans are very aggressive. In fact, you said they are the most aggressive people in the world. And you suggested that this is because of certain complexes of guilt and social obligations. Turning to the problem of channeling this type of aggression toward work, you suggested ways of making education more efficient in terms of producing people who are more adaptable to the work situation.

Why haven't you considered an alternative? Why not suggest that education should attempt to *reduce* these complexes of guilt and social obligations, rather than turning out people who are more efficient in channeling their energies into work situations? Why not think of the educational system as a way of reducing aggressiveness by reducing the guilt and social obligations?

KIMBALL: It all depends on what kind of society you want.

STOIKOV: Yes, but you haven't considered the alternative.

KIMBALL: I do not understand why it is that Navajo children grow up to be Navajos and Hopi children grow up to be Hopi, or why Peruvians grow up to be Peruvians. I don't understand the process, but each new generation does resemble the preceding ones. Americans grow up to be Americans. From the manifestations of behavior, we can arrive at certain conclusions about our society. We examine the organization, the kind of people and their values; and, in addition, as I was attempting to make explicit, we examine the kind of psychic organization associated with other aspects. This society has been one that has given us an immense growth in the area of technology, which means that, for example, your food can be refrigerated and airplanes will carry you from one place to another. But, our society is also one in which violence erupts from time to time and will continue to erupt. We may view these disturbances as evidence of tensions at the psychic level as well as on the social level.

So the question arises as to what kind of world you want? My point, and this is a position that anthropologists defend, is that there is a relationship between the psychic orientation and the cultural and societal aspects of a given people. So, even if you could do what you are proposing as an alternative, I would ask whether this is desirable, because this inevitably would move us in directions other than those in which we are now moving and from which we have come.

CANNON: What Mr. Stoikov is suggesting is really the main drift of federal policy in the past couple of years. The federal government isn't aiming to promote congruence with business, but to redress the balance, to get rid of social tensions, and so on. So, if I hear you correctly, we are doing wrong. Or do I hear you correctly?

KIMBALL: No. You may hear me very correctly. But I also made the statement that one aspect of American society is that it does a remarkable job of handling its tensions and of handling its aggressions through the definition of our activities as games with rules and with the need to have these rules both observed and enforced.

CANNON: I am trying to suggest something broader and maybe it isn't true. What your paper describes, it seems to me, may be the output—the result—of the educational system of the past half century.

KIMBALL: It isn't the educational system that can be held accountable for the characteristics of our society.

CANNON: I conceive of the educational system as an instrument of government that is used to obtain certain social objectives. The ones you are suggesting have been attained, or nearly so. But there are still huge areas of social and individual change, which the educational system is now turning to.

KIMBALL: I think this is excellent, but it doesn't necessarily eliminate the aggressiveness. All it does is open up new channels for constructive use.

CANNON: I am really shooting at your theory of congruence—of what is to be congruent with what.

LECHT: Along the same line, it seems to me that discussion of organizational systems leaves a lot of problems unresolved. Certainly, our kind of society is characterized by complex organizations: educational systems, corporations, universities, and government. The problem is not simply how individuals relate themselves to these organizational systems, but what impact these organizational systems have on individuals. How can individuals be educated to protect themselves or their personalities in a culture characterized by giant bureaucratic organizations?

KIMBALL: I have hesitated to try to state what the values of American society are, except as I attempted to formulate what I believe to be the emerging world view. It was my belief that such a statement would lead to a discussion of another order. It might be useful to say something about the Protestant ethic as an expression of values of an earlier age. The Protestant ethic did not encourage the accumulation of material goods merely for the comfort of mankind. It assumed that material welfare was a corollary of the spiritual, which was the ultimate goal. Part of its argument held that, if human beings could be provided with adequate food and housing and the drudgery required in their acquisition was reduced, then the human spirit could address itself more directly to the higher values associated with God.

American society, since the period when the Protestant ethic was dominant, has become secularized. Even though our view of spiritual welfare is no longer supported by supernatural sanctions, it seems to me that we have not lost this basic value, which now finds expression in humanitarian terms.

Whether our system or any other can make it possible for all people to develop their capabilities fully is another question. But, it seems to me, the policy that attempts to broaden the base by which larger numbers of people can realize their full potentialities is now widely accepted. Whether the document produced by President Eisenhower's Commission on National Goals should be taken as a final statement is arguable. But that commission, if you will remember, said that the goal of American society is the self-fulfillment of the individual, and such an objective is identical with the basic thesis of the Protestant ethic as stated earlier. It should be emphasized that self-fulfillment cannot emerge where there is poverty, ignorance, or oppression. The means and measures by which we eliminate these social wrongs need to be developed.

There is a difference between evaluating ethics and values and advocating them. I have tried, however, to be more analytical and less hortatory in my statements. My choice of the analytical statement does not deny that our system is far from perfect. But it does indicate my belief that our system has self-correcting mechanisms. We may be slow in putting remedial measures into operation through legislation and other means. But the point is, we seem to be doing it.

2

Attention to Social Detail
in an Economically Developed Society

FRED L. STRODTBECK

During the past thirty years, we have witnessed the increasingly widespread acceptance of Keynesian cash-flow economic theory. In the application of this theory, economists have made enormous gains in their ability to predict, guide, and control the direction and well-being of the economy. The theory, itself, holds that we are now sufficiently developed as an economy to use government spending to increase the cash flow within the economy and, thereby, to raise the level of consumption and reduce the level of unemployment. It is, of course, only because we have developed production capacity that we can expand the gross national product (GNP) without causing crippling inflation. Nevertheless, what was once a radical economic theory has now evolved into a working system; we now accept the theory that a careful attention to economic indicators will allow us to guide the economy and prevent disastrous swings and the dislocations consequent upon them.

The larger question this paper raises is whether we have a theory that will permit us to use social-process indicators for guidance in formulating a similar, radically new theory of social welfare. Is there any way that we can move from a sort of balance-sheet candor about the organization of social enterprises to a set of cumulative indicators that can be used to shape national policy? Is there some social process that can be stimulated as cash flow has been, which will have a comparable capacity to contribute to the social good? As I raise these questions, it is my intuitive feeling that we must approach the inquiry from the lowest level, that we must attend to the social details. It is as the role of pin factories in the wealth of nations: We must move from single family units toward concern with the health of nations.

To shift from the cash matrix of an economy to the noneconomic concerns of society is difficult because of the lack of consensus about measures. One of the characteristics of national economic policy-setting is that it is a roughly specifiable system which may be indexed by wholesale indexes, exports, tariff collections, stock prices, and so forth. There is a lot of redundantly interrelated information, all of which is reducible to a common denominator of economic relevance. It has only been through the compression of information, both practically and theoretically, that the system characteristics have been recognized, and, once recognized, it is an almost unique phenomenon that the economic policy of a nation is made by such a relatively small number of men who share the professional knowledge of the same discipline.

In social welfare, the problem will certainly be much more complicated. It is our guess that a society must first establish a stable government, then relative economic stability, before it is freed to turn, in the detail here contemplated, to the social welfare of the larger society. Since the first third of this century, particularly since the elaboration of the income tax and the public supervision of the sale of corporate stock, there has been full information concerning economic affairs. But, at the moment, we are just standing on the threshold of what might be done to check undesired social consequences. It will take courage to cultivate the consensus that would permit us to use modern technology to obtain and process information on selected social behavior. At the moment, the consensus about the degree to which all aspects of welfare are interrelated is increasing, but with macro-orientations there comes a kind of heroic pose. If our process is to work, it must be valid at the level of basic detail.

Let me offer an illustration of what I mean by attending to

social detail. In the Social Psychology Laboratory at the University of Chicago, we have taken great pains to maintain easy access to urban dependent families. One of our projects is a reading-readiness nursery for four-and-one-half-year-old children of female-based Negro families supported on Aid to Dependent Children (ADC). The illustration I have in mind involved a Negro mother whose child was in this nursery and was about to celebrate his fifth birthday. The mother wanted to make cupcakes to bring to the nursery. According to her report, she went so far as to buy the mix at the supermarket, but she could not find the cupcake liners. At this point, an information failure occurred. She had seen paper wrappers around cupcakes, but she didn't quite understand the rest of the technology. She did not conceptualize the cupcake containers as muffin-tin liners—she didn't own a muffin pan. Now, our question is: Why was she unwilling to ask the clerk where to find the liners and how to use them?

In her area, the tension between patrons, who know they are being overcharged, and store representatives, who know that pilferage is widespread, is high. This was a part of the background of the unasked question. Our experience suggests that, time and time again, the socially deprived person is prevented from asking for, and using, the help and resources of others because of fear of losing still more status by revealing his need. For this mother, a contemplated step toward meaningful participation in a social ritual with her child's teacher was in this way stopped. The nonperformance, in this instance, reduced the probability of further interaction, and it is our guess that, along with this reduction, the possibility of other positive effects was lost.

Conversation opportunities in which something really meaningful arises are rare; the chance of their occurring depends upon a running background of benign talk about parallel activities. It is almost that people talk best when they are in some degree looking the other way. The careful study of how interaction between people with different resources can best be sustained is an instance of attention to detail which, once the principles are established, must be carefully watched in thousands of contexts. Can you imagine a time when we check the "conversation index" in the same way we now check the cost of living index?

The one context in which we have shown some concern about the social-process consequences of a government program is in the field of low-cost, subsidized housing. Multistoried, homogeneous occupancy public housing represents a considered effort by urban communities to deal not only with housing but with some of the negative consequences of poverty. But in the "before and after" studies of the effects of public housing, in Baltimore, on a carefully chosen sample of 600 people moved from crowded tenements to public housing, the expected changes in social behavior did not materialize. Wilner's report states: "In general . . . it is not clear . . . that the change from bad to good housing has brought . . . distinguishable alteration in relations among persons within the family."[*] There was no greater freedom from illness, no difference in the rate of pregnancies, no improvement in the children's mean arithmetic and reading test scores. There was no change in concern for the larger community, no improvement in self-concept, and very little heightening of aspiration for the husband's job or the children's education. This study does report that the rehoused group liked the space they occupied better and their neighbors more—findings which, though positive, certainly fall below the community's expectations of what might be accomplished by improving housing at great public expense.

THE SOCIAL EFFECTS OF DENSITY

In view of the failure of public housing to produce any dramatic changes, it might appear doubly futile to turn more intensively toward considerations of interpersonal effects associated with population density for guidance in understanding the dependent poor. Nevertheless, I'm going to persist in this direction, because I believe that we are too reluctant to view man as a biological organism limited in the range of conditions to which he can adapt and stay healthy. We believe, quite correctly, that

[*] Daniel M. Wilner *et al.*, *Housing Environment and Family Life: A Longitudinal Study of the Effects of Housing on Morbidity and Mental Health* (Baltimore, Md.: The Johns Hopkins Press, 1962), p. 159.

man, with his culture, is able to adapt over a very wide spectrum of conditions. However, if we think of the range of conditions to which man can adapt as being codetermined by his social organization, it is then possible to believe that the conditions which will permit the forms of social organization desired are more limited than those which will support biological functioning.

One need not raise old issues involving the contrast between the "ideal farm existence" and the "evil city life"; nor does one have to think about travel in space. One can look very narrowly at the chronically dependent in our cities and ask whether their existence is the product of a competitive process we know only in land-value terms—not in social-value terms. Can one say that the middle class, as we know it, is dependent upon a lower-lower class that is defined as a contrast conception? A lower-lower class like our own is what one produces, according to Kluckhohn,* if the middle class of a society is future- and doing-oriented, individualistic, and holds a man-versus-nature outlook. In such a society, it is predicted that the lower class will be present- and being-oriented, collateral (or lineal), and subjugated to nature. Stimulated by such assertions, one is disposed to grant that the pattern of land use in the city indexes many social processes, and effects are not hard to conceptualize. It is sometimes difficult to place one's finger on the facts that cause one to conclude that system effects have produced a given result, but we are motivated to understand this better because, in the case of Keynesian theory, those conclusions which made sense for the nation would have ruined the corner grocery. So may it be in the area of *our* concerns.

For constructs with which to discuss competitive processes in systems, I wish to introduce the recent work of John Calhoun,† an animal-ethologist and psychologist. His work makes quite clear the generality of the Wynn-Edwards proposition that biological populations are not limited by food, but by the aversive social effects of density. For example, Calhoun demonstrated

* Florence R. Klockhohn and Fred L. Strodtbeck, *Variations in Value Orientation* (New York: Harper & Row, 1961).

† John B. Calhoun, *The Ecology and Sociology of the Norway Rat*. U.S. Department of Health, Education, and Welfare, Public Health Service Publication 1008 (Washington, D.C.: GPO, 1962).

that the progeny of 5 pregnant Norway rats with plenty of food and no pressure from predatory animals evolved a population that never exceeded 200 and stabilized at 150 per quarter-acre area. If the 10,000 square feet had been used for pens 2 feet apart, 5,000 rats could have been kept in health; in cages 8 inches square, 50,000 could have been maintained. The question is, why did the population level off at 150?

To answer this, Calhoun built pens open to observation through one-way glass windows. This arrangement permitted observers to have a complete view of the lighted pens at any time of the day or night without disturbing the rats. Each pen was a complete dwelling unit containing a food hopper, a drinking trough, places to nest (skyscraper-type burrows for observation), and nesting materials. Ramps over an electrified fence connected the pens, which were arranged four in a row. If they were equally divided, each pen could have accommodated a colony of twelve rats—under natural conditions, this is the maximum size a group of Norway rats attains before serious stress from crowding occurs.

To begin his studies, Calhoun placed one pregnant female in each of four pens and removed the ramps. He allowed the young to mature, then removed the mothers and replaced the ramps over the electrified grids. A balanced sex ratio was maintained by removing excess animals, and the first series began with thirty-two rats. After the ramps were replaced, all rats were allowed complete freedom to explore all four pens. From this point on, human intervention ceased except for the removal of surplus infants. Calhoun's strategy was to maintain a population in a stressful situation while three generations of rats were reared, so that he could study the effects of stress not only on individuals but on several generations.

In order to grasp Calhoun's idea, we need to begin with the moment the young rats are given their freedom and follow them in their development and behavior. In doing this, one is looking for contrasts with what their behavior would be if they lived in a normal, uncrowded state. Even in nature, there is a short period when the young, but physically mature, male rats fight with each other until they establish a fairly stable social hierarchy. Once this is established, the rats form into groups of ten to twelve hierarchically graded members and live in a common territory, which they defend. Each group is dominated by one mature male and is made up of varying proportions of both sexes. High-ranking rats do not have to defer to other rats as much as low-ranking rats. Their status is indicated, in part, by those areas within the territory which are open to them. The higher the status, the greater the number of areas they may visit.

Both male and female Norway rats participate in nest-building, but the female does most of the work. Nesting material is carried into the burrow, piled up, and hollowed out to form a cavity to hold the young. Normally, females work hard to keep litters sorted out and if a strange rat pup were introduced into the nest, the female would remove it. If a nest were uncovered, the young would be moved to a new location that was more protected.

Courting and sex among Norway rats normally involve a fixed sequence of events. The male rat has to be able to make three basic distinctions in the selection of a mate. First, he has to make the usual male-female distinction and, at the same time, differentiate between mature and immature females. Then, he must find a female in a receptive (oestrous) state. When this combination appears within his visual and olfactory field, the male rat chases the female. She runs, but not too fast, and ducks down into the burrow, turns around, and sticks her head up to watch the male. He runs around the opening of the burrow and performs a little dance. When the dance is over, the female leaves the burrow and mounting takes place. During the sex act, the male will grasp the skin on the female's neck gently between his teeth.

In Calhoun's rat pens, as in our great cities, some came to live with ample room and others were crowded into undesirable areas. Strong males accumulated a harem at either end of the four-pen area, and population built up in the middle area; along with this build-up came very gross distortions of behavior. For example, dominant male rats in the dense area were unable to establish permanent territories. Each subgroup was dominated by a single male and, within the group, these males were equal to each other in rank. But unlike normal hierarchies, which are extraordinarily stable in nature, social rank in the dense area subgroups was very unstable. Three times daily there was a tempestuous "changing of the guard" around the eating bins, which involved fighting and scuffling. In addition, at regular intervals during the course of their waking hours, the top-ranking males within subgroups engaged in free-for-alls that frequently culminated in the transfer of dominance from one male to another. This social churning produced broad social effects.

Mothers were no longer good housekeepers. They could be seen carrying a piece of nesting material up a ramp and suddenly dropping it. Material that reached the nest was either dropped in the general area or added to a pile that was never hollowed out, so that the young became scattered at birth and few survived. Litters became mixed; the young were stepped on and often eaten by hyperactive males who invaded the nests. When a nest was exposed, the mother would start moving the young but would fail to complete some phase of the move. Young carried outside to another nest were often dropped and eaten by other rats.

Even the routines of sexual behavior were severely disrupted in the crowded areas. The hyperactive subordinate males spent their time chasing females. Three or four might tail one harassed female at the same time. During the pursuit phase, they would fail to observe the amenities; instead of stopping at the burrow entrance, they would follow the female inside so that she had no respite. During mounting, these male rats frequently maintained their grasp on females for several minutes instead of the usual two or three seconds. There were also pansexual males who tried mounting anything: receptive and nonreceptive females, males and females alike, young and old. Any sex partner would do.

Some males withdrew from social and sexual intercourse and went abroad chiefly at the time when other rats slept. The passive males avoided both fighting and sex. Only the aggressively dominant males, and there were only three of these in the dense area, exhibited normal sexual behavior.

As Calhoun watched his population through time, he noted that, within the dense group, the rats formed into classes with shared territories and similar behavior. A further increase in density led to an increase in the number of classes and subclasses and, in the final stages, there was a class of hyperactive males that ran about in packs—pushing, probing, exploring, and testing. Not only did these rats invade the burrow when chasing females but they violated other territorial mores.

As one reads Calhoun, there is an Orwellian echo of delinquent gangs in the city. The thought is not that human life is like an "animal farm"—as Orwell might have had us believe—but, rather, that there is a degree of psychological vulnerability which, when exceeded, brings in its wake animal-like behavior, perhaps even among humans. What one can't do is to ask Calhoun's rats where they place the blame. To discover the rhetoric of motive, one must turn to human informants living under circumstances that approximate the threshold where something like "pansexual and sadistic" accommodation to the competition for desirable space in the city occurs.

THREAT IN THE SLUMS

Without elaborate development, I state categorically that there is a widespread sense of threat in slum life. There is symbolic meaning in the triple locks Chicago's Negro slum-dwellers place on their doors. I quote recorded selections spontaneously offered during child-rearing interviews:

Concerning rape. "We had that two times since I've been in the building, but that's in the back apartment where you can see the husband—or whatever man is sleeping in—leave. The first time, the man came on the first floor. He came through her kitchen window and he had a knife against her child and told her if she said anything he was going to kill her and so he tried to do it to the mama and she screamed and he went to get the child and that's when she got to the door. When she got to the door she left him in there with her child and that's the part I wouldn't have done. He'd just have had to kill me. She got the husband of the girl across the hall to go down there and get that man out of her house. So when they got down there, he was gone.

Concerning transiency. "As soon as someone moves out, someone else moves in. Before you can get acquainted with them, they're moved out. They don't be there long enough for you to know their names. All the old tenants from when I moves in there are gone."

Concerning fear of disaster. "Because so much fires breaking out, I don't want to leave the children. It's hard to get somebody to keep them: it's dangerous to leave them by themselves. So that means I don't hardly get a chance to go nowhere. I'm scared to leave them at the house by themselves because so much fire breaking out. I just sit at the house all day long with the children. I just never go nowhere. I suspect that when I get around people I get nauseated, just nauseated. I just can't stand a crowd of people. I would like to go back to school, but my nerves are too bad. I don't think I could take it. If I was there, my mind would be right back at home with my girl, she's a young lady now, and I'd be afraid to leave her in the house by herself."

The uneasy strategy that emerges is one of not getting too involved. One ADC mother stated it very reflectively: "I just visit a few people. If the group gets too big, there's confusion. Now I have coffee every couple mornings with just two. I used to be guilty of visiting around out of loneliness and lack of self-control. You need people around to do favors and fight loneliness." The general view is that if you are too close to people, you can become overwhelmed by demands they might make in times of great need. A child can be taken care of while a friend comes in for a nap, but more complicated actions relating to guards or signal systems at the door seem bafflingly difficult to arrange.

The strategy concerns are not geared to positive ends but, rather, to reducing threats from neighbors. For example, a mother says: "When I go to the store I tell the children, don't open that door for Jesus. And they won't, 'cause I know my worker came and he wouldn't let her in and she said but I'm Mrs. X and he said I'm sorry, but you can wait outside and she'll be back, and sure enough, I came in before she left the building and she said he wouldn't let her in and I said if he lets you in he might let someone else in. I told him don't open that door for Jesus. You know what that means. He's a spirit and that's the only thing that can go through. Anybody can say I'm the case-worker."

This distrust of others prevents a spontaneous growth of ways of coping that is based on cooperation with others. The reactions of these mothers to participating in a cooperative-living project offers an illustration of this point. This hypothetical project would have involved private apartments for the mothers and their small children and dormitories for the older children. A common kitchen was suggested to reduce the labor of food preparation. The mothers' reactions to this plan were unremittingly negative. Of nine mothers given a standard interview on this possibility, all rejected the idea of a common kitchen. They didn't trust others; they were concerned about the stealing of food, and the possibility that some people would fail to carry their share of the responsibilities was, for them, a near certainty. Seven of the nine rejected having their older children sleep away from them on the grounds that they would learn bad practices from others and this would lead to fights between the parents, and that it would require excessive supervision. Even the two mothers who did not object on the basis of anticipated impulse-control problems were still not favorable. One mother felt that it might not be sanitary and the other thought the children might not like it.

THE DOMESTIC VIEW OF ADC MOTHERS

It is my observation that the mothers' philosophies of the good and bad in their lives turns quite narrowly upon the situation within their own homes. I will illustrate this by reading the comments obtained when one mother was asked to listen to the recorded comments of other ADC mothers. After listening, the mother commented without interruption, but with encouraging nods and agreements from the interviewer.

You know . . . I think the trouble with the failure of our marriages nowadays is we go into it for the wrong reasons. Very few marriages are for love. Most of them are for convenience, for escape from the home . . . you know, feelin' grown-up too quick or just the *idea* of wantin' to be married for itself. People indulge in too many marriages for convenience—I don't mean just financial—I mean just like I say, to get away from home. Some of them marry to stop loneliness. Well, all these . . . marriage is not the answer to all these things and naturally, like I say, the average person, they're not gonna find it. I think it's truer more in men than in women, though. I know I'm prejudiced about this so I don't know if this is a good answer or not, but I *know* I'm prejudiced where men are concerned. I don't think men have the stayin' power nowadays that they once had. They have no tolerance and now they have no feelin' . . . they don't have the same feelin' of responsibility that our fathers had. I *know* this to be a fact because one thing, the way our society is set up, it doesn't teach them any responsibility and that's one of the major disapprovals I have of Aid [Aid to Dependent Children]—that it's really robbin' our men of any sense of responsibility at all. Why should they stay with the family and support it when they can sneak around and enjoy the family and have none of the responsibility for it. Aid is really killin' the family life in our society now. I don't know—I guess everybody else knows that, too, but it's really a very, very bad thing in that way. It's really very bad for our family life. I mean, 'specially in our race—I don't know about the other races, I can't speak for them—but, in our race and the society and the circles I travel in, it's killin' any chance for a marriage. Why should a man stay and support a family when he don't have to—when he can sneak around, you see—and the women are discouraged and not so much they immoral or anything, but it's a problem they don't *know* what to do about. It's a problem of our kind.

Then another evil of our society, most of our children—a *lot* of our children—are raised in broken homes and children (I notice about my girls) they play house; look at children when they play—they play just like they live. When I was a little girl, we had to have a father to play house. The little girls in our buildin' don't and they have those little purses and high heels and they say, "loan me some money until I get my check." You see what I mean? They play the way they see you live. And it's sad that we don't recognize it. The man in the home is not exactly satisfactory. It's far superior to none in the home, I'll tell you that, because it's like bein' in a whirlpool—it just takes you. I know my life is like that. I keep makin' high standards for myself. I try to live up so hard as I can, but every now 'n then you find yourself bein' pulled down. Children seein' these different people trampin' in and out of the home, you know, and then the girl, right away, she doesn't give her marriage too much of a chance because mama didn't have a husband. So, as soon as she can get rid of hers, if he gives her too much trouble, she'll do it, and the same with the boy. Daddy didn't take care of him, so why don't he run around and enjoy hisself and just . . . well, I got a child on *this* street and I got a child on *that* street—seem to be the trend of our times. It would be good if we could get away from it and back to family life.

Now, my Geraldine's father—his job moved out of town and he

just hasn't been able to do any good for hisself. They had us in court and they went for him and threatened to arrest him and everything. Well, he started to—it was so hard for him—so he didn't show up for his last court date; that was way before she was two years old. I didn't care. I *really* didn't care, because it was so unfair, you know. The judge said, "I have had a parapalegic [*sic*]—whatever it is that's paralyzed that they call a paralyzed person—that come to the city and *he* found a job." Well, naturally, probably somebody helped him. I know for a fact he [the child's father] paid people when he got his little service pay from the army. He paid people who carried him out on the dock. He took three civil service examinations—he didn't pass; he tried to get on at the stores downtown. These are things I know and he did get on at Goldblatt's for a little while and they were paying him less than $50 a week for six days and I didn't report it 'cause what could he give? He had his own expenses—you know? I just heard from some of his people, 'cause he just got discouraged and, you know, every now and then he'd send her [the child] something or send a message to her or ketch her on the street and see her, but I don't see him much now—it's just strictly a financial and a thing like that because he's fifty-two, I think. Well, a man that age—it's sometimes not even worth it for him to fill out an application, and from what I can hear from his people, he's still tryin' to find employment. So you see how they work against family life. The case-worker asked me once why we wouldn't get married. That's the reason.

This mother's comment is quietly eloquent, it is easy to understand, it is easy to agree that something is wrong, and it may be as she says—the men just do not have enough staying power. On the other hand, if the Wynn-Edwards thesis is correct, her theory would give no guidance as to the type of social intervention which would be maximally effective in restoring human dignity. This mother is obviously observing the scene from the vantage point of one who is familiar with a more ordered life. Let me quote another mother who demanded less. It is as if she had been able to move back from the scene, to talk about it as if it were a kind of dream.

I've been on ADC for six, seven, sixteen years. . . . I would sneak out and do a little work, and I'm not—I wasn't supposed to and they punished me for it once. But . . . it was just impossible to make out on what they had, and I was so nervous. Oh, I was so nervous, I shaked and trembled, and my heart it just . . . I just stayed out of breath. Oh I was. . . . Oh, I was like that for years. I'm still like that, but . . . and that was one thing that worried me. I have never, never been able to relax and I couldn't dress my children up in a complete outfit. And, oh, it just hurt me that I wanted to see them with all new clothes on, even. . . . I didn't like cheap things. To me those old two-dollar dresses or a dollar dress, I just hated them; I couldn't stand to see them with a dress on like that. I always want to see them with five- or six-dollar dresses on. And sometimes I managed to get a dress and a pair of shoes and it was, I mean, then I would be so tired, I mean just about ready to drop. And I *was!* I was real, real sick for a long time. No, I never could manage on that. It seems, like I was saying, I had those hangers-on, and it's a funny thing, they come around and they want to socialize when I got . . . when I have. . . . They keep up when you get those checks. Oh my, oh no, they really kept up with it. And so I didn't realize it, but I . . . so I'm a little "feeble-ated." They come, they grab you: "Buy me a drink!" I don't drink. I never asked them to buy me one. They just try to take it—take my money, and I. . . . That was when I tried to find out who . . . who lived in the neighborhood. And so a lot of people accused me of only socializin' with bums. And a lot of those fellows are very weak and they did get drunk. They were chasin' balls all the time. But after I got to know them, I got. . . . They noticed how I could keep off of that liquor. It never interested me. I don't know. Now one of my children's fathers just died at thirty-eight. His alcohol really killed him, 'cause he had been told to stay off of it, but he wouldn't. And he, . . . But, now, he was a man—he didn't know how to manage his business, and he . . . I'd try to help him and I'd give him some of my money, but he got . . . but he took the whole bill, and we suffered terrible for a while. When my daughter was graduatin' from high school, he took all my gas money and went off and squandered it. And he . . . I don't know. But he was a person. He wanted to come back. Wanted for me to come back—to clean up my house. He knew I had a problem keeping my house clean and he come by and clean up the whole house, mop it and everything. And . . . I don't know if. . . . He knows. . . . Among some of those fellows, they feel that if they come in and clean up your house you should pay him for it. So, but he. . . . We had talked. We was talking about goin' back together, but I think he was kind of confused. Because I know he was, 'cause he was . . . socializin' with a lot of people, and these people would. . . . They were drinkin' once. And I heard that when he took that $22 that I gave him to pay my gas bill, he went and gave another woman some. But yet she wouldn't . . . she wouldn't help none like I did.

THE INTERACTION OF DOMESTIC WORLD-VIEW AND EXTERNAL THREAT

Is the larger society, in its role as its brother's keeper, performing like Mr. Calhoun with his animal populations? Are we providing food and shelter, but giving no thought to details? Is there encouragement for the type of social organization which multiplies the strength of one individual by giving him access to the adaptive information distributed among the network of other persons in the group?

This is of crucial importance to education, because the most profound insight we have into the recurrence of the syndrome of poverty and low educability is through the linkage of the Negro mother's fearful world views and her actions to socialize her children. She weans her children later, but more abruptly; she starts bowel-training later, but takes less time than the white middle- and lower-class mothers studied by Sears, Maccoby, and Levin.* Her children are more frequently enuretic and continue to be so at later ages. The Negro ADC mother is less responsive to crying and less punitive toward dependency. She exerts strong pressure against masturbation and sex play and is strict in modesty-training. She is not permissive of aggression toward parents and siblings and she places more restrictions upon physical mobility. Although she expects less of the children in terms of performance of household tasks, she is stricter about obedience.

The ADC mother's training techniques include more physical punishment and little use of praise, positive models, and reasoning. Isolation and withdrawal of privileges are rare. She rewards and punishes her children immediately and her children are rarely required to delay gratification. The failure to discipline in terms of language symbols as well as the related dependence upon physical means of punishment reduces the necessity for cognitive

* R. Sears, E. Maccoby, and H. Levin, *Patterns of Child Rearing* (Evanston, Ill.: Row, Peterson, 1957).

mediation in impulse control. The child gets much less assistance in discovering the relationship between his behavior and the responses it is likely to elicit.

Much of the Negro ADC mother's energies go into admonishing the child to "be good" instead of rewarding and punishing for acts freely entered into. In the context of an overcrowded living space, being good means being physically inactive and verbally nonparticipative and nonobservant. It is not that the achievements of the child are negatively viewed; rather, it is the trouble achievement activity may lead to that is so consistently avoided. A mother who is extremely vulnerable to serious and unpredictable threat teaches her children—above all else—to be generally fearful rather than selectively cautious. In the unspecific admonishment to be good, there is a threat to the educability of the child.

THE ORGANIZATIONAL LINK

The stable lower class in our society have just enough resources to meet the minimum spectrum of social expectations. To do this, they must expend all of their resources. They are able to do so because, behind their own nuclear family, there is a reserve set of social relationships. Muir and Weinstein* describe the behavior of the lower-class person as he attempts to evolve a way of life that will reduce his insecurity and enhance his power by means that do not depend on achievement in the universalistic sector or on command of a rich and sophisticated variety of perspectives. He does this by forging a network of relationships with people similarly circumstanced, which is in some ways like a mutual insurance scheme. People linked by such a network provide one another with a sense of status and worth and, also, with aid and support in time of need. Such a network differs from a conventional insurance scheme in that the kinds of benefits to which one is entitled are not specified in advance, but consist broadly of help in time of trouble and of doing whatever one can when another is in need.

* D. E. Muir and E. A. Weinstein, "The Social Debt: An Investigation of Lower Class and Middle Class Norms of Social Obligation," *American Sociological Review*, XXVII, 1962, 532–39.

If such an individual has a sufficiently extensive network of such obligations and has honored obligations in the past, there is probably someone he can turn to, if ever he should need help, until he is "back on his feet." Title to these benefits is not tied to incumbency of specific roles, approaches through prescribed channels, or conformity to legalistic requirements. On the contrary, the relationships are valued precisely because they are not hedged about by such conditions, they are diffuse, reciprocal, durable, and particularistic.*

In contrast with lower-class persons, the dependent poor in the great cities do *not* have this security network and suffer the even greater deprivation of being fearful of their neighbors.

There was once a tendency to act as if the courts were equally available to all in our society. We now understand that use of the courts implies sophistication and the resources to be litigious. The proper use of the power of redress through the courts requires some segment of the society to seek out clients and encourage them to use their prerogatives. With regard to fearfulness and to the effects of social isolation, those who suffer most from them are the least able to make known their needs. By partitioning family life from school life and job life, we have made it progressively more difficult to get a complete picture of how an individual is functioning before a crisis has occurred. Our slums have many people whose primary lifetime accomplishment is keeping out of trouble.

The argument of this paper is that there could be specialists, with responsibilities for particular areas, who would circulate to increase the interaction between clients and service institutions and among the service institutions themselves. Instead of sending home report cards, schools might initiate a program of exchanging information with parents. If schoolwork improved, parents might be asked if they noticed anything at home that could account for the improvement. Wouldn't that be a switch on the present state of offenses? Whatever stressful school interclass rituals, like proms, were coming up, parents could be gotten together at school, with their children, to try to reduce the stress. The most likely location of every out-of-school adolescent in a

* *Ibid.,* p. 538.

community could be determined from relatively simple contacts in peer-association sites. With better assessment, communities that now know the per cent of their steel-making capacity may some day know the percentage of the capacity of their adolescents they realize. And, when this comes to pass, then every man in the community can begin to play the game of speculating about what might be done to raise the percentage. Community policy could then be directed toward those characteristics of social process that are analogous to cash-flow—the meaningful transactions between people of different classes, who are related in a stable organization, for the purpose of achieving common objectives. Men will then have to begin to collect and tabulate information that they do not now know about, information they may consider to be as much a private matter as we once did income. The good teacher, who now masterfully manages the atmosphere of his classroom, will then have to accept a criterion of good education based not on what's done in the classroom but, rather, on what's done, and not done, in the community. In this process, segments of the large high school and junior college, so well suited to upper-lower- and middle-class needs, will have to be reshaped into continuing education programs in the community centers of depressed areas. To the degree that education can be considered to be expanded because there exists easy access to someone who knows, continuing education should have, as an explicit goal, community reassurance that every undereducated person has at least two opportunities a week to interact in a small group with a college-trained person—a person able to answer some questions that fall outside the assignment. With appropriate attention to the detail of social auditing, the negative effects of slums are as preventable as the negative effects of bank failures.

DISCUSSION

BEASLEY [presiding]: We are ready for questions and comments.

LLOYD: It seems to me, Mr. Strodtbeck, your paper delineated several psychic patterns rather than a simple psychic pattern. In the Kimball paper, I felt we were given a portrait of middle-class America—which is numerically, of course, the largest social class. Your paper presented patterns, or a pluralistic portrait, rather than a one-dimensional portrait. Am I right about this?

STRODTBECK: Yes; certainly, there is a way of looking at life that is sufficiently different from the middle-class orientation to make it possible that middle-class persons will understand the motivation of the lower-lower-class person.

BUSHNELL: Earlier, you and I had a chance to talk a little about the experience of the West-Coast Japanese relocated during World War II. They were exposed to arduous conditions of confinement, immense deprivation, and considerable crowding at relocation centers. Would you care to comment on their ability to respond and survive under those conditions and on what happened to them after the war? Evidently, they were able to take advantage of educational opportunities and have continued to do so. The children continued to have a low delinquency rate and became quite stable members of the community after release from the centers.

STRODTBECK: Yes. The situation involving the Japanese-Americans is quite interesting. If we take a two-dimensional perspective and plot the age at which certain child behaviors are expected against the amount of n Achievement* present, we find that the earlier the age of the expectations, the higher the n Achievement. The behaviors in question were making one's own friends, finding one's way about the community, and so forth. The earlier the parental expectation of mastery, the higher the n Achieve-

---

* The phrase is taken from H. A. Murray, *Explorations in Personality* (New York: Oxford University Press, 1938) and means "need to achieve."

69

ment of the child. The average age of mastery of these behaviors is about six for Presbyterians and Jews, and their *n* Achievement on an arbitrary scale is around 3.6. It is just beyond eight years for Italian-Americans, and their *n* Achievement goes down to approximately 3.2. The age of mastery is about ten years for Japanese-Americans, and it is at this point that there is a delicate tension in theory. As Mr. Bushnell has indicated, the adaptations of the Japanese-Americans have been remarkable. Yet, will their *n* Achievement be low, as predicted by the child training theory? And, if so, what implications does this have for McClelland's thesis,* which relates early child rearing and the inculcation of *n* Achievement?

Well, in fact, it is lower. The Japanese-American *n* Achievement scores are clearly lower than those of Italian-Americans. In the face of these low scores, one seeks other reasons for their adaptiveness. One asks: "What is the role of social organization in the adaptations they have made?" Our inquiries have indicated that one of the things that took place during the relocations was that, contrary to government policy, the Japanese settled largely in Chicago. The second largest number were clustered in New York City. Once there, remarkably enough, the traditional lines of deference to older persons were brought into being to the degree necessary to provide the resources for reorganization. Their adaptation reveals a hidden element in the patterns of reciprocity in Japanese society that is sometimes not well understood. We all know that it is the responsibility of these children to take care of their parents, but I think that we are less acquainted with the fact that it is the responsibility of their parents to relinquish control, or resources, for a system of this sort to work. In fact, those people who have made detailed studies of the Japanese-American adaptations after relocation have found that younger persons did, however politely, take the reins of control. Thus, it was assured that an intact community organization could be asked to provide the resources for the highly remarkable adaptations which took place. Without re-

* David A. McClelland, *The Achieving Society* (Princeton, N.J.: D. Van Nostrand, 1961).

location, Japanese-American community organization might have continued to weaken as acculturation continued, in the way that it has developed for most ethnic groups in this century.

I might add—since we are talking about these camps—that experiences in them do support my contentions about density. In the crowded living conditions of the relocation camps, there were sharp and fierce riots at times, comparable to the response of almost any human population under the pressure of great population density.

FOLGER: You made a substantial point of the density part of the problem. But, when you left the rats and began talking about people, this turned out to be mostly a question of whether they had an adequate network of interpersonal relationships. In the Lower East Side of New York City, where there has been about the same level of density for nearly a hundred years—or, if not that far back, for a long time—such limited indices as we have indicate that a great deal more social disorganization exists there today than at the turn of the century. The common explanation is that this is part of an ethnic succession from a Jewish slum to a Negro and Puerto Rican slum, although there are still some Jews in the area. So I wonder, how important is density alone as an explanation?

STRODTBECK: Mr. Folger has called attention to an aspect of my presentation which I think was patently confusing. I was not talking about physical density per se. Let me cite some other examples. Around the periphery of Santiago, there is a slum area called the Callampa. If you visit there, you can see the women standing out at the bateas, washing and talking. You ask them, "When you leave your house, what precautions do you have to take?" People who have lived in the area more than four years, in most cases, express no concern about the violation of their property rights when they are away.

In the *favelas* in Rio, you can walk through a large slum, right by the football field, where the houses are so close together that your shoulders brush them on either side of the path. Small dwellings not much larger than a chicken coop sometimes contain two families. There again you may ask, "How long have you lived here?" The individuals living in the central portions—who now have access to the networks whereby one family gets an electric meter and then sells the prerogative of using one bulb in another house—say they have been there sixteen or eighteen years. I think there are approximately 15,000 people in this particular *favela*, and there are more than 500 little grocery stores that carry people on credit. Living more than ten years in a community, even under very harsh conditions, brings about a very great reduction in the sense of threat.

More than that, I know of no social welfare legislation in these Latin countries that says you cannot have more than two generations living in the same house. There is no disposition to shear off the kinship network as we do, particularly with Negroes in our urban slums. And I will make the assertion, until someone corrects me with a better example, that no people, at any time, have ever lived with as much shearing off of the support to be derived from kinship as do urban Negroes at the present time.

So, with these examples, it becomes obvious that I am not talking about—and there is a sense in which even the animal ecologists are not talking about—physical density per se.

Ross: Many of these women, the ADC Negro mothers, are from the South. I think, in southern rural or small town areas, the density is not so great and the kinship structures are maintained to a greater extent. The element of fear is still very great, and the major rule the mother teaches the children is to stay out of trouble—that is, to be passive, unaggressive, unobservant, and so forth. Isn't there a background of that, under circumstances that are rather different, in the northern ghettos?

Strodtbeck: Mr. Ross is, essentially, asking, "If the situation is as you observe it to be, Mr. Strodtbeck, couldn't it be so because the mode of adaptation developed in the South has been carried over to slum-living in the North?"

Ross: Of course, in the North, I think there is more fear of other Negroes; in the South, the fear is of whites. But, certainly from what I know of southern Negro families, there is still the same emphasis on instructing the young to stay out of trouble.

Strodtbeck: Yes. And I think that your own phrasing catches it very nicely. In one situation, you had an enemy who could be identified by his white skin. In the northern cities, there are two enemies, and fearfulness of one's own neighbor is an accentuating characteristic.

BEASLEY: I wonder if you would elaborate on your suggestion about specialists. How can one increase effective interaction between people in these circumstances? Is it the job of the social agencies, of the schools—or do you see it as being necessary to institutionalize selected families?

STRODTBECK: Some of you may have encountered the book I did with Jim Short last summer.* The information for this volume was obtained through the cooperation of the YMCA in Chicago. The YMCA agreed to assign twelve or fifteen detached workers in the city at places that suited the requirements of our investigation. We had the opportunity to interview the detached workers for several hours every two weeks. In addition, we gave extensive personality tests to 600 boys and watched a sample of more than 400 boys over a three-year period.

In the process of this investigation, we actually saw the role of detached worker emerge and become defined and established in the larger cities. I have recently been on a consultation visit to Monterey, California, where school officials are very much concerned about the excessively high dropout rate in that salubrious and romantic county. Obviously, the kind of contact with their community that these schools need will require people who are not so shaped by professional expectations as to be impeded from relating to nonschool adolescents. Such people need to be free to go out in the community and find where the students are and what they are doing. This means that the educational systems will have to shake off their intramural bias and recognize that new kinds of people have a legitimate role to play in educational service. The middle-class women who now do most of our teaching are, by occupation and identity, precluded from circulating in ways that are necessary. Their service should be supplemented by the employment of people who can. It certainly would seem to me that, if one kept the full spectrum view of the responsibilities of a modern junior high school in mind, 12 to 15 per cent of its personnel would be engaged in community organizations

* *Group Process and Gang Delinquency* (Chicago: University of Chicago Press, 1965).

and detached work—not as a new service but simply to enhance the effectiveness of what now is supposed to go on "within the walls."

TAYLOR: Was the YMCA's detached worker identified with the institution, or was he more of a free agent within the community who tended to identify with his clientele? I am wondering about his problems in establishing rapport.

STRODTBECK: The largest problem in the management of detached work is to extend a sense of organizational efficacy to the detached worker, to support him on his detailed assignments. Any person who is called upon to work in the evenings and on holidays and late at night, when respectable people of the community are with their families, needs to have very, very special kinds of support. It takes a new kind of man. Detached workers were not good if they had been trained as teachers, but they were impossible if they had been trained as social workers.

CANNON: This is the point, really. In the near future, there will be published a study showing a shortage of 12,000 social workers. This is going to generate tremendous pressure to get a big social-worker bill up and passed. Are you arguing that the detached worker would be much more cost-effective than the traditional social worker?

STRODTBECK: I may not fully understand your term "cost-effective," but I think I agree.

DAVID: I wonder if it is fair to recast your arguments in an economist's terms and say what you are really pointing out to us is that we have to invest in a communication-information network, just as we would invest in physical capital machinery, and that we want indices of what this network is doing for us, just as we have productivity indices of labor and capital?

STRODTBECK: Exactly.

FOLGER: The turnover rate in schools in these neighborhoods is very high. It may run from 200 to 300 per cent per year. How does one establish *any* kind of network with all this mobility?

STRODTBECK: Well, you will find, if you examine the turnover statistics, that while people move far enough to change the elementary school they attend, they really don't get out of the slums. It would mean, I think, a program of busing those children who get dislocated during a particular year, so that they can complete that year with their classmates.

We have a program in which we take twelve children and operate with them, for thirteen weeks, in our nursery to see what contribution we can make to the improvement of their school adaptability. We find that, in thirteen weeks, perhaps two or three of these children will move outside the convenient route of the bus that picks them up. I think that a proper study of small-scale mobility would lead to a recognition of the contribution of classroom stability to educational advancement. If one decided to get those children who have moved back into the classroom with the same teacher, a number of inexpensive devices would help. Each teacher could have a phone in her classroom, so that the mother could call and tell her when she is going to move. It's now usually a couple of weeks after such moves before you can locate the family. There are other, similar kinds of practical investments in information flow, which I think would make unanticipated contributions to reducing the sense of threat.

DANIEL: Is the roving-leader idea part of what you are advocating? I know of a situation where the workers—young men— have the title "roving leader." They are on a project that is related to the schools, but they are not schoolteachers. Some are college graduates who, by personality or by inclination, seem to relate well to boys. They themselves are moving about, getting into gangs, learning the gang structure, and so on.

STRODTBECK: Yes, that is the kind of position I'm alluding to, but it is not the exact description of the situation in Chicago. In Chicago, the coordination of the detached worker and the school is not close. One might suggest that all education students, between their third and fourth years, should spend at least three months in an apprenticeship relationship to other social-service agencies in urban communities. The degree to which their own sense of efficacy within the school systems would be enhanced by their greater knowledge of the operation of other formal bureaucracies in the city would justify this. If this is done, teachers will have to be taught how to relate to detached workers. This will enhance the teacher's own sense of potency. If the teacher knows that a detached worker is going to walk through the school once each day and that she can stop him at the classroom door and say, "Look, such and such is happening here. What's going on in that area?," she will be better equipped to do a professional job.

Ordinarily, the detached workers in the large cities are given station wagons. The agency pays half of the cost; the worker pays half. The workers are paid $8,000 to $9,000 a year and operate $3,000 to $4,000 station wagons. They then must be brought into very frequent contact with potential employers of large numbers of workers in the community and with people who have their fingers on sources of power. The way in which they can translate the perspective of people who need the employment services to those who have the resources is a further instance in which detached workers create a channel of communication where none existed before.

They don't believe that they are going to "psyche out" the neurotic problems in any boy. What they are going to do is done largely by being available. It stops intergang fighting very quickly. With a little organization, you can, by giving $10 a month to a boy, cause him to be one of your agents in an area; so that, with a relatively small expenditure of money, a detached worker can maintain a much wider network of contacts. Whenever any boy is "going wrong" in an obvious way—such as brandishing a gun—he can be identified and contacted within a few hours. When you find a boy in a stolen car, you get him out of the car and the car back to the police. In this way you prevent the stigma that being apprehended for the theft would otherwise cause—a stigma which would complicate your subsequent work with the boy in question.

The police are extremely appreciative of the flow of firearms that the detached workers bring into them. This is a kind of symbiotic relationship built upon something that most people do not understand. Police, in most urban areas, have been in those areas for periods of from five to twenty years. If given a little greater social-psychiatric insight into their potential use, they are potentially important for a community. The way in which detached personnel and police who work in the same areas can be taught to cooperate with educational objectives of all schools is an unexplored frontier in urban America.

KIMBALL: I wonder if you have any comments on the nature of the differences between what you are describing to us and their consequences, and those of the operations of Saul Alinsky.

STRODTBECK: Well, Saul Alinsky would hold that there is no person who could be a spokesman, as I am, for the greater exchange of information who would still be able to make that message heard clearly. Therefore, he really believes that protest—rubbing raw the sores of discontent—is the way to do the job. And, you know, if I were playing "Big Brother" to society, I'd put a little money in his pot—but a little more in mine. I think that both methods probably are going to be required. I would hope that one of the accomplishments that might come from this symposium is a heightened awareness of the social importance of information exchange, to the point where it can become a positive objective recognized by that segment of our society that controls the resources for bringing it about. So, far from wanting to quash protests, I want to beat the protesters at their own game with another technique.

KIMBALL: Is there another element here in which there is really great similarity, or at least a tangential similarity, between what you are talking about and what Alinsky is doing? At least as I read about it, he is saying that only through participation—by which he means heightening the intensity of interaction—can you build the kind of strength that will give you the capability to meet problems.

STRODTBECK: My study of the people in Woodlawn who have had an opportunity to be exposed to Mr. Alinsky's program convinces me that those who can gain from participation in his program are the relatively more privileged. My concern in Woodlawn is for persons who are less visible and less accessible. Some of these, for example, are the vegetative, passive women who sit on the edge of the bed with little children climbing around them, as if they were the old lady who lived in a shoe. Many of these children, whose mothers have exempted themselves from a Negro identity, still do not come to the nursery ill-fitted for early training. The interaction with their peers has prepared them for many of the early experiences of education. But, they are very poorly fitted at a later time. My concern is for the kinds of domestic organizations which will, in some way, get this woman up off the side of her bed. She doesn't pay any more attention to Alinsky than to astronauts. Both are beyond her sphere of concern at this time.

TAYLOR: Let me return, for a moment, to our earlier discussion. It seems to me one of the critical points here, in the detached worker's role, is the degree to which he can establish rapport, gain trust, and be accepted by this group. The discussion of Alinsky leads me to ask what kind of institutional affiliation you would suggest for the detached worker? Can he be attached to the schools? What insights, in terms of background and preparation, do you suggest so that he can achieve the kind of rapport necessary if he is to effectively perform this role?

STRODTBECK: When you want to relate to a Negro gang in Chicago, you go and stand on the corner. They ask you if you want a woman. You indicate to them that you don't. Then they check on interest in a homosexual contact. If you decline, they suggest dope. And if you are not interested in dope, they begin to really wonder what in hell you are there for.

TAYLOR: Then one approach is to arouse their curiosity.

STRODTBECK: That's right. They provide the opportunity for a mutual movement over the threshold of personal threat. One quickly finds out how starved for attention these boys are. That is the secret of the contact. Many of the people who would do very well as detached workers would find it a little difficult, at this time, to circulate in and out of good junior high schools. I think their position will have to be reinforced by periodic meetings with the school superintendent and the board, and regular contact with a few other people. The degree to which the legitimation of their activity must be taken out of the certification mold of the state requires a positive conception of how they will expose themselves to review and guidance. If you were to ask me, "Who is the specialist whose services you first need to facilitate the utilization of detached workers in connection with education?," I would respond: "A person who understands administrative law; someone who would take your school codes and draft the necessary provisions for incorporating people whose training is atypical in this closely guarded prerogative of contact with the young."

KLEIN: Your point about the need these groups feel for recognition is so essential. In five years of working in Harlem and in the southeast section of the Bronx, in schools servicing this population, I found that all they were looking for was someone to listen and to recognize that they were human and had feelings. They were not recognized, so they rebelled, and this went on and on until they committed an act that brought the authorities into the picture.

If these nets were established, I feel the incidence of crime would be drastically reduced, and we would see the beginnings of some integration into the society.

FOLGER: How long, in your judgment, would a person have to serve as a detached worker in order to be maximally effective in setting up a network? Haven't the experiences with somewhat similar roles shown that these people tend to get into conflict situations, conflict over identification with the boys and the established authority?

STRODTBECK: I can be optimistic on this, for I watched it in connection with the YMCA. They started talking about the suppression of corner boys' smoking and drinking. Now the YMCA is collaborating in the operation of youth locations where light wine and beer is sometimes on the premises. The degree to which the board members were startled by accounts of "freight-training" [successive intercourse with the same girl by a group of boys] and other sexual exploits was high at first, but these early concerns were relinquished in a search for the significance of the background factors. It is essential to recognize that, in a relatively small period of time, a network can be established— by paying $10 and $20 a month to boys who are critically located in the peer networks of the gangs. It can be assumed that, when a problem is sensed, you can locate it; sometimes, sufficiently in advance to take corrective action. The consultants themselves may become reinvolved in delinquency; though they then lose their stipend, contact is ordinarily not lost and they can be reinstated later.

Gang fights were virtually eliminated in Chicago prior to the mobilization of gangs in aspects of the Negro protest movement. No action that has been taken thus far has materially reduced strong-arming. It's hard to touch, through group activities, the motivations of a couple of boys who go out on their own to strong-arm. So, while detached work is not a device for handling strong-arming, when boys get venereal disease, when they need help to get into the army, when they need to be placed and re-placed and re-placed in a job—here, detached work is most valuable. With detached work, these things can be coordinated in ways that previously were not possible at all. The patent gain from such operations is such that there is no real tension in Chicago between the police officers handling juveniles and the detached workers. There seems to be no "Officer Krupke" bucking the detached worker in Chicago at this time.

If we are to insist that the corner boy do his homework and never strong-arm, smoke, or fornicate, it will require another wave of organization, which goes well beyond what I think can practically be done at this time.

McLure: Where is this $20 coming from?

Strodtbeck: The YMCA has its local resources for 50 per cent of the costs; it also has had some National Institutes of Health money and it may now have poverty money. The Chicago project is parallel to similar projects in New York City.

McLure: Is there a danger of organizing and formalizing this structure by supporting it adequately?

Strodtbeck: No, it works out to have the opposite effect. The detached worker discourages the gang treasury. Adequate support is essential because the network does not have the symbols that would enable it to keep a large, aggressive group of boys identified with one another as club jackets or raincoats would. It is not that kind of activity. And the YMCA has discovered that it is not wise to organize highly competitive games. Competition on the playing fields of Eton implies adherence to norms that are a part of middle-class society. The gang boys release tremendous internal organizational conflicts whenever they lose and this moves programmers toward kinds of athletic intervention that reduce the possibility of losing.

Another implication in Mr. McLure's question is whether there is any really effective contact between the detached work and the school. The answer is no. There is no reason why other communities in America needing programs like this can't start them on some basis that will increase the effectiveness of the contact between the programs and the schools—make it greater than it has been in New York, in some degree, and in Chicago, in particular.

McLure: That is the real question I was coming to. Can the schools really move in to develop this organization and employ the kind of worker you have described?

Strodtbeck: Consider this question: How could they pay him if he were not certificated? I'm afraid the whole of the paraprofessional's role in the schools is, right now, in a real muddle. But these are primarily organizational matters, which will require redrafting of school codes.

For example, I have consulted with members of the poverty program about the rate of remuneration for paraprofessionals in the schools. I suggested that teachers who supervise paraprofessionals have direct responsibility for setting their level of pay. This was so inconsistent with the teacher's desire to *not be* in business for herself that the whole discussion just stopped at that point. Most needed is a change in the teacher's conception of herself as a professional.

I had one consultation in a rather unusual "deteriorated area" —Mount Kisco, in Westchester County—where the schools were involved with a detached-worker program. The detached workers in the program were instructed in group dynamics. Even the principal came to understand that when she and her teachers talked about ways of giving greater assistance, she must relinquish her role of giving nods of affirmation to indicate what was or was not to be done. The principal in question said, "It took me literally weeks to learn that I should just look down, until finally someone in the group would mention something they could do personally. Then we would support him in that activity."

The big concern of the detached workers was how to go out and say to a mother, "We are trying to give special services, like a trip around Manhattan Island, to a child—like your son—who is educationally deprived." When they first tried it, there was no problem, because the mothers told them, "Oh ho, you're trying to help those of us who have large families," and the teachers were immediately relieved to accept this definition.

The health coordinator, in her extramural work, was tremendously concerned because there were people who, to her knowledge, bought clothes and cars but didn't get the caries in their kids' teeth fixed. She had no framework whatsoever for thinking that there could be a rational allocation of consumption resources that would cause people to buy clothes and cars *before* they got teeth fixed. One of the problems was to give to her a model of what happens in middle-class adaptations. In my contact, I suggested that there was a whole spectrum of consumption needs encountered by a family. What most of us spend most of our time doing is balancing these needs. We have the orthodontia, the car, the living room, and so forth. We make expenditures on any one of these in spurts. But people who are pushed down far enough can't delay and optimize their gratifications over this spectrum of demands.

This interpretation of the economic consequences of status defensiveness needs to be understood within schools before schoolteachers can begin to understand that some of the interventions of detached workers are more than the result of too little professional training. Detached workers do not give the kinds of help that require the lowering of status defenses. While such help may, at times, be required, one has to have continuing contact to bring it about.

KLEIN: Would you comment on your other point dealing with our society's view of ADC? I am referring to the need to promote the integration of the family and what this means in regard to breaking this recidivism.

STRODTBECK: The support of a kinship structure rather than restriction to a family is the answer. The way we administer public relief cuts away at kinship structure. We do not build dwellings that are designed to accommodate three grown sisters and their elderly mother. We insist that a mother and her children, with some exceptions for one grandparent, be in a particular unit. Do we know what forms the basis of the social attraction that causes people to want to live together and help one another? Can we take 1,000 families who have this desire and facilitate their finding units of residence which will thus enhance kinship structure? The middle-class nuclear family has developed in response to the need for people to be maximally mobile—to shift in accordance with the demands of a changing technology. These needs may not be present, to the same degree, for service workers in the city.

DAVID: You have said there is a tremendous feeling of threat in the lower-lower class—due, in part, to the fact that the poor have hostile economic relationships with all the people they deal with, both on the consumption side, with the shopkeepers, and on the income side, with the welfare authorities. In terms of the income side, a current topic of interest to economists is whether an effective way of reorganizing the income structure is to provide a payment by right—a guaranteed income of some kind, or a negative tax credit—which would, presumably, vastly increase the resources of these people on an unconditional basis. Would such an income reorganization help them to extend their network of contacts or will this take something else as well?

STRODTBECK: The degradation from the receipt of public relief is greatest among those persons who are most prepared to leave public relief, so that the program you mention is like Alinsky's program. It is my opinion that you will be hitting one level higher than the level of my own greatest concern, so something else will surely be required.

What we find, in studies of this question, is that the degree of protest that a mother feels about the way in which her personal prerogatives are hedged by the regulations surrounding relief moneys is directly related to her degree of integration into the local Negro society. The mother who has come up from Mississippi, has self-hatred for Negroes, thinks of herself as white, and continually moves from houses with noisy neighbors, does not protest. Life on relief with her three or four children, in Chicago, is just very much better than it would have been in Mississippi. This mother is not in a position, at the present time, to think that free access to her relief check is going to mean anything to her, psychologically. If you were to ask what percentage of the

ADC mothers I have contacted are presently in a position to really feel a positive psychological effect from this reorganization of the check, I would doubt that it would be more than 20 or 25 per cent. But, for that proportion, the change might be quite important.

LECHT: This problem of communication with people of other classes, particularly with the really poor, has come up in other programs, such as the new federal government programs for retraining. There was a very interesting study done of attempts to get Negroes to undertake retraining in Richmond and Norfolk, Virginia. The government retraining agency sent out invitations advising these people of the opportunities. Very few responded. Then they sent the local ministers to find out why; they found that, when the recipients got this letter, they felt it was a threat. They interpreted such letters as either a bill or a summons to come to court or to some government agency because of an involvement that spelled trouble. It wasn't until the retraining agency actually got people from their own community to contact the prospective retrainees, in pool halls and on street corners, that they got them to undertake training.

STRODTBECK: Your point is very, very much in the spirit of this argument, Mr. Lecht. Everyone understands, from "West Side Story," that people have territory and protect it. Almost no one intuitively and easily understands that anyone who protects his territory assumes that others do likewise and is, therefore, fearful of leaving. That is exactly the point of detached work. You have to pay the fellow $10 a month to get him to distribute, among his friends, tickets to a jazz concert. That is, you need help to get them from their ghetto to a place where the jazz concert takes place. You have to give the same kind of support to interest them in the local ball teams.

When the Chamber of Commerce in Ticul, a peasant commercial trading center in Yucatan, brought in Oaxaca potters—whose reputation gives them a certain status—to give demonstrations, none of the local potters, who are of the low status class in Ticul, would come to the demonstrations. The problem we have of getting people to exchange information across classes is quite universal. The solutions that are worked out, if we pay attention to these details, can be world-wide in their implications.

CANNON: You are talking about Negro mothers and not a word about fathers. Is there any significance in that?

STRODTBECK: I have not done research on fathers. I am really talking about the chronically dependent people who not only are dependent but who are socializing their children in such a way—so it appears to us—that the probability of *their* becoming economically independent is low. These are people I see as falling one step below stable lower-class persons.

CANNON: Are you talking about the case where aid is given to a child in an intact family?

STRODTBECK: The techniques we follow in this kind of inquiry involve asking: "Was Michael's father living with you when Michael was born?" We don't ask, in the first instance, who a child's father is. The degree of instability in the marital relationships does not preclude there being some instances of better organized families that do have sufficiently stable relationships—so that the father is present in the home. But the number of mothers that we contact in our research who have such arrangements is very, very small.

Our reading-readiness program has been running continuously now for about four and a half years, so much of our observation was done before the current Social Security Administration efforts to make the program less divisive had become effective—if they have. I lack empirical experience—with cases involving fathers—that would reveal the effects of change.

BUSHNELL: One of the more viable concepts in curriculum development today is the use of games in the classroom. I would be interested in your comment. Do you feel this is an appropriate way to help a deprived child develop coping skills that will make him more capable of interacting with his environment?

STRODTBECK: That's a very good question, but I feel I'm not well enough informed to respond to it.

BUSHNELL: Let me give you an example, if I may. You probably know about the career "game" developed at Johns Hopkins University by Saran Boocock and Jim Coleman. It was designed to assist and to develop the career decision-making process and is oriented to teen-age girls. This is done by letting students take on responsibility for making certain decisions about a hypothetical girl of seventeen who comes from a background like their own. They are asked to make choices, starting at age seventeen and continuing through fifty. Their answers are fed into a computer, which cranks out certain results or "life experiences." Is this the kind of experience that would make a real difference in a deprived child's ability to make appropriate career decisions, substituted for the usual kind of counseling given in schools?

STRODTBECK: I think it is a fascinating idea. I think that, probably, it will have more effect on the middle-class people who hear about the experiments than it will on the children who participate. Occupational decisions are made by persons with too little information, and, once they are made, they are irreversible in their effects. Middle-class children will certainly learn from such games.

However, I must say that when we ask the lower-class gang boys, the lower-class nongang boys, and middle-class boys their evaluation of a boy who studies, a man who works hard, and so forth, there really is no differentiation in the evaluation of positive adaptations by strata. But, when we ask about pimping, strong-arming, and so forth, there is much more positive evaluation by persons in lower-class positions. This suggests that the games, if they are flexible enough, can be used to determine class-specified values; once these are known, possible interaction could be considered.

One almost has to spend time around a Negro home to learn why a mother doesn't use her money to put lots of things in the "fridge." Her control is so low that people, in all probability, would just eat the food too quickly. So one of the things the mothers do is send the child out to buy groceries before almost every meal. When the time of the month comes when money is running low, there is a great dependence upon some friend dropping in. If he drops in with groceries, it is very essential to *be* there to participate in the meal. There is a little whiskey and older children must play outside for a while, but such details should not obscure the degree to which just being around the home is rewarded. The adventitiously delivered meal is a reality that middle-class people might not intuitively appreciate.

There is sometimes a reciprocal dependency on the part of a mother who wants her children to stay with her for reasons she can't easily explain. Her own personal isolation is so great that she has come to need close, almost physical contact with her children all of the time. The interpersonal dependencies this creates are negative and slow to yield to cognitive attacks offering greater information about career lines.

KLEIN: You discussed the possibility of establishing communication and breaking down distrust. How do you do this?

STRODTBECK: People make a fatal error in attempting to give service to those who are educationally deprived: They believe that there must be greater intervention in the lives of the educationally deprived. Some of you may know of my analysis of the so-called hidden curriculum in the middle-class home. We conclude that, in the middle-class home, expenditures are made in successive lump sums, so that, at any point in time, there are a number of obligations that people are sustaining under norms of reciprocity and that are going to be balanced in some later expenditure.

I think, in the handling of lower-class children in educational contexts, you cannot just give them more of the kinds of educational training given to middle-class children. The elaboration of the verbal skills that comes from the preparation in the middle-class home is not there. One of the things that has to be done is radically to revise the school system, so that there is much greater autonomy in decision-making by the children in the school context. This is necessary if you are going to develop the requisite compensatory skills.

DAVID: Is the use of time by these children sufficiently different from the middle-class child? Is this another matter the educational system should take into account?

STRODTBECK: The problem is how to conceptualize the distractability of the lower-class child. Time has a different meaning if you are subject to interruption at any point than it does if you can assure yourself of privacy for continued attack on a problem. The meaning of time has two implications. First, middle-class kids will work longer at tasks without becoming distracted. Second, they work at more tasks. It is one of the anomalies that "to those who have will be given," because a busy person can always do one extra thing. As you force on the lower-class child the necessity of organizing several activities, he will meet much more certainly and rapidly the frustration that comes from failure to fulfill expectations.

SNIDER: Do these children you are talking about go to kindergarten?

STRODTBECK: Very, very extensively. The mothers want to get the children out of the home. They will get the children to kindergarten for that purpose.

BUSHNELL: Do we need a Presidential advisory board, such as a Council of Behavioral Sciences, to interpret information developed by behavioral scientists?

STRODTBECK: I would not feel that my attention to such problems has been serious enough for me to give very much counsel. It is sobering to think how late in the day we have developed the competence to use social statistics. But it is imperative to create information and make it publicly available, and then hope that someone will have the temerity to relate it to public policy and that public discussion will grow. When that discussion grows, the people with the necessary competence to check one another's interpretations will emerge.

BEASLEY: I have been reading, recently, that the Negro father in the South is never the real head of the family so far as passing down moral judgment and setting the tone of family behavior is concerned. He is the man who hoes and harvests the potatoes. When he moves to the large city, he loses even this function. His means of economically relating to the livelihood of the family is removed because his lack of skills prevents him from getting a job. In the South, there is a matrilineal relationship, but at least the father stays with the family. In the large city, he leaves the family because he cannot, economically, support it. If the father had a guaranteed income, would this reverse the procedure and bring him back with the family?

STRODTBECK: I don't know.

KIMBALL: I think a mythology about the Negro family in the South is being circulated. There are all kinds of Negro families, and there are many traditions in various parts of the South.

Another undeciphered problem is the extent to which there is a cultural continuity of behavior among American Negroes similar to the cultural continuity among some whites, in various parts of the country, that I was describing. Several scholars are now in the process of attempting to decipher this problem of cultural continuity among whites.

There is very good reason to believe that, once we get an explanation of the problem, the same thing will appear with regard to the American Negro. He may be heir to a diversity of African cultures. Some of these were highly paternalistic in organizational pattern and some were highly maternalistic, particularly the Ibo of Nigeria. Among the Ibo, the women were the dominant personalities within the tribal system. The Ibo had a tribal system of dispersed families in which women controlled the purse, carried the excess products to market, and developed high mathematical skills. It is entirely possible that this mathematical skill may be a kind of residual cultural factor that we have not yet tapped in their American descendants. The Ibo not only sent their own people into slavery—they raided each other—but, also, their territory was a passageway for slave traders coming from the interior of Africa and moving people to America and other countries.

A similar situation exists in Brazil. You discover there that, with certain peoples of African descent, the female is the dominant figure. It appears that these cultural characteristics had nothing to do with the plantation system in the South. Similarly, you discover peoples of other backgrounds in Brazil who carry a very strong male tradition.

So, the point that I am trying to make is, it is very dangerous to generalize until intensive study of cultural continuities makes clear what I think we will discover—namely, that there is a tremendous diversity of Negro life.

BEASLEY: I think nothing I have read has traced it back to African origin. Most studies begin with the plantation Negro and bring him forward to the urban centers.

KIMBALL: I think that argument is on shaky grounds.

ROSS: Aside from what may have been the influence of African cultures, hasn't the family structure of the Negro been nurtured by several hundred years in the New World?

KIMBALL: I am sure it has, in the same way that the family

structures of other traditions that have come to America have been nurtured and modified.

Placing a family within a structural position of either deprivation or advantage has an effect upon the nature of the relations among the members, irrespective of the kind of background out of which they come. But, the anthropologist would still insist that, until you look into the historical aspects of cultural groups, you don't want to make final judgments.

STRODTBECK: The principal finding, in my studies of gang boys, is the degree to which the motivation for many of their activities seems to grow out of fear. For example, you fight only when the ratio is six or seven to one in your favor. There are many other manifestations of the way in which being dispossessed and low in status causes one to be fearful. But, in our laboratory, we are also doing more fundamental studies of sex role identification. Our technique is to use elaborate tests, some of which discriminate between boys and girls at various ages. We ask questions of such nature as: "Does spit on the sidewalk offend you?" "Are you frightened by thundershowers?" "Do you like to drive a racing car?" It is obvious how a boy wishing to protest his masculinity would answer these questions.

At the same time, we have drawings that are incomplete and we search them for instances in which the completions by boys are different from the completions by girls. By utilizing the unconscious and conscious measures together, we have a particularly powerful technique.

We find, for example, that a person who responds as being unconsciously feminine and consciously masculine is much more punitive toward a defendant in a trial if the defendant is alleged to be homosexual in character. We find that there is a tendency of persons who are unconsciously and consciously masculine to search for different strategies in a broad variety of decision-making circumstances.

For example, we are doing some work now on reactions to water pollution and we describe the situation as being serious to half of the people and nonserious to the other half. We tell half the subjects they can do something about it and half that they cannot. When seriousness and efficacy are present, willingness to act is always high. When seriousness and efficacy are absent, willingness to act is low. But, there is an interesting difference related to the sexual identity of the participant. People who are consciously and unconsciously feminine are much more moved by those situations described as serious when they cannot be efficacious in doing anything about them. We look at this response as an insight into the origin of enthusiasm for lost causes.

At the other extreme, those who are consciously and unconsciously masculine are very much more disposed to act, even though the situation might not be serious, if they can be efficacious in carrying out their actions.

The demonstration of some strategic implications from this aspect of identity places the situation of the Negro boy who is socialized in a female-based environment in quite a different light. When we talk about masculinity and femininity, we are not talking, necessarily, about wearing pants or making out with the women. We are talking about strategies of thinking. Any mother, Negro or white, can tell a boy he shouldn't wear a dress and other matters of that nature. But, if there is an unconscious disposition, on the part of any child, to pattern his way of thought after the example of that person who controls resources in his presence, then it is quite clear that we are producing, on the part of Negro lower-class boys, dispositions toward problem-solving in which they tend to emphasize the primordial recurrent rhythms that are like kitchens, kin, and relationships of that sort. They can be predicted to have a lesser disposition to move into an environment where many people are competing; where they have to watch without emotional commitment until the time arises when they make a decision; where they would maximize a short-term gain and then move out of the field.

These matters I am talking about are related to identity processes. They are related to fearfulness and to inherent masculinity and femininity, but not exactly in the way that Moynihan suggests [in his study of the Negro family, written in 1965 for the U.S. Department of Labor] and not, in any sense, in the way that a term in the army could correct.

DEITCH: Could you, perhaps, specify for us the precise sense in which you speak of masculinity and femininity?

STRODTBECK: I have to preface my response by saying to you that, in a pluralistic society like our own, if it were not for the fact that certain boys get caught up with an enthusiasm for lost causes, we would be the worse for it. A willingness to sacrifice oneself to end war, to try to help other people in trouble—these are the sources of motivation which get one hooked in collective activities. These activities insidiously move one toward the professions, and this will cause one to make more money later in life. The enthusiasm for lost causes that I am talking about is an exceedingly important problem orientation to develop in any society. It is extremely important, therefore, that we have some people who are not sports car addicts. That is a part of what I am talking about.

But, in the absence of a context in which energies can be directed toward collectivity-oriented activities, the same psychological problem-solving disposition might manifest itself in the use of marijuana in a lower-lower-class context.

To give you one dramatic insight: Being a good mathematician means that you have to take a walk alone as you review various alternative solutions in your mind. It just happens that, if you were to ask me, "Where is the greatest untapped reservoir of mathematicians in America?," my answer would be that it is among Negro females. They are a sigma-and-a-half higher than Negro males in mathematical ability.

These are the kinds of distinctions in psychological make-up that are intertwined with family functional and social position.

DEITCH: The only point I want to make is that "lost cause" is not a perfectly unambiguous concept. Today's lost cause may very well become tomorrow's victory. Consider, for example, those people currently protesting about the war in Vietnam. Is this a lost cause? Suppose their efforts do effect a change in American policy. In that case, speaking realistically, their cause would become very much won. At the outset, it is very difficult to know whether one is fighting a winning or losing battle.

STRODTBECK: You understand that lost cause, as I used it, is a metaphor to lead people into a richer understanding of social functioning.

KIMBALL: Are you also saying that this is a phase in the life of a person, as he moves into a lost cause and then beyond? So, therefore, it hasn't anything to do with lost causes. It has to do with the individual's development.

STRODTBECK: It's according to where he is located. Sometimes, it really may be a lost cause.

KIMBALL: You mean the individual is lost.

STRODTBECK: That's right. That the cultural context that surrounds the motivations is important. If you are a little more privileged when you start, disregarding consequences and continuing to plug at something because of identification may lead to accomplishments the society prides itself on, but it may not. I am saying that, consciously and unconsciously, feminine persons are more disposed to get hooked on situations they think are related to current social sentiments, even if they cannot be efficacious. On the other hand, the boy from a stable, hard-working home, who is consciously and unconsciously masculine, will be more likely to go out and see what the job is, find out whether he can do it, and, if he can, move out and get that job done. Many important aspects of the economy turn on there being such people.

McLURE: We have one line of inquiry in which the anthropologist says there is something in the cultural residue which helps to explain the projection of a culture. The psychologist has another line of inquiry, which produces evidence that there is something in the environment which may be culturally transmitted as a result of the effect of the environment. If each of these is partly correct, then how do we explain the emergence of large middle-class and upper-class Negro groups? The question I am raising relates to processes of change.

STRODTBECK: As Frazier argues in *Black Bourgeoisie,* the Negro middle class is not giving the leadership that is required.* Wilson made the same point in *Negro Politics.*† Is this true? There is a real scarcity of Negro leadership. The notion is that that scarcity will be reduced. Current Negro leaders have been recruited from

---

* E. Franklin Frazier, *Black Bourgeoisie* (Chicago: The Free Press of Glencoe, 1957).

† James Q. Wilson, *Negro Politics* (Chicago: The Free Press of Glencoe, 1960).

those families where the parents have been very largely sustained on civil-service jobs. With the increase of such families there may be a sufficient basis for this leadership in the future.

It certainly was clear to us, as we worked with middle-class Negro boys in connection with the programs reported on in *Group Process and Gang Delinquency,* that their attitudes were not those of persons excessively concerned with normative conformity. So far as these boys were concerned they were, as predicted from Frazier's *Black Bourgeoisie,* "living it up." No adolescents that I know have more access to indulgent gratifications than the middle-class Negro boys whose parents run beauty parlors, funeral houses, and so forth. They have adequate ability, but very little motivation to go on to college.

The absence of an effective Protestant ethic at the middle-class level is undoubtedly a product of past discrimination and it is also undoubtedly one of the factors in the gap in leadership in the Negro community. But, it is quite clear that one of the routes through which stable middle-class life has been achieved by the generations of Negroes we are now encountering in the large cities has been through the civil service, through the protection from discriminatory processes that civil service employment offers.

Ross: I think there are two ways in which the term middle class can be used. *Black Bourgeoisie* referred to Negro business, which has been a pretty marginal thing, as you indicate—beauty parlors, funeral houses, and that sort of thing. The more significant Negro middle-class members are those in white-collar occupations. I would say that the government has been a very important factor there, in more than one way: partly, because the opportunities in private employment have increased somewhat as a result of government pressure; partly, because governments make war and that creates opportunities for Negroes; and, partly, by direct employment.

The percentage of Negroes moving into middle-class occupations, in that sense, is greater and it is going up slowly. It is certainly true that the great bulk of Negroes are in the proletarian occupations.

Strodtbeck: The Otis Duncan studies show that, if you look at income as a function of education, the gap between expected income and education is greatest for Negroes who are high school graduates.

Ross: That is correct. Of course, one reason is that the high school degree is not necessarily the same thing from one school to another.

3

Full Employment: The Role of Government and Education

ARTHUR M. ROSS

Current experience reminds us of the ironic fact that government does the best job of promoting full employment in periods of wartime. During the past generation, work has been available for substantially all job-seekers only during World War II (including the postwar reconstruction period, 1946–48), the Korean conflict, and, now, the war in Vietnam.

The unemployment rate for the civilian labor force fell to 3.7 per cent in February, 1966. Although the Employment Act has been in effect since 1946, and 3.7 per cent does not constitute full employment in any absolute sense, we must go back to 1953 to find a rate that low. It is still to be established that the United States is able to maintain full employment without the stimulus of defense production, the enlargement of the military services, and the expectation of price increases that accompany a war.

THE HEIGHTENING OF THE COMMITMENT

Irrespective of military demands and influences, the government's responsibility for the amount of job opportunity is undoubtedly becoming more serious and comprehensive as time goes on. Over the past generation, we can identify a number of basic, and irreversible, reasons for the heightening of this responsibility.

Demonstration Effects

Prior to the 1930's, it was generally believed that a depression was the result of maladjustments in the cost-price structure, which would have to work themselves out over the course of time. Government interference, no matter how well-meaning, would only make matters worse. Many conventional theorists refused to recognize unemployment as a disease of the system as a whole and preferred to regard it as a result of indolence and prodigality. It was assumed that any necessary relief assistance would be supplied through private charitable organizations; each local community and religious group would "care for its own." Government would make its greatest contribution toward recovery by reducing expenditures and finding new sources of revenue, thereby balancing the budget. This action would set a good example for households and private business and maintain confidence in the soundness of the dollar.

The only significant intellectual opposition, aside from some disreputable "underconsumptionists," within the ranks of the economists came from the socialists. Marxist theory held that periodic crises and a growing army of the unemployed were the essence of the capitalistic economy. The only cure, in this view, was to socialize the means of production.

The New Deal of the 1930's was not socialist; the stated aim was to revive the private enterprise economy by "priming the pump." Numerous expedients were tried during the first two terms of the Roosevelt Administration: monetary manipulation; business "self-government" under NRA codes; farm production controls; direct relief to needy individuals, in cash and in kind; work relief projects administered directly by government agencies; public-works spending on highways, bridges, schools, and housing; enactment of minimum wages and maximum hours; and establishment of the social security system. In the late 1930's, Keynesian economics began to supply a systematic account of the relationship between public spending and private economic activity. But the fact is that the pump was never primed very well. The government spending programs of the New Deal made important contributions to employment in their own right, and probably prevented a complete collapse of the system. Yet, it was not until 1940 that Gross National Product per capita (in constant dollars) reached the 1929 level. The unemployment ratio stood at 14.6 per cent in 1940, which was higher than in 1936.

Thus, it was World War II that demonstrated what the government could do to establish full employment. This episode involved an eightfold expansion of federal spending, as well as the creation of a military establishment with 11.5 million men in uniform and a degree of regimentation that would not have been acceptable in peacetime. Nevertheless, by the end of the war, the conviction had taken hold—not only in the United States but throughout the industrialized world—that government must assume responsibility for the level of employment. The Employment Act of 1946 was paralleled by similar legislation in other countries, and the Charter of the United Nations declared that that organization would promote "higher standards of living, full employment, and conditions of economic and social progress and development."

In the United States, the commitment to full employment was not really tested during the first decade of the Employment Act. It is true that prosperity was maintained, except for moderate and relatively brief downswings in 1949 and 1954. But 1946–48 had the stimulus of accumulated wartime shortages, and 1950–53 was affected by the Korean conflict. It was about 1957 that the immediate postwar era—which had been marked by frequent supply shortages, a persistent investment boom, and a favored American position in world markets—came to a close. There followed some six years of economic slack, with unemployment ratios between 5.5 and 7.0 per cent and much higher rates for the less favored groups in the working population.

Meanwhile, however, the nations of Western Europe and Japan were presenting a dramatic demonstration of how full employment could be maintained more or less indefinitely under conditions of peace. Some of these countries—such as France, Sweden, and Great Britain—from time to time used the language of economic planning. Others, such as Germany and Japan, cultivated the ambience of free enterprise. But, regardless of rhetorical or institutional differences, all of them were able to avoid serious or prolonged unemployment for a period of time that became increasingly impressive as it moved into the second half of the second postwar decade. To decision-makers in the United States, this demonstration was undoubtedly more eloquent than the much-discussed economic growth rate in the Soviet Union.

The Role of Social Protest

The civil rights movement has been a second factor sharpening the awareness of responsibility for employment. The Negro protest, to be sure, has been directed toward numerous objectives, including voting rights, access to civil accommodations, and the integration and improvement of education and housing. Yet it cannot be denied that the central aim has been more and better jobs. The unemployment ratio for Negroes remained above 10 per cent throughout the period between 1958 and 1963; it was much higher for those less than twenty-five years of age; it was evidently astronomical in many of the big-city ghettos, although specific information concerning these central-city areas is very poor. Furthermore, the employed Negroes were heavily concentrated in unskilled, poorly paid, and irregular jobs in agriculture, household work, common labor, and manufacturing and service industries. Considering the stimulus that Negro protest has given to the full-employment responsibility, it is ironic that Negroes have not yet benefited as fully as whites from the economic improvement of the past three years.

The discovery of the poverty problem in the United States has had a more complicated impact. The poverty program, in its origins a few years ago, was not a response to overt manifestations of discontent; the poor, as such, are characteristically passive and withdrawn.

About 1960, there began a period of sober stocktaking in the United States. It reflected a reaction against the complacency of the Eisenhower period and an awareness of the altered structure of world politics. It moved on to successive waves of concern over the growth rate, the unemployment problem, the Negro protest, and, finally, poverty.

Concern for the poor, at this time, was similar to concern for labor exploitation during the Progressive era of 1905–14. Although progressivism was essentially a middle-class movement, the working class benefited modestly and temporarily. The first workmen's compensation laws were passed by the states, industrial safety programs were initiated, and employers began to think of their workers as human beings rather than "hands." Some legislation to protect working women and children was passed by the states. These labor aspects of progressivism illustrate the potentialities of charitable or humanitarian reforms, actuated by a troubled conscience and adopted for the benefit of a relatively inert or powerless clientele. Helping such a clientele is deeply satisfying because it fulfills the instinct of *noblesse oblige* without letting things get out of hand and because quiet pathos is more appealing than unmannerly protest. At the same time, there are certain limitations from the standpoint of the beneficiary. The improvements are confined to what seems reasonable and proper to the benefactor, so that nothing very basic is changed. The charitable format must be preserved; if the clientele begin to demand as a matter of right what is being offered as a matter of grace, or to seek more than is given, all the rules of the game are broken. Finally, episodes of this type tend to be temporary because nothing becomes so quickly obsolescent as a troubled social conscience.

The anti-poverty movement of the 1960's would not have lasted so long, nor could it have generated so much pressure on behalf of job opportunity for the disadvantaged, if it had not been merged, to a very large extent, with the Negro protest movement. Negroes make up only a small proportion of the poor, as officially defined. But a high proportion of all people enrolled in Project Head Start, the Neighborhood Youth Corps, the Job Corps, the work-study program, and other poverty programs are Negro children, teen-agers, and young adults from urban areas. Thus, it is continuing Negro protest that has generated the continuing political energy on behalf of job opportunity for the poor.

Intellectual Tools

In the United States, which never would have resorted to socialization of industry except under almost inconceivable stress, implementation of the full-employment objective has required a more sophisticated understanding of private economic activity as well as of the relationship between public policies and private decision. This is not the place to elucidate the "New Economics," which have recently broken out of professional circles into more popular circulation. Suffice it to say that, while the formulations of Keynes and his contemporaries are still fundamental, theoretical concepts have been greatly elaborated and refined since the 1930's. Econometrics and computer technology have gone along hand in hand with theory building. Sharper tools of economic theory, the profusion of statistical measurements, and the great possibilities of automated data processing combine to provide the basis for systems analysis of the whole economic process.

The intellectual tools of the full-employment commitment also include policy concepts. The Council of Economic Advisers, in its 1966 report, describes the elements of "revised economic policy" as it relates not only to "high employment levels" but also to "steady balanced growth" and "essential price stability."

> First, it [revised economic policy] emphasizes a continuous, rather than a cyclical, framework for analyzing economic developments and formulating policies. . . . Second, in this way, it emphasizes a preventive strategy against the onset of recession. Third, in focusing on balance of the economy, this policy strategy cannot give top priority to balance in the budget. . . . Fourth, it considers the budget and monetary conditions in the framework of a growing economy, recognizing that revenues expand and thereby exert a fiscal drag on demand unless expansionary actions are taken. . . . Fifth . . . manpower policies, selective approaches to control capital outflows, as well as general fiscal and monetary measures, are all part of the arsenal. Sixth, it calls for responsible price-wage actions. . . . Finally, it makes greater demands on economic forecasting and analysis. The job of the economist is not merely to predict the upturn or the downturn but to judge continuously the prospects for demand in relation to a growing productivity capacity.*

Attenuation of Ideological Conflicts

Traditionally, the relationship between business and government in the United States made it virtually impossible to implement an effective full-employment program. Communication was carried on in primitive clichés, which served only to befuddle the policy issues. Business and government operated with different systems of economic doctrine, while labor had yet a third; although the United States had more economists per capita than any other country, it could not be said that the educated public

---

* *Annual Report of the Council of Economic Advisers* (Washington, D.C.: GPO, 1966), p. 180.

was sophisticated on economic questions. An administration—like that of President Roosevelt—attempting to innovate boldly in the economic field, created a crisis of business confidence, which tended to dry up the flow of private investment. A business-oriented administration—like that of President Eisenhower—pursued deflationary policies, which reduced production and employment as the price of retaining "confidence" and "stability." Endeavors to develop more intimate consultation between government and business have, in the past, run into a wall of mistrust and a suspicion of economic planning.

These ingrained attitudes were clearly self-defeating for both parties. For example, a principal reason for the failure of New Deal policies to reinvigorate the private economy was that private investment never recovered. In 1939, after six years of pump-priming, gross private domestic investment (in constant dollars) was less than in 1930 and only three-fifths of what it had been in 1929. And this was despite a threefold expansion in federal spending and a sizable increase in consumer spending. Suspicion and hostility between business and government, symbolized by mutual expression of belligerence and contempt, prevented the investment recovery which normally would have been expected.

Compare this situation with the business-government relationship in the Kennedy and Johnson administrations. We may note the investment tax credit, more liberal depreciation rules, the reduction in corporate income taxes, the absence of any punitive spirit in the regulatory agencies. Profit is no longer an ugly word. In contrast to other periods of war in the twentieth century, today there is little discussion of excess-profit taxes. While businessmen do not operate the government, they are treated with unfailing respect and solicitude. And, if the attitude of government has mellowed, so has that of the businessmen. The reluctance toward any outright confrontation with government since the steel-price episode of 1963 does not indicate the full extent of accommodation. No longer do government and the big corporations speak two different languages, though this is not true of the "Main Street" small business.

Of course there is a great deal of bargaining over who should pay higher taxes, who should get the benefit of tax cuts, who should be asked to show restraint, and so on. But the differences are no longer ideological absolutes. I am not suggesting that business would willingly go all the way into formal planning or joint price review; but surely there has been an acceptance of the government's active responsibility for employment which could not have been foreseen a decade ago. And why not? Enough time has passed to convince the more sophisticated executives that business can hold its own in a regime of high-employment policies and come out with its fair share of the gains. That this confidence is not misplaced is shown by the record of corporate profits, which have risen from $50 billion, in 1961, to $73 billion, in 1965.

PROBLEMS OF EXECUTING THE COMMITMENT

The Employment Act of 1946 emerged from a bitter political controversy between liberals and conservatives in Congress. The former wanted a full-employment bill with a strong commitment to the principle of compensatory spending. The latter wanted to emphasize the need for price stability and to express a cautious attitude toward government intervention.

The resultant statutory language was worded with unusual delicacy:

> It is the continuing policy and responsibility of the Federal Government to use all practical means consistent with its needs and obligations and other essential considerations of national policy . . . to coordinate and utilize all its plans, functions, and resources for the purpose of creating and maintaining . . . in a manner calculated to foster and promote free competitive enterprise . . . conditions under which there will be afforded useful employment opportunities, including self-employment, for those able, willing, and seeking to work, and to promote maximum employment, production, and purchasing power.

Thus, the Employment Act of 1946 emerged from a political controversy that made it necessary to retain significant ambiguities as to the nature and extent of the commitment. These ambiguities persist today despite the strengthening of support for full-employment policy, and the development of better theoretical and operational tools during the past two decades. The unresolved political issues are clustered around two related questions:

How is full employment to be defined, and what is the proper "trade-off" against other objectives, particularly the objective of price stability?

The Employment Act, as already noted, did not speak of full employment, but the omission has ceased to be important except to the historian. I doubt that any President or Council of Economic Advisers would adopt any policy goal less than full employment in one sense or another.

What Is Full Employment?

The classical definition given by Sir William Beveridge is that a country has full employment when the number of job vacancies equals or exceeds the number of unemployed workers. This definition is oversimplified; it says nothing about the characteristics of the vacancies and of the unemployed. If all vacancies were for heavy construction workers and all the unemployed were middle-aged women, the equality in their number would not be especially significant. It is the task of labor market policy to reshuffle the labor force and produce an accommodation between job specifications of employers and personal qualifications of workers. In any case, we do not yet have comprehensive job vacancy data in the United States, although the Department of Labor hopes to launch a nationwide program this year.

Experimental surveys have been made by the National Industrial Conference Board in Rochester, New York, and by the U.S. Department of Labor in sixteen other areas. These surveys indicate that the number of job vacancies tends to equal the number of unemployed in an area when the latter is in the neighborhood of 2.0 or 2.5 per cent of the labor force.

A second concept, more familiar to American economists, is that full employment is reached when there is no lack of effective demand for labor. In such a case, the residual unemployment is the result of frictional factors such as movement in and out of the job market, labor turnover, and seasonal fluctuations of output. As a practical matter, there would also be a residue of the hard-core unemployed whose handicaps are so great that they are unacceptable to employers even when labor is scarce.

These factors are not as self-contained as they may seem. Seasonality of production is distinctly related to the strength of effective demand. The same is true of the rate of labor turnover and of the length of time it takes to move from one job to another. There is no clear line between employability and unemployability; much depends on what the alternatives are as seen by the employer. Moreover, the "irreducible minimum" also depends on the extent of governmental assistance and control in the operation of the labor market. During World War II, for example, the unemployment ratio fell to about 1 per cent in a regime of compulsory controls over hiring and job-seeking.

Some reasonable calculations can be made, however, based on our knowledge about labor turnover and movements in and out of the labor force, together with some plausible assumptions concerning the average amount of time required to find a job, or fill a vacancy, in a period of high demand. These approximations would indicate an over-all rate of about 2 per cent in a month of minimum seasonal unemployment, such as October. Greater amounts of seasonal unemployment during other parts of the year would have to be averaged in, and account would have to be taken of the perhaps 200,000 virtually unemployable among the ranks of the unemployed. The sum and substance would be a rate of about 2.5 to 2.8 per cent, corresponding to a "full effective demand" concept of full employment.

The third concept of full employment has been the most important from an operational standpoint. In this view, full employment is attained, for practical purposes, when inflationary tendencies become so strong as to require fiscal and monetary policies that slow down the economy. The Eisenhower Administration thought the economy was overheated, in 1957, when the unemployment rate fell to about 4 per cent. This is now almost universally viewed as a mistake; but some conservative economists stated, in February, 1966, that the dangers of inflation were so great that unemployment should not be pushed below the most recently reported 4 per cent rate—which had actually fallen to 3.7 per cent.

Clearly, this concept of full employment is judgmental and political rather than statistical. Aside from the fear of inflation, several other factors tend to stop an expansion short of providing job opportunity for all who desire it. Many people feel that, so long as jobs are available for married men with families, residual unemployment among women and young persons is really not too serious. At an over-all unemployment rate of 4 per cent, the rate for married men is about 2 per cent, reflecting mainly seasonal and frictional influences. If economic need is to be one test, the fact is that a great many women need jobs just as much as the married men. Many high school and college students need part-time work in order to stay in school. Whether a high school graduate can find work is of the utmost importance, even if he lacks a wife and children.

Below 4 per cent, the mismatch between the characteristics of labor supply and demand becomes more serious and requires more strenuous efforts if it is to be overcome. At the same time, unemployment is not high enough to generate much political pressure. Complaints begin to mount that the unemployed— except for those involved in a speedy transition from one job to another, or affected by seasonal fluctuations—are deficient in intelligence, education, training, experience, and work discipline. Naturally, this is true of a greater proportion when the rate is 4 per cent than when it is 6 per cent.

It is important to keep clearly in mind the distinction between the "full opportunity" concept of full employment, equivalent to 2.5 to 3.0 per cent under present conditions, and the "practical limit" concept, which depends on the views of those who must make the decisions.

The Trade-off Between Employment and Inflation

The importance of the practical limit concept makes it necessary to confront the problem of inflationary tendencies that emerge as full utilization of economic resources is approached more closely. This problem involves questions of fact, questions of policy, and questions of value.

A great deal of research has been done in an effort to establish the relationship between levels of employment and rates of change in wages and prices. Thus far, no precise correlation has been found. Wages and prices increased more rapidly in 1956 than in 1965, although unemployment was reduced to a lower level in the latter year. Still, there can be no doubt that upward pressure on wages and prices is accentuated as the level of unemployment falls to 4 per cent and below. This being the case, it is necessary to ask what can be done to postpone or mitigate inflationary pressures so as to permit a closer approach to full-employment opportunity.

Probably the most important step is to break the bottlenecks in labor supply that are bound to develop while many workers still cannot find jobs. When unemployment has fallen to a low level, the residual unemployed (aside from those in transition from one job to another, or those affected by seasonal influences) are relatively unattractive to employers because of deficiencies in education, experience, and work discipline. It is at this point that manpower programs for basic education, training, retraining, and work experience have their greatest application. There is still much misunderstanding of manpower programs in the United States. Many people regard them as necessary when unemployment is excessive, but dispensable when conditions improve. If a choice had to be made, the opposite proposition would be more correct.

The wage and price guideposts are designed to alter the relationship between employment increases, on the one hand, and wage and price increases on the other. As a practical matter, the guideposts have been most effective in industries characterized by a few large and profitable companies, industrial unions, and national multiplant or multiemployer agreements. They offer some possibility of restraining cost-push inflation induced by the exercise of market power on the part of these companies and bargaining power on the part of these unions. The federal government has also been able to apply the guideposts to its own employees. The guideposts do not restrain a demand-pull inflation resulting from the impact of bargaining demand on limited supplies. Neither do they have much meaning in small-scale, competitive industries with narrow profit margins, such as consumer services, apparel, and retail trade, or in nonunion situations. Even within their proper sphere of influence, the stabilizing effect of the guideposts is subject to much argument. I believe they have made a sizable contribution in recent years, but I am probably among the minority of economists in holding this view.

Although the Council of Economic Advisers stated, in its 1966 report, that manpower programs and the guideposts had been sufficiently effective to permit the dropping of the former "interim goal" of 4 per cent, the fact still remains that complete price stability and full-employment opportunity are conflicting objectives. No modern nation has been able to achieve both. Sooner or later, the time comes when a choice must be made.

In the United States, it seems clear, more weight has been given to price stability than has been the case in Western Europe or Japan. After the middle of 1957, unemployment rates remained two or three times as high in this country. Most of the other countries encountered substantial price increases year after year, but they apparently were not greatly concerned.

It is true that the foreign-exchange balance was a more serious problem for the United States as a result of economic and military aid, foreign investment, and tourist expenditures. Above and beyond this difficulty, however, it is fair to conclude that, in the United States, we have placed more value on price stability as an end in itself; we have been more concerned about increases in the federal debt, even though the debt has born a declining relationship to the annual output of the economy; and we have been more distressed about the impact of price increases on domestic income distribution.

Probably there has been some re-evaluation of the conflicting objectives during the past two or three years. Right now, of course, the situation has changed; as a result of the war and the capital boom, there is a real concern over the possibility of an inflationary spiral. When more normal conditions have returned, we will have a better test of whether the United States is willing to accept price increases of 2 per cent or more annually as a necessary cost of fuller employment.

THE ROLE OF GOVERNMENT

We may turn now to specific government policies for promoting full employment in the United States.

Prevalent theory and techniques are addressed primarily to promoting and sustaining high activity in the private sector of the economy. In contrast to the New Deal period, there is little emphasis on large-scale work relief or public works. While the total number of wage and salary earners has increased about 10 million since 1960, the federal civilian payroll is only 100,000 higher. State and local government employment has risen rapidly, it is true, but the purpose has been to cope with the rising demand for education and other public-service functions, and not to create jobs.

Aggregative and Structural Theories

A vigorous debate has raged concerning the causes and cures of the excessive unemployment that persisted in the United States after 1956. According to the structuralists, the principal explanation was to be found in the rapid transformation of economic activity and occupational structure. They pointed to the declining importance of goods-producing industries, the shrinkage of blue-collar occupations, and the changes in the geographical pattern of economic activity. They held that, as a result of these changes, imbalances developed between labor demand and labor supply. Many of the displaced workers did not have the education, training, and experience to qualify for the new jobs becoming available, so that manpower bottlenecks would choke off economic expansion even before the interim 4 per cent goal was reached.

The aggregative theorists argued that the basic cause of unemployment was not structural transformation but insufficient aggregate demand on the part of consumers, business firms, and government. They recognized the existence of structural differentials in employment, but pointed out that these differentials had always existed; blue-collar workers and young people, for example, always suffered more unemployment than professional employees and middle-aged persons.

The debate had considerable political significance until quite recently. The structuralists focused on retraining the displaced, on education and counseling of young people, and on area unemployment, worker relocation, and other like measures to increase labor mobility. Their opponents emphasized policies geared to increase effective demand—expansionary fiscal and monetary policies, in particular.

Actually the controversy was unnecessarily sharp in that differences in emphasis were made to appear like differences in principle. At any event, it is obvious that the basic problem was indeed a deficiency of demand. The investment tax credit of 1963, the income tax reduction of 1964, and the expansion of federal expenditures—from $106 billion, in fiscal 1962, to an estimated $154 billion in fiscal 1967—combined with the war in Vietnam and a massive capital boom, have clearly been the principal factors in the expansion up to now. Yet, the expanded manpower programs have been essential in providing a sufficiently qualified labor force for the rapid expansion of employment. The "Great Society" spending programs have had a substantial effect of their own. Direct involvement of young people in the Neighborhood Youth Corps, the Job Corps, and similar programs accounted for perhaps one-third of the total reduction of unemployment during 1965.

If fiscal and monetary policies were paramount until the beginning of 1966 when unemployment fell to 4 per cent, manpower policies will be equally crucial in permitting a further decline, toward 3 per cent or below. While the labor force has shown its usual flexibility, up to now, in adapting to changes in the structure of demand (which were not so great as some writers anticipated), the manpower bottlenecks are real and manifest at the present time. The supply of trained, experienced, adult men is stretched thin. Additional employment growth means primary reliance on young people, women, part-time job-seekers, and many less attractive candidates with educational deficiencies and personal handicaps. The situation is aggravated by enlargement of the armed services. But the situation would not be too different if the unemployment rate were to move substantially below 4 per cent in peacetime. No one should assume that we can attain full employment without the most vigorous efforts to correct the mismatch between manpower requirements and supply that eventually emerges.

Doubtless, there are some job-seekers whose handicaps are so great that they are unlikely to secure private employment except under conditions of unlimited demand, which only present themselves in a total military mobilization. The question of using the government as the "employer of last resort" for this group will be discussed in the final section of this paper.

The Thrust of the Federal Government in the 1960's

It is not my purpose to present specific legislative, programmatic, or statistical details of the federal government's activity in pursuance of its responsibility for employment. Any such account would necessarily be encyclopaedic and would leave no room for interpretation. A historical treatment of the origin, subsequent development, and present status of the commitment to full employment seems more useful.

In this section of the paper, therefore, I will mention only briefly the principal classifications of federal activity in this field.

Aid to education.   Federal assistance for education is not new. It began with the Morrill Act of 1862, which provided land grants and funds for state colleges to train youth in agriculture and the mechanical arts. It was extended to vocational education in the secondary school system by the Smith-Hughes Act of 1917, which was modernized and expanded in the Vocational Education Act of 1963. It was culminated, a century after the Morrill Act, in the National Defense Education Act of 1958, the Higher Education Facilities Act of 1963, the Health Professions Education Act of 1963, the Nurses Training Act of 1964, and the Higher Education Act of 1965.

Assistance to education has not usually been thought of as a means of encouraging full employment, yet it is crucially important in an economy undergoing rapid changes in technology and occupational requirements. The economic function of education has had more explicit attention in connection with developing countries, where it is regarded as a form of "investment in human capital." This repellent phrase indicates that, when economic resources are agonizingly scarce, the allocation of substantial funds to education must be viewed in terms of the contribution to economic growth and employment goals.

The role of education in preparing young people for the employment opportunities of the future becomes clear when we compare projected manpower requirements for 1975 with those of 1964. In order to achieve and maintain an unemployment rate of no more than 3 per cent, there will have to be 89 million civilian jobs in 1975. The distribution of these jobs can be predicted on the basis of trends in technology and in consumption patterns. We have calculated that the attainment of 89 million jobs will require increases (over 1964) of 54 per cent in the number of professional and technical workers, 37 per cent in the number of clerical workers, 35 per cent in the number of service workers, and 27 per cent in the number of skilled craftsmen. These net increases do not begin to picture the demands on education during the next decade, for many millions of highly educated people will be needed to replace losses due to death and retirement.

Vocational training and retraining. The need for federal support for vocational training has several roots—the low estate of apprenticeship in the United States, the absence of alternative methods of effecting the transition between school and work, the large number of undereducated job-seekers, and the rapid obsolescence of skills in the wake of technological change.

Despite decades of dedicated promotion by employers, unions, and government officials, formal apprenticeship programs turn out only about 25,000 journeymen per year. Many others are able to secure employment in trades without completing their indenture, yet the fact remains that apprenticeship is not a major source of trained manpower in the United States.

Private employers do a considerable amount of training with no government involvement, in order to improve the performance and potential of their own employees. In normal times, however, employers tend to expect that they can find job-seekers with the desired qualifications. In periods of high employment, a mismatch develops between the qualifications employers seek and those the unemployed possess. During World War II, a massive "training within industry" program was sponsored by the government; a similar effort would seem logical today.

Direct federal involvement, in recent years, has been concentrated on training and retraining for the unemployed. Begun on a small scale under the Area Redevelopment Act of 1961, this activity expanded considerably under the Manpower Development and Training Act of 1962. Last year, some 100,000 unemployed were enrolled in MDTA programs conducted in public vocational-education facilities, and another 10,000 in federally subsidized on-the-job projects. Sweden, which has had a well-integrated manpower program for many years, counts on retraining about 1 per cent of its labor force every year. This would be equivalent to about 800,000 workers annually in the United States.

Unemployment insurance.   The central purpose of unemployment insurance is to cushion the individual and his family against joblessness of short or intermediate duration. But unemployment insurance has an economic function as well. By maintaining the incomes of hundreds of thousands of laid-off workers, the program helps to prevent a cumulative decline in spending and economic activity. In periods of high employment, the reserves are rebuilt. Accordingly, unemployment insurance is known as a built-in stabilizer.

Actually, the economic function is not performed as well as it might be. The ratio of benefits to average wages has slipped steadily over the years; many workers are still not covered, and the duration of benefits is too short in the majority of states. A recent study indicated that, as a result of these deficiencies, only about 20 per cent of wage losses from unemployment were being compensated.

Employment services.   That unemployment rates are chronically lower in Europe than in the United States is, in part, due to management of labor-market processes. Earlier, I estimated that seasonal and transitional unemployment, plus a relatively small group of almost unemployable candidates, would yield an over-all rate of 2.5 to 2.8 per cent in the United States. But countries such as Germany, France, and Sweden have enjoyed much lower rates, year after year. A considerable part of the difference is surely due to the weakness of the public employment services in the United States, from the standpoint of helping young people into the world of work and of cutting down the length of time required to locate an acceptable job for workers who have been laid off, have moved into new areas, or have decided to seek better opportunities. Of course, there will always be a great deal of trial and error, since an employer-worker relationship is sensitive and unpredictable. Yet, it seems clear that the whole process of matching jobs and workers could be done much more efficiently if the public employment offices were the true centers of manpower activity in each community.

Fiscal and monetary policies.   Even the greatest support of education and training, and the most effective labor-market arrangement, will be of no avail if there is insufficient demand for the resulting supply. It is the task of monetary and fiscal policy to regulate the amount of effective demand. Monetary policy is too complicated to discuss here. Fiscal policy embraces the taxing and spending decisions of government. While federal spending has been increasing, to finance military and social objectives, conscious fiscal strategy has stressed the tax mechanism in recent years. New concepts have included the full-employment surplus and the fiscal drag, both characterizing a tax structure that defeats its purpose by pulling down the economy in a period of prosperity and thus inducing recession and the accompanying federal deficits. The importance of private investment as a key factor in a healthy economy has, likewise, been emphasized.

Among the specific changes in recent years have been the investment tax credit, which has played an important role in the subsequent capital boom; more liberal depreciation rules; the $16 billion income tax cut of 1964; and the excise tax cuts of 1965 and 1966. Fiscal policy is, however, now moving in the other direction.

These strategic uses of tax policy constituted a brilliant innovation, which contributed greatly to the economic improvement that began early in 1964. Until that year, the employment situation had hardly improved at all, despite President Kennedy's diligent efforts. The rapid economic growth of 1964 and 1965—much of which would have occurred even in the absence of the war in Vietnam—emphasizes the crucial importance of fiscal policy in the full-employment strategy.

Unfinished Business

Much water has gone over the dam since the Employment Act of 1946. The commitment to full employment has been strengthened; old issues have been clarified, and new programs have been launched. Improvements in fiscal and manpower policies, in the 1960's, represent a more serious response to the challenge than had been given during the preceding fifteen years.

Despite this progress, a number of basic questions are still unanswered. At present, they are considerably overshadowed by the war in Vietnam. But, eventually, these questions will have to be confronted:

Is the country prepared to do what is necessary to maintain full employment, in the sense of fully adequate job opportunity, even without the urgencies of a war situation? It is still not established whether we are willing to accept the inevitable price increases of 2 per cent or more annually and to deal with the awkward imbalances between manpower supply and demand that will gradually emerge as the unemployment rate sinks below 4 per cent.

Is the country prepared to make the extraordinary efforts that will be necessary if Negro workers are to be accorded their full share of job opportunities in the future? Changes in the occupational structure will magnify this task in the next decade, because the occupations slated for the greatest growth are those in which the Negroes have made the least inroads up to now. We have calculated that if the occupational distribution of the Negro labor force should be the same in 1975 as in 1964, then the Negro unemployment rate would be four times the white rate. If Negroes should increase their penetration into white-collar and professional occupations at the same speed as in recent years, then their 1975 unemployment rate would still be twice the white rate. Up to the present, there is no evidence that the Negro's progress is being accelerated sufficiently to carry out the promise of full employment in the foreseeable future.

What should be done with those job-seekers whose accumulated handicaps of illiteracy, poor health, apathy, and discouragement are so great that they are unlikely to secure decent jobs even in a period of widespread labor shortages? It can be estimated that there are perhaps 200,000 of these severely disadvantaged individuals among the unemployed today, and others outside the labor force. We may hope that, in another generation, this outcast group will not exist. Meanwhile there are three alternative social policies: (1) to regard them as economic casualties and to retire them from the labor force, regardless of age, on some type of social security allowance; (2) to subsidize them in private employment; and (3) to use the government as "the employer of last resort," as proposed in the February, 1966, report of the President's Commission on Automation and Technology.

Can we develop "rites of passage" from youth into working life, which will eliminate the excessive unemployment rates for young persons under twenty-five years of age? Throughout the postwar period, unemployment among the 16–24 year age group has been more than double that of the mature age group. We tend to take this situation for granted, but there is no natural law that requires it. In the European countries that have been enjoying full employment, as well as in Japan, youth employment opportunities are as plentiful as those for adults. The difference is that we do not have effective institutions linking together school and work. The young person leaves school, with or without a diploma or a degree, and thenceforth he is on his own, to compete with experienced adults for regular jobs at regular rates of pay. But, often, he is not ready to make his own way. We have yet to develop the proper combination of education and work, the entry jobs reserved for young persons, and the special guidance and protection, which have constituted the rites of passage in most societies.

These are some of the questions that must be answered, some of the problems that must be solved, before we can be sure that the commitment to full employment has been fully accepted. It is clear that continued collaboration between government and the educational system will be an essential ingredient in the development of solutions.

DISCUSSION

ARNESEN [presiding]: I am sure Mr. Ross will be glad to enter-
tain any questions, comments, or observations.

CORREA: Could we say that inflation has brought benefits to the
labor force as a whole because of increases in employment? Are
these group benefits more important than the individual disadvantage brought by higher prices?

ROSS: Inflation has redistributive properties and, of course, it
would work to the disadvantage of anyone whose income goes up
less and to the advantage of anyone whose income goes up more.
It is to the advantage of people who otherwise wouldn't be working to have an income even with some price inflation. It is better
than to have no income, or to be on relief.

DAVID: I would like to focus on the note with which you ended
your talk. What can education do to help promote a situation of
full employment? It seems to me you stressed the fact that we
need to have two things, training and basic education. But, what
kinds of institutions are going to deliver these goods? Is it going
to be done locally, through the public education system? Or will
we have to develop new institutions?

ROSS: Well, beyond what I've already mentioned, I really
couldn't say. I do think that we should re-examine the system of
apprenticeship. In the United States, apprenticeship is quite a
vestigial institution. There are really only a very few thousand
people who complete formal indentures in this country every
year. In countries like England and Germany, apprenticeship has
a much more general significance than in the United States. Our
apprenticeships are in the printing trades, building trades, and
metal trades; in Europe, the young are apprenticed in almost all
kinds of occupations.

In Japan, where there is full employment for youth, wages depend on age and length of service, rather than on job duties. The
industrial worker goes to work after finishing junior high school,

the rank and file white-collar worker after finishing college, and each at a time- and age-graded rate of pay. This is contrary to the American concept of payment according to job duties. These young people in Japan make hardly anything, but they are all working. Of course, it isn't terribly important to economize their work. If you go into a store, there are pretty girls all over the place opening and closing the doors. It takes three or four girls to wrap a package and another one thanks you for making a purchase and hopes the service will be better next time. That sort of thing.

They are paid very little, but they do have a work connection. They are starting to see what work experience is. They have identification with some enterprise. They are still living with their parents, because the age of marriage in Japan is generally rather advanced. So that's another kind of institution. In the United States, we lack the means of easing the passage from school, which is preparation, into the world of work.

KLEIN: You commented on European apprenticeship. The ILO, under a U.S. Labor Department grant, has just published a report* dealing with apprenticeship in Europe. It is the most extensive review we have of rites of passage and it gives a very good synopsis of changes taking place in European apprenticeship programs today.

STRODTBECK: One of the unanticipated effects of programs set up to induct young people into the labor market is that there is virtual absence of the real, rough type of juvenile delinquency that we have in this country.

ROSS: That's right. You can certainly see that in the countries I mentioned. There seems to be a tendency in the United States to say, "We have to extend the period of education. We are getting into very complex technology and everybody should have at least two years of college." I don't really like the idea of boys and girls getting to be nineteen or twenty and never having worked.

STRODTBECK: The Negro boys in Chicago who drop out of school face a five- or six-year period when they are not going to be employable. The contrary notion can be found in England.

---

* International Labor Organization, *European Apprenticeship* (Geneva: ILO, 1966).

There, a boy will be taken on at places where I am sure the employment is not conceptualized formally as an apprenticeship; it is several steps higher. But he will be taken on as a wrapping clerk and be paid really a very modest amount. It's that latitude for paying according to the economic contribution of the worker, which our legislation restricts, that I think is crucial. To a degree, the youth centers I visited in Europe caution a boy not to take a job that is only summer employment with high pay. The accepted pattern is for him to go to an employer who can keep him working all year round even though it may be at a more modest rate.

I visited some of the industrial schools in England and talked with the boys about their occupational aspirations. I found that, by far, the highest aspiration some of them have is to be a lorry driver, because it is the practice in Britain to let a man be the sole operator of a given vehicle; to get out of London and be able to drive up to Scotland and back in a vehicle that is identified with you seems to be a unique privilege. By our standards, it's a modest reward for a job well done.

In this country, there are some developing models, such as the Antioch College plan, which might apply more generally to high schools and junior colleges through arrangements with employers. Every summer, there are youth-employment campaigns under the sponsorship of the President and the Vice-President and others. The big corporations are beginning to feel that it is their responsibility to provide jobs, and I think this can be regularized and institutionalized. If we are going to have long summer vacations, obviously we don't need all youth for farm work any more. I think work opportunity should be lined up. I haven't really thought it through, but it seems to me that many of the problems of youth are connected with the absence of a work connection.

LECHT: If we wanted to institutionalize this, wouldn't it be necessary to modify the minimum wage law?

Ross: Yes. It would be necessary to make the law compatible with such programs. Again, that is being done in some cases. For example, under the Neighborhood Youth Corps, a youth has a combination of work and training. He is paid $1.25 an hour for time counted as work, but not for training hours, so that the income he receives for total time spent is a good deal less than the minimum wage. I suppose, if arrangements could be worked out with private industry and the desire were not to subsidize private industry by giving it a substandard labor supply, it would be a matter of conceptualizing how much of it is training, which would not be paid for, and how much of it is work. These things are subject to negotiation.

BUSHNELL: I might mention that there has been, for some time, in vocational education an emphasis on work-study arrangements. While such programs have not been given wide recognition, they exist in many school districts, frequently in such occupational areas as office education. One of the real utilities of this type of arrangement has been the opportunity for the vocational teacher to place his better students in full-time jobs that were originally obtained on a part-time basis while the student was in school.

BEMIS: I would like to call your attention to a 1962 Phi Delta Kappa-sponsored casebook of work-study programs for alienated youth,* which describes nine programs in our country for youngsters who couldn't qualify for the kind of work-study program that you have just discussed. These are for youngsters who are, in most cases, below even high school age. That is, they are of typical junior high school age.

SNIDER: How does your department determine how many people would be placed in these training classes throughout the country? For instance, we read in the paper that a certain town is starting a course for fifty automobile engine repairmen, or maybe sixty-five secretaries; or we read about jobs in training programs that run over a period of several months. How do you determine how many of these people are needed?

ROSS: I'll let Mr. Klein answer that one.

KLEIN: What we do is to make a local market survey of availability of supply and demand based on employment-service records, a sample of employers of the area, a judgmental factor, and a survey of the existing educational facilities and programs.

DEITCH: Can you give us your thoughts on this empirical matter of measuring unemployment? Do you think, as we now do it, we get an accurate index of what we are trying to measure?

* George W. Burchill, *Work-Study Programs for Alienated Youth: A Casebook* (Chicago: Science Research Associates, 1962).

Ross: I would say yes, except that unemployment is a social fact. It is not like a tree or an apple, which are physical facts. It is a man-made social category and most of the confusion about it results from different concepts of how it should be measured, not from any problems of using a given measure.

For example, some people think that a measure of unemployment should represent only people in economic distress. They say, "Well, here are some middle-aged women who are looking for work. They don't really *need* jobs." But, of course, we don't claim that all the unemployed are in great distress. I think we have done a lot to clarify the statistics, in the past few months, by giving more of the details. We have put a lot of emphasis on distinguishing between a part-time and a full-time job-seeker and I think that has clarified it considerably. We are also making more complete breakdowns by age, sex, and race. I would say the primary difficulty is taking a rate like 3.5 or 4 per cent. It's a perfectly good rate, except that it throws together such heterogeneous elements that if you want to understand it you must understand the components.

There were studies, a few years ago, showing that the lower unemployment rates in Europe were not due to different methods of measurement. For example, there are many people *we* count as employed who are getting only part-time work although they want full-time work, so there is a little ragged edge there. Any social definition like this has difficult borderlines. The unemployed are supposed to be looking for work. But, of course, some may not be looking too hard. For example, cannery women typically work in a cannery nine months a year and go on unemployment insurance for the other three months. In fact, there may be no other jobs in their communities. It's awfully difficult to say, "Are they looking hard enough in San Jose?," if those are the only jobs for them.

An unemployed person is supposed to be employable and, as I emphasized in the paper, there are certainly many people on the borderline. They may be unemployable one year, yet, if demand increases enough, employers may begin to use them the next year. Or, they may be unemployable until the Poverty Program or the Labor Department does something to rehabilitate them.

So, I think the employment measures are good. The sample method is always a better method than an enumeration. I would say, for example, that the figures we get from our monthly sample are better than the census figures or other censuses of unemployment. Many countries now are shifting over to the household survey sample method. We may lose some individuals who aren't connected with any household. I just don't know much about this. We are told that, in ghetto communities, there are some youths who just do not have a household. They live on the streets. I don't know that there are enough to affect the figures.

STRODTBECK: Do we have a systematic way of eliciting information about unfilled jobs?

ROSS: No. People have been requesting what is called the Job Vacancy Data Program. We have, before Congress, a proposal that would give us a nationwide system of job vacancy data. If we get the appropriation we'll put it into practice. We have been making experiments in sixteen areas and, thus far, these show it to be practical and useful.

STRODTBECK: I would say that a choice between greater precision of unemployment statistics and fuller information about unfilled positions would give me, as an executive, an easy decision. I think greater knowledge about the unfilled positions is essential in planning.

ROSS: Yes. It would certainly indicate more clearly what has to be done to get the unemployed into these positions, and that's often not a direct transaction. It often takes several intermediate steps, including upgrading those who already have jobs and moving the unemployed in at the bottom. That is more apt to be true with those currently unemployed. Today, we say that we have 3 million unemployed. But that really isn't a net 3 million. About 400,000 of them are just seasonally unemployed, like the building tradesmen, and they will go back to work in the spring and summer. Then, about 2 per cent represents normal labor turnover, and people in this position are not really a net surplus.

Out of this 3 million, perhaps about 1 million might be considered a net surplus and, on the whole, they are not very good job candidates. They don't have the qualifications for the vacancies that are hardest to fill. Many of the vacancies they can fill are transitional or seasonal. But the problem vacancies are, to a large extent, in some of the chronic labor-shortage professions and skilled trades—such as metal trades—and your hard-core unemployed cannot be put directly into these positions. So, it is a point of knowing your vacancies in situations where you can't engineer a direct transfer.

BEASLEY: Does the Department of Labor ever attempt to find out how many people are working more than one job, the so-called moonlighters? How do you handle them, statistically?

ROSS: Yes, we have made special studies. We released a report, in the February, 1966, *Monthly Labor Review,* which had complete estimates of the number of moonlighters and how much they earn.

BEASLEY: Is this number significant enough to affect the employment market—if these jobs could be allocated to the unemployed?

ROSS: No, because most of the moonlighters don't work very many hours on the second job. Moonlighters would include the college professors who, maybe, do one day of consulting a week. In Washington, I notice quite a few of the lower-paid government people drive taxis for two or three hours after work.

I suppose you could put these jobs together to make a number of full-time jobs, but I'm not sure of it. It certainly isn't in our tradition to have a law that people can do only a certain amount of work.

CORREA: Is there, in the United States, the problem of underemployment and do you have a method of measuring it?

ROSS: The answer to both questions is yes. Underemployment is a problem in two respects. One of them can be measured and the other can't. There is a problem of underemployment in the sense that some people would like full-time work but are getting only part-time work. We have measures of that. I think it was 1.8 million in February, 1966. And we do know just how many hours less than full time they are missing, on the average.

The other type of underemployment is really not measurable. It involves people working below capacity; that is, people who are not doing the job for which they were trained. Many people have the capacity to do a responsible job but haven't been pushed up to it. One of the benefits of a high-employment or full-employment situation is that the employer is apt to push a man (even if he hasn't received a college degree) up to a new job he can do perfectly well and give him whatever additional training is necessary.

STOIKOV: At one point, you suggested that we do not have a very good indication of the relationship between unemployment and price increases in the United States. On the other hand, you said that full employment will require a 2 or 3 per cent price increase. Where did you get that figure?

ROSS: Well, this is my judgment. I suppose half of the Ph.D. candidates in economics have been doing research on the relationship between the employment level and the wage-price trend. If I had to give a figure for full employment, I would estimate it to be 2 to 2.5 per cent and I would say that it's likely that you would have a concurrent annual price creep of about 2 per cent. Now you may ask, "Where did I get it?" It is just a judgment from having studied the problem for a long time.

LECHT: Along that same line, you pointed out that in other than periods of war in the recent past we haven't had anything close to what most people consider full employment. You also mentioned government as an employer of last resort. I wonder if there isn't some kind of connection here that might result in full employment without full inflation or in full employment with much less price increase. We look at our cities and see how badly kept many of our streets and parks are. At the same time, unemployment is concentrated among the unskilled. These are the people who are hard to reach. I wonder if considerable expansion in public services and facilities isn't the least inflationary way of increasing employment, because it is such a highly labor-intensive approach.

ARNESEN: Mr. Ross, do you want to comment on this question, on the possible role of governmental agencies in taking up some of the slack in employment?

ROSS: I don't really know whether I need to. It's a question that has been debated for years by Galbraith and the neo-Galbraithian writers. I don't think I have anything terribly original to add to it.

SNIDER: I'd like to go back to the job vacancy question. Earlier, Mr. Klein explained how your department determined the placements in training classes. Why couldn't the department do the same, then, to determine what the job needs are throughout the country? Does it take too much time? By the time the department got the survey finished, would it be out of date?

Ross: It takes quite a bit of money, and also there is a general drive, you know, to eliminate the paperwork jungle and not to keep asking employers to fill out more questionnaires. You have to get the approval of the Budget Bureau and of Congress to initiate a big data-collection program.

Snider: I think this is very important.

Ross: I think so too. You should have heard me before the House Appropriations Committee. I don't know if they were impressed. In the past, both management and labor have been lukewarm. Labor didn't like it because they were afraid that figures on job vacancies would be used to dilute or to detract from the unemployment statistics and they thought they were getting a lot of mileage from the unemployment statistics. Management was afraid they would be asked to use the public employment offices, or told, "We want you to hire some Negroes." So both have been a little lukewarm.

Some of the economists have felt that there was ambiguity about the concept of job vacancies. I think we have done a pretty good job of clarifying this. We have shown that job vacancies can be measured—employers know what you mean when you ask them to report their vacancies. We have shown that you can get the wage rates and the occupations, so that you don't misuse any gross, undifferentiated total. We have shown that you can have the employer check a box if he wants help; if he doesn't check the box, nobody so much as telephones him. So, I think the opponents are down to some arguments that aren't very persuasive; still, we might not get that appropriation.

Snider: We sometimes feel, in the public schools, that we are operating in a vacuum. In some areas, we train many people who are not needed. This certainly adds to the feeling of operating blind.

Ross: There are some things to go on. Mr. Klein referred to the job orders employers place with the Employment Service. These are not representative, but there are many of them. That is one helpful source of information. Then, there is a list of critical occupations, put out in Washington for the benefit of the Selective Service boards. And there are some things that are matters of public knowledge, so I wouldn't say that the schools were entirely in the dark. Of course, job-vacancy statistics would have many uses even if they weren't needed for guidance or training programs.

KLEIN: What we have found, by conducting surveys of the local labor markets and of smaller community segments, is that a pattern is beginning to emerge. There are certain occupational titles with high demand frequencies. This data should be available shortly,* for use by the educational planner.

Ross: May I add one comment on Mr. Snider's point? For career planning, I don't think the short-term vacancies are so important as the long-term outlook. You are probably familiar with the *Occupational Outlook Handbook*.† I think we are going to sell about 100,000 copies this year. It really does have a pretty good write-up of career prospects and it is based on a careful study of demand, technology, and other factors affecting career prospects.

I think if counselors and youths read this book, they would have a good basis for making some decisions.

TAYLOR: In your paper, Mr. Ross, you referred to some limitations, or weaknesses, of the public employment services in introducing youngsters to the world of work. I wonder if you would elaborate? What do you see as some ideal types of changes that would aid in this transition period, changes on the part of your Employment Service and of the schools?

Ross: I don't know that I could say much more than we said a little while ago. I think we talked about work and training combinations, or various types of apprenticeship—aside from the very narrow and minute apprenticeship program that we have in the United States—and summer work programs in which the employers in a community take on responsibility to provide opportunities for the youth of the community. I think this could all revolve around the Employment Service.

We have a bill in the Congress not to federalize but to step up

---

* N.Y. State Department of Labor, *Manpower Projections for New York State 1965–1975* (Albany, N.Y.: N.Y. State Printing Office, 1967).

† *Occupational Outlook Handbook* (Bureau of Labor Statistics Bulletin No. 1450) (Washington, D.C.: Department of Labor, 1966–67).

the activity of the U.S. and the state employment services. The general aim is to make them community manpower exchanges rather than concentrate solely on unemployment or unemployment insurance matters.

FOLGER: I would like to go back to two points you made about the government's improved ability to fulfill its commitment to full employment—one being intellectual tools and the other, reduction of ideological conflicts. Then you went on to make the point that manpower policies will be more important than fiscal policy in reducing unemployment, or in keeping it below 4 per cent.

ROSS: At the moment, we have the aggregate demand. The problem is to bridge the mismatch between the workers and the jobs.

FOLGER: My question is twofold. Do we really have the intellectual tools, and do we have an ideological problem in introducing manpower policies?

ROSS: On the manpower side, I don't think there has been much of an ideological problem. In fact, the conservatives in Congress really went for the training programs more easily than they did for the tax cut a few years back. At the present time, whenever there is discussion of a tax increase we can expect to hear the argument that if we are going to increase taxes we will have to cut domestic spending programs, including manpower programs. That, I think, would be a terribly misconceived idea. I am not sure whether that is ideological or political. I don't see any real ideological problem, as such, about manpower programs, because America has always, you know, spent a great deal of money on education.

FOLGER: In your paper, you talk about the undesirability of planning for people. This is a recurrent theme that some people use in objecting to the notion of the government planning anybody's career for him.

ROSS: Well, I don't think you have raised a real issue there, because we are not talking about compulsory manpower planning, where somebody would plan your career against your will. All of these things are services or facilities. I did express some distaste for the concept of "human investment" or "human resources."

STOIKOV: Is your objection made on esthetic grounds?

ROSS: I have an esthetic objection to considering man as a tool or an object, which I think is sacrilegious. But that would not be of

great policy importance, in most cases. In other words, the manpower planning we are talking about has nothing to do with compulsory direction of manpower, if that's what you're thinking
about.

FOLGER: I am just asking whether you think there are any ideological issues in this area.

ROSS: No. I thought you were going to talk about fiscal policy,
the New Economics, Keynesianism, and so forth—which I think
have raised greater ideological problems than the manpower policies.

FOLGER: I think, actually, there are probably some latent ideological conflicts. Whether they will emerge will depend on how
much government intervention there is and what sort might be
necessary to make a match between people and jobs, as the occupational structure speeds up in its rate of change.

ROSS: I would say that, so long as the manpower policies are
putting people in private employment, I don't believe you will
really hit an ideological impasse. If it comes to the concept of the
government as employer of last resort, or to a subeconomy of people being hired, at great economic disadvantage, for public service
tasks, then you may run into grave ideological conflict.

MCLURE: You quote a figure of 1 per cent for retraining in
Sweden and apply that figure as the per cent of the labor force that
it is necessary for us to retrain. Is the educational question one
we should decide by inference from the trends of such statistics?

KLEIN: There is one basic area that has been left out of the discussion. That is the private sector and its tremendous investment
in training. It does this both internally and externally. The investment is huge and continues to increase. Contrary to popular belief,
the work force is adjusting to technological change. The key is to
provide appropriate time intervals for the transition.

ROSS: Well, I think there is another point to be made, though,
in response to Mr. McLure. The product of a good education
would have the personal flexibility or theoretical breadth or whatever it would take to be able to adjust as job requirements change.
I suppose, perhaps, that is the distinction between education and
training. I don't know. I am really not expert on this. But I don't
think of education as merely fitting a person into a momentarily

conceived job definition. At the same time, I think there has been some exaggeration of the extent of change. It is now fashionable to say that everybody will have to have three entirely different and separate types of careers in the future. I don't think this is correct.

It is true that what goes on within a career is becoming less traditional. In other words, to be an engineer for fifty years probably means that you have to keep on learning and changing. Or, to be an economist—if you got your degree when I received mine—you either have fallen far behind or have had to learn quite a bit since then. So I would guess that, even with an advanced education, it is a matter of building in some process of keeping up with change.

DAVID: There is one other matter that I think is important, which hasn't been given any emphasis at all. You can also solve the unemployment problem by encouraging people not to be in the labor force. We recognize that students are perfectly valid as a socially desirable category of people not necessarily in the labor force. We also recognize that there is an age of retirement beyond which people are not necessarily in the labor force.

However, I think that the retired have a real problem of disorganization. Society must develop some purposeful role for these people. The educational system may define ways in which individuals can assume new roles that are outside of this traditional concept of the labor force.

CORREA: I want to make a point that was mentioned earlier with respect to manpower planning. Do you include, in your definition of manpower planning, planning of the educational systems in order to produce manpower for economic development? Do you think that, in the United States, there is the intellectual and ideological basis for planning the educational system?

ROSS: I don't see any great ideological problem. Traditionally, we have not thought of education as a manpower function, the way it might be conceived in a new African state, for example. It certainly is if you try to conceive broadly the manpower program of a country. In education efforts, it would include long-term, as well as short-term, training.

Education is very decentralized in this country. There are thousands of school boards and all kinds of political jurisdictions. I find it hard to think of planning in any monolithic way when I see how many states, localities, school districts, vocational-training authorities, apprenticeship authorities, agricultural-extension people, and other different agencies are now involved in manpower training.

STOIKOV: This is not necessarily what one means by "planning." Clearly, you can influence hundreds of units through federal spending of one type or another: This is planning, in the sense of looking forward to certain kinds of demands.

ROSS: If you have the money to pass out, you can influence the activity of these different units. However, looking at it from the national viewpoint, it might seem necessary to move people from one state to another, or from one section of a state to another. But, the local people might not want to lose their labor supply. Or, in another case, it might seem necessary to train a great many more building craftsmen, but the trade unions might not see it that way.

I think that long-term planning to meet the demand for Medicare, for example, will certainly call for a great many more medical schools. But we have not had much enthusiasm, in the medical profession, for establishing new medical schools. This is a decentralized country with a tremendous number of interest groups and a great deal of political differentiation; that situation does affect the possibility of centralized planning, even on a voluntary basis.

KIMBALL: I have two or three things to discuss. First, some of the South American countries are developing, or have developed, a different approach to manpower training and the educational system. I am acquainted with two systems, one in Brazil, which is of fairly long standing, and the other in Peru, which is of more recent origin.

Under these systems, manufacturers pay a special tax—assessed on the basis of the number of workers and, I think, by some other formula—into a program that is cooperatively operated by industry and the state. The program helps to train or upgrade workers in industry.

The philosophy behind this is that the public school system should provide the general education for a population; that industry should bear its share of the cost of the special training that is for the benefit of industry. Of course, there is an ideological problem here. How does one determine how much responsibility is owed by industry and how much by public institutions for manpower training?

KLEIN: The concept is taken even further in some countries where, when the economy indicates a decline of aggregate demand, training is used to bring about changes in the system.*

KIMBALL: My second point is that I want to compliment Mr. Ross on his use of the term rites of passage. This is the first time I have heard an economist use that particular term and I think the whole notion of rites of passage could very easily be brought into economic training in a very fruitful manner.

My third point is of another kind and it carries with it a question. In this country, we have hundreds of thousands of people who are volunteer workers, who contribute to the GNP through their services. They are represented by the Boy Scouts, by Red Cross workers, by volunteer workers in hospitals, in schools, and in many other public and private programs. May I ask, do labor and government economists attempt to take into account the number of people who are thus engaged and the relationship of this kind of activity to preparation for paid employment?

ROSS: The answer is, not in general, because both the concept of production and the concept of employment for commercial purposes mean payment of wages. It is certainly true, as a practical matter, that many things people do without pay are very valuable. I suppose that is certainly true of the mothers who instruct their children. They are not counted as employed, nor is the value of their instruction counted as part of the gross national product.

Certainly, as more leisure becomes available, as social problems become more complex, the value and the worth of what these people are doing must be recognized. This is particularly true for people who need to have a job to identify with. It can be among the most valuable and satisfying kinds of work. Many of these activities will turn into gainful employment. We are seeing the development of new professions. I have heard some terms today I hadn't heard before, such as detached worker.

SWANSON: There is such a thing as a distribution of aptitude on the supply side of the employment market and a distribution of

* See the National Market Board, *Modern Swedish Labor Market Policy* (Stockholm: The Swedish Institute, 1966).

aptitude on the demand side. How close together are these two distributions? Are they moving apart or together? And what part of this is served by what you call the government as the employer of last resort?

Ross: The closer you come to full employment, the more discrepancy develops between the residual supply and the unfilled demand, and the more need there is for government activity. But even so, the government activity can only be a kind of pump-priming. When all is said and done, most of the adjustment is accomplished within industry and much of it is a natural reaction to economic changes. I think more can be done by the government to stimulate it and, perhaps, subsidize it. But for every person we train institutionally under MPTA, I suppose there are quite a few industry would train and upgrade.

Swanson: In reference to the distribution of aptitude on the supply side of the employment market and the distribution of aptitude on the demand side: There are those who say that, on the demand side, there is a distribution of aptitude that is much higher than the supply side is prepared to offer.

Folger: I would argue that there is no evidence to verify this. Of course, everyone would like to have more bright people working in his area.

Swanson: I think there is supporting evidence. I think a school superintendent who has a thousand graduates from his school can show you that there are people above the median who are drained off and move into college and get fellowships and so on.

Folger: I thought you were saying that we are running out of talent in the country, and I would say that there is very little evidence that we are running out of talent.

Ross: Everybody wants the best people. You are always going to have more competition for the better people.

Klein: I would like to give some illustrations of this matching of supply and demand.

In a study* conducted by the New York State Department of Labor, an attempt was made to identify that part of the population employed as technicians. For definition, we used the standard that

* N.Y. State Department of Labor, *Technical Manpower in New York State* (Albany, N.Y.: N.Y. State Printing Office, 1964), Vols. I–II.

the person had to have some knowledge of math and science and had to apply this in some way in his work situation. The study revealed that 2.5 per cent of the work force met that criterion. There was a ratio of about 1.19 technicians to one engineer. What was discovered, in many instances, was that the employer hired engineers who were functioning at the technicians' level. In estimating growth in the technicians' category of employment, even if we take a very liberal position and state that the aggregate technician employment would double in the next decade, it still would only represent 5 per cent of the work force. However, this doubling is not likely to occur.

We came to the conclusion that the majority of the jobs within the state could be handled adequately by people with less than a high school education if there were some acquisition of skill on the job. What is occurring, however, is that the minimum acceptable standard for admission is a diploma from high school.

FLANIGAN: I should like to remind you all that, if we are going to do a real job of planning, we are running a big chance of letting the 1970 census go by with some very crude job titles, along with the standard major classification—which is now either "public" or "private" worker. There is no nonprofit entry, though the department gets to it in a very roundabout way by asking the name of the employer. I have already written the Census Bureau a letter about it and I hope everybody else will.

4

Manpower Needs, National Goals, and Educational Policy in the 1970's

LEONARD A. LECHT

As a nation, we are probably more concerned now with the relationships between our educational system and the labor market than ever before. In this paper, I propose to explore some of these relationships, from the perspective of our society's estimated manpower needs in the next decade. The projections I will offer refer to manpower requirements for a broad spectrum of national objectives in the private and public sectors of our society, rather than to estimates of need in individual areas, such as health or education. The estimates are based on the preliminary findings of a study being conducted by the National Planning Association's Center for Priority Analysis for the U.S. Department of Labor's Office of Manpower Policy, Evaluation, and Research.

Many economists, many people in education, and a great many other individuals are concerned with our nation's future manpower requirements. The U.S. Department of Labor prepares estimates indicating probable employment opportunities in different types of occupations. We now have such estimates for 1970 and 1975. For the professions, the National Institutes of Health publish projections of manpower needs in the health occupations, and the U.S. Office of Education prepares similar ten-year forecasts of requirements and supply for teachers.

Of course, meeting manpower needs is not the only function of teaching and learning. Education is important for many reasons, not the least of which is that it provides a means for the enrichment of personal life and is a prerequisite for intelligent social and political participation in our complex society. Education not only serves to develop our human resources, it transmits our culture and provides the foundation for our technological dynamism. And it should not be forgotten that expanding educational opportunity has become the strategic ingredient in the nation's programs for coping with poverty and racial discrimination.

But, viewed from the vantage point of the labor market, the educational system diffuses social and economic opportunity by educating and training people to become participants, or more productive participants, in gainful employment. The farm boy who becomes a physician, the girl from the poor family who becomes a teacher, or the graduate of the local community college who finds rewarding employment as an electronics technician are the living illustrations of the success of the system.

CHANGES IN THE RELATIONSHIP BETWEEN WORK, EDUCATION, AND EMPLOYMENT

Both educators and economists have observed, in the past decade, that the relationship between work, education, and employment has been undergoing a significant change. The impact of this change has been to accentuate the premium on formal schooling and to increase the economic penalties for lack of sufficient education. The changes in the relationship between work, education, and employment have been responsible for much of the discussion of the manpower revolution, school dropouts, and automation. In 1964, President Johnson observed that "the education . . . of many of our people has not prepared them adequately to qualify for today's jobs, to absorb skill training, or to capitalize on new opportunities."[*] The Job Corps, the National Defense Education Act, and the legislation enacted several years ago providing federal aid to support education in low-income areas are probably the forerunners of many new programs intended to alleviate the economic penalty of inadequate education, or to help assure that the supply

[*] *Manpower Report of the President,* XIV (Washington, D.C.: GPO, 1964). Henceforth cited as *MRP.*

of physicians, engineers, teachers, and other professional and technical workers will increase as needs increase in the future.

School dropouts are not a new phenomenon, of course, and they make up a smaller proportion of the young adult population than they did ten, twenty, or fifty years ago. What is new is the greater economic penalty attached to being a school dropout and the virtually nationwide consensus that the federal and state governments should embark on large-scale programs to provide facilities and financial support to encourage all young persons who have the capacity to finish high school or college.

Underlying these concerns is the substantial evidence that social and technological changes since World War II have greatly expanded employment opportunities for the well educated. The same changes have curtailed opportunities for persons with limited schooling.* The number of occupations that now require a high school diploma has been expanding rapidly. The same is true, to an even greater extent, for college degrees. Between 1947 and 1964, the employment of white-collar workers increased by two and one-half times the percentage increase in over-all civilian employment. During the same period, employment for professionals and technical workers increased even more rapidly—by 125 per cent, compared with 22 per cent for all civilian employment. Job opportunities for those having less than a high school education—blue-collar jobs and farming—increased very little and, in some instances, they have actually been decreasing. The correlation between education and job opportunity has one major exception. Jobs for service workers have increased by about the same percentage as those for white-collar workers. However, in absolute amounts, these jobs increased by less than a third as much. These percentage comparisons take into account the modest increase in blue-collar employment that occurred between 1961 and 1964.

These figures in the *Manpower Report* are supplemented by our information on the association between the level of educational attainment and unemployment. In 1964, 7 per cent of the white males who had completed eight years of schooling or less were unemployed; only slightly more than 1 per cent of those with four or more years of college education were unemployed. The risk of

* For a summary of these changes, see Table A-10, *MRP* (1965), pp. 202–3, from which the information that follows was drawn.

joblessness was over five times as great for males with only a grammar school education as it was for individuals who had completed four years or more of college.*

Some economists and other social scientists fear that these tendencies will accelerate in the next decade or so and that their net effect will be to divide the labor force into two groups. One group will be made up of individuals with limited schooling and occupational skills; this group is expected to be characterized by unemployment and underemployment. The other will consist of highly educated professional and technical people, and it is anticipated that our ability to educate and train sufficient people in these areas will frequently lag behind the growth in the demand for their services. If this situation were to materialize, far-reaching changes could be anticipated in our educational institutions, our government's policies, and in our social structure. One of the solutions, proposed by individuals who expect these tendencies to accelerate markedly in the next decade or two, is for the government to pay a guaranteed income to the large numbers of people they anticipate will be without work or income in the not too distant future† I do not share these anticipations. However, I agree that the underlying changes they stem from are likely to be influencing our economy in the 1970's—although with somewhat different consequences than are taken for granted in this version of the future.

What do the changes in the occupational pattern of employment mean for young people who will be entering the labor force in the next decade?

Between 1964 and 1975, the labor force is expected to increase by an average of 1.5 million a year. Will there be enough growth in blue-collar and service employment to absorb new entrants into the labor market who have limited schooling? Will our schools be graduating enough educated and trained people to fill growing needs in the white-collar occupations and, especially, in the professional and technical field?

To provide a basis for our opinions about the future, it would be

* See Denis F. Johnston, *Educational Attainment of Workers, March, 1964* (Bureau of Labor Statistics "Special Labor Force Report" No. 53) (Washington, D.C.: U.S. Department of Labor, 1965), Table 5, p. 521.

† For a presentation of this point of view see Robert Theobald (ed.), *The Guaranteed Income—Next Step in Economic Evolution?* (Garden City, N.Y.: Doubleday, 1966).

useful to indicate the strategic variables that have been changing manpower needs and job requirements since World War II. While technological change is the variable usually singled out for most emphasis, and it is certainly important, it is only one of several factors that have been influencing manpower needs. Others that should be considered include the impact of higher family incomes, the influence of rising levels of educational attainment, and the consequences of pursuing national priorities. All of these factors interact to produce the changes already noted in the nation's pattern of employment. By 1975, employment opportunities in the different occupations are also likely to be significantly affected by these four variables.

Technological changes, and especially those associated with what we have come to term automation or cybernation, have received widespread attention as the cause of the slow growth in blue-collar employment and the elimination of many routine clerical jobs. We are all familiar with the example of the large petroleum refinery operated by a dozen employees and a computer, or with the data processing equipment that has taken over the record-keeping operations in banks and insurance companies. The phrase manpower revolution has received much of its impetus from concern with automation, and it is concern with the impact of technological change that prompts the fears of those who anticipate a future society with sharply diminishing employment opportunities for blue-collar and routine clerical workers.

In practice, it is often difficult to disentangle the effects of technological change on employment from the influence of other factors that also affect the occupational distribution. Some of the changes in employment opportunities attributed to automation are probably due to changes in consumer spending brought about by rising family incomes. Between 1947 and 1964, average family income, in dollars of 1964 purchasing power, increased from over $5,600 to over $7,800. As our society becomes more affluent, the majority who share this affluence spend a smaller share of their income for food, clothing, or housing, and a larger share for services. Spending rises more than proportionately for visits to physicians and dentists, for vacations and travel, for books and education, and for the services of beauticians and gardeners. These changes in family expenditures also help account for the rapid growth in the professional and service occupations.

The greater importance attached to education also influences job requirements. Discussions of the relationship between education and the labor market sometimes take it for granted that changing manpower needs make up the independent variable and that education is the dependent variable. The educational system, we are told, should adapt to labor market needs. Yet, the opposite is also true. Rising levels of educational attainment have probably caused some of the changes in job requirements.

TABLE I

EDUCATIONAL ATTAINMENT OF EMPLOYED MALES 18 YEARS
OLD AND OLDER: OCTOBER, 1952, AND MARCH, 1964

Occupational Group	Per Cent Completing 8 Years of Elementary School or Less		Per Cent Completing 4 Years of High School or More	
	October 1952	March 1964	October 1952	March 1964
All Occupations	41	26	40	55
White-Collar Workers:				
Professional and				
Managerial Workers	17	10	71	81
Clerical and Sales Workers	17	11	66	75
Blue-Collar Workers:				
Craftsmen and Foremen	41	29	34	46
Operatives	50	34	24	38
Laborersa	67	47	17	27
Service Workers	53	38	27	40
Farm Occupations	67	58	21	27

a Excluding farm and mine laborers.

SOURCE: Denis F. Johnston, *Educational Attainment of Workers, March, 1964* (Bureau of Labor Statistics "Special Labor Force Report" No. 53) (Washington, D.C.: U.S. Department of Labor, 1965), Table 6, p. 522.

The educational level of the entire labor force has been rising markedly since World War II. (The changes between 1952 and 1964 for employed males eighteen years old and older are highlighted by the data presented in Table I.) It has increased rapidly for operatives, laborers, and service workers. These are the occupations that have provided the bulk of employment for persons with less than eight years of education. As a majority of the employees in these jobs come to have at least a grammar school education—and many come to have a high school education—individuals with lesser schooling will be at a disadvantage in obtaining employment. Similarly, 75 per cent of all clerical workers have now completed at least four years of high school. Potential clerical employees with less than a high school education will find it increasingly difficult to find jobs. The more skilled clerical jobs, such as secretaries, are likely to draw heavily on those who have some college education, many of whom will be graduates of local community colleges.

The expression that "supply creates its own demand" is a truism in economics. But, the economic relationships this expression summarizes are likely to have far-reaching implications for job requirements in the future. As the supply of well-educated people increases, their greater availability to employers becomes a factor in raising entrance requirements for many types of work.

The nation's priorities also exert a significant influence on manpower requirements and this, in turn, greatly affects education. During the past decade, Sputnik, the civil rights movement, changing manpower requirements, and the war on poverty have led to substantial increases in the share of the nation's resources devoted to education. Growth in the population of young people has accentuated these increases. Total public and private expenditures for education have increased from $14 billion, in 1954, to $34 billion, in 1964. This represents an increase from just under 4 per cent of GNP, in 1954, to almost 5.5 per cent of the larger GNP in 1964.*

As a consequence of our population growth and growing concern that more and better educational opportunity be made available to Americans, the educational system has become a massive consumer of manpower. Thinking of education as an industry, in 1964 it employed some 4 million people. Of these workers, 1.5 million were employed in some capacity other than professional and technical work. The education industry, in 1964, for example,

* *Trends* (Washington, D.C.: U.S. Department of Health, Education, and Welfare, 1964), p. 59. Henceforth cited as *Trends*.

employed over 600,000 service workers, including almost .4 million janitors and sextons, and over 100,000 cooks.*

Most people in education are employed by state and local governments. Between 1953 and 1964, state and local government employment increased by almost seven times the rate at which total employment grew.† About 60 per cent of the employees in education are professional and technical workers. Pursuit of our nation's objectives in education has been a major force in increasing the demand for white-collar workers and, especially, for professional employees.

Similarly, in the decade after 1953, expenditures for research and development in the United States tripled, rising from $5 billion, in 1953, to $17 billion a decade later. Most of this growth in R&D spending represents public expenditures associated with the pursuit of national goals in defense, space, atomic energy, and health. Changes in the tempo of these programs have created "shortages" and, less frequently, surpluses of scientists and engineers.‡ The pursuit of our goals in R&D or in education primarily affects employment for professional and technical people. Vigorous pursuit of our objectives in housing, in urban development, or in reducing the prevalence of poverty could play a significant role in creating job opportunities for blue-collar workers in the building trades, in manufacturing, in transportation, and in trade.

PROJECTIONS INTO THE FUTURE

It is reasonable to anticipate that the forces that have been changing manpower requirements since World War II—technological change, larger family incomes, rising levels of educational attainment, and the pursuit of national priorities—will continue to change manpower needs in the next ten years.

By 1975, the GNP is expected to increase, in dollars of 1964 pur-

* Unpublished data from the U.S. department of Labor.

† See Table A-1, *MRP* (1965), p. 193, and *Statistical Abstract* (Washington, D.C.: GPO, 1965), Table 592, p. 440.

‡ For a discussion of the relationship of national priorities to "shortages" of scientists and engineers, see Gerhard Colm and Leonard Lecht, "Requirements for Scientific and Engineering Manpower in the 1970's" in Committee on Utilization of Scientific and Engineering Manpower, *Toward Better Utilization of Scientific and Engineering Talent* (Washington, D.C.: National Academy of Sciences, 1964), pp. 71 ff.

chasing power, to over $1 trillion. This assumes a reasonably optimistic GNP growth rate, averaging slightly over 4 per cent a year, in the next decade. The average annual income of American families, again in 1964 dollars, is expected to increase to about $10,400. The civilian labor force is likely to receive an additional 17 million people—an increase from 4 million, in 1964, to the 91 million anticipated in 1975 by the U.S. Department of Labor.*

As the typical American family reaches the $10,000 a year income group, it is likely to find that expenditures for services have probably increased more rapidly than the growth in income. Spending for items of durable equipment, which have become symbols of American affluence, is also likely to increase substantially. By 1975, it is anticipated that over 40 per cent of the families in the United States will own two or more cars. The spending patterns resulting from these higher incomes will tend to increase the share of the labor force in the service occupations, in auto and home equipment repair, and in the professions.

By 1975, according to U.S. Department of Labor estimates, 60 per cent of the civilian labor force will have completed four years of high school or more. For workers in the 25-34 year age group, this proportion is projected to reach 70 per cent.† Older workers, who typically have had less schooling, and young school dropouts are likely to find that the disadvantage of inadequate schooling, in obtaining a job or in getting promoted, is greater than it was in the 1960's.

What about technological change? The most important single measure of the impact of technological change is the increase in output per worker, usually measured by the annual percentage change in GNP per man-hour. In the past two decades, GNP per man-hour has been increasing by just under 3 per cent a year. The productivity gains in the next ten years are expected to increase by slightly more than 3 per cent a year. [In Chapter 6, Dr. Colm will discuss the reasons why the technological changes anticipated in the next decade are unlikely to make for a discontinuous increase in productivity.]

The degree to which we pursue our nation's goals, in the 1970's,

* See Table E-6, *MRP* (1966), p. 217.
† See Table E-7, *MRP* (1966), p. 218.

will be an important element in determining whether we make adequate use of our society's human resources, or whether we overstrain or underutilize them. Vigorous pursuit of the nation's unfinished business in health and education, in building viable urban communities, in encouraging research and development, or in reducing the prevalence of poverty, could fully occupy a labor force using the technological advances anticipated in the next decade. Attempting to achieve all our aspirations at once would probably lead to severe labor shortages. Our manpower projections for the 1970's are, therefore, related to the requirements for achieving national objectives in the next ten years.

These estimates of manpower requirements are the sequel to a study of the dollar costs of achieving national goals in sixteen areas in the 1970's. That study was conducted by the Goals Project of the National Planning Association's Center for Priority Analysis.*

Our study of national goals has used the work of President Eisenhower's Commission on National Goals as a point of departure.† Space goals were added in 1961, when President Kennedy proposed that it become a national objective "to put men on the moon and bring them back." We interpreted this to mean embarkation on a sustained space research program.

The sixteen goals, which figure as the basis for our manpower estimates, are listed in Table II, along with actual expenditures in 1962 and projected expenditures—based on an estimate of the cost of achieving them—for 1975.

To reflect the trend in the consensus of informed opinion, the standards for the goals were based on the reports of expert studies, on legislative enactments, such as the Hill-Burton Act in hospital construction, and on the recommendations of public bodies, such as the National Academy of Sciences and the National Institutes of Health. The study also estimated costs, deriving these from the quantitative relationships goal achievement would require. The improvements considered in the education goal, for example, have been translated into ratios of teachers per 1,000 students, changes

---

* See *Goals, Priorities, and Dollars—The Next Decade* (New York: The Free Press, 1966).

† *Goals for Americans: The Report of the President's Commission on National Goals* (Englewood Cliffs, N.J.: Prentice-Hall, 1960).

in the compensation of faculty, and into the additional classroom, laboratory, and dormitory space needed for the greater percentage of the eligible age groups assumed to be attending school by 1975.*

TABLE II

EXPENDITURES FOR GOALS: ACTUAL 1962 AND PROJECTED 1975
(IN MILLIONS OF 1962 DOLLARS)

Goal Area	Expenditures in 1962	Projected Expenditures for Aspiration Goals in 1975
Consumer Expenditures	$355,050	$659,600
Private Plant and Equipment	48,900	151,600
Urban Development	64,200	129,700
Social Welfare	37,800	92,400
Health	32,300	85,400
Education	30,400	82,100
Transportation	35,100	75,400
National Defense	51,450	67,550
Housing	29,400	62,000
Research and Development	18,300	38,850
Natural Resources	5,900	16,700
International Aid	5,100	13,150
Space	3,250	9,350
Agriculture	7,200	9,200
Manpower Retraining	100	2,850
Area Redevelopment	350	950
Gross Total	*724,800*	*1,496,800*
Minus Double Counting and Transfer Adjustments	164,500	369,800
Net Cost of Goals	*$560,300*	*$1,127,000*

SOURCE: L. A. Lecht, *The Dollar Cost of Our National Goals* (Washington, D.C.: The National Planning Association, 1965).

As a democratic and relatively wealthy nation, we shall very probably be pursuing all the goals on our list in the 1970's. It is also likely that some new goals will emerge and that present standards will be raised. As in the past, how and where we assign our priorities will be determined partially by political processes and partially by the market, which reflects decisions of consumers, firms, and trade unions.

* An abstract of the standards for each of the goals is appended to this paper. See pp. 153–55.

To bring out the impact of pursuit of our goals for manpower requirements, Table III presents two projections for 1975 and the corresponding actual data for 1964. One projection indicates the anticipated manpower requirements for achievement of all our goals in 1975. The other represents the U.S. Department of Labor estimates of employment by broad occupational group in 1975. The Department of Labor projections are based on an assumed 3 per cent unemployment rate, which implies an anticipated volume of unemployment of 2.5 million in 1975.

TABLE III

LABOR FORCE AND EMPLOYMENT, 1964, AND PROJECTED 1975

	Number Employed (in Thousands)				
	1964	Projections for 1975		% Increase, 1964–75	
		Department of Labor	Aspiration Goals	Department of Labor	Aspiration Goals
Total Civilian Employment	70,350	88,700	101,200	26	44
White-Collar Workers:	31,100	42,800	48,900	38	57
Professional and Technical Workers	8,550	13,200	15,600	54	82
Blue-Collar Workers:	25,550	29,900	34,050	17	33
Operatives	12,900	14,800	16,600	15	28
Laborers	3,600	3,700	4,800	3	33
Service Workers	9,250	12,500	14,650	35	58
Farm Occupations	4,450	3,500	3,600	21	−19

SOURCE: Table E-6, *MRP* (1966), p. 217.

What do these numbers mean? According to the Department of Labor estimates, total employment in 1975 would be about 18 million greater than in 1964, an increase of 26 per cent. To fully achieve our goals by 1975, an increase in employment of 31 million would be involved. This is 44 per cent more than the 1964 level. If the civilian labor force were to grow only to the 91 million total anticipated by the U.S. Department of Labor in 1975, attempting to achieve all our objectives at once would involve a serious labor shortage.

Estimating manpower requirements for achieving our nation's objectives ten years from now involves considerable elements of uncertainty. We do not know which combinations of goals will receive first claim on the nation's resources in the 1970's. However, the exercise points to a conclusion. As we utilize the economy's growth in resources to transform more of our society's aspirations into reality in the next decade, our manpower problems are likely to concern ways and means of improving education and training, or of encouraging mobility, rather than the issues posed by the existence of a large mass of unskilled, poorly educated, and unemployed Americans.

It is interesting to note that, for both estimates, the largest percentage increases in employment are expected to occur in the white-collar group and, especially, among professional and technical workers. Large increases are also listed for service workers. The major break from the experience since World War II is in the blue-collar area. The projections for both lists contain a larger percentage increase in requirements for blue-collar workers than was the case between 1947 and 1964. These estimates are in keeping with the upswing in employment in blue-collar occupations since the early 1960's.

Increasing the volume of production, construction, research and development, teaching, and other services, because of more vigorous pursuit of our objectives, would be especially significant for the groups that include large reserves of underutilized and unemployed manpower—nonwhites, women, teen-agers, the handicapped, and older workers. For nonwhites, achievement of the sixteen goals is estimated to involve an increase in employment of 52 per cent as compared with the 44 per cent increase projected for over-all employment. The largest percentage increases for nonwhites would be in the white-collar occupations and in the skilled crafts.

What about the manpower requirements associated with the pursuit of certain individual goals such as urban development, social welfare, or health? As part of our study, we attempted to estimate the manpower needs for achieving some of these. The changes in manpower requirements that are needed if we are to achieve these goals in full can also serve as indicators of potential areas of expanding employment opportunities and job development needs, which would frequently arise as we pursued our objectives even if we adhered to levels consistent with the available resources and other national priorities in the next ten years. The manpower impacts for achievement of urban-development and social-welfare goals provide an illustration of this point.

TABLE IV

MANPOWER REQUIREMENTS FOR ACHIEVEMENT OF URBAN DEVELOPMENT
AND SOCIAL WELFARE GOALS, 1962, AND PROJECTED, 1975

| Type of Employment | Number Employed (in Thousands) | | | | | |
| | Urban-Development Goal | | | Social-Welfare Goal | | |
	1962	1975	% Increase	1962	1975	% Increase
Total Employment	6,336	10,175	61%	4,592	8,442	84%
White-Collar Workers:	2,264	3,788	67	2,081	4,257	105
Professional and						
Technical Workers	695	922	33	634	1,438	127
Blue-Collar Workers:	3,691	5,831	58	1,421	2,236	57
Operatives	1,204	1,896	57	744	1,164	56
Laborers	662	938	42	176	324	84
Service Workers	245	428	75	674	1,423	111
Farm Occupations	136	128	−6	416	526	26

SOURCE: Table 15, *MRP* (1966), p. 47.

By 1975, it is anticipated that 75 per cent of all Americans will be living in urban areas. Rebuilding our urban centers into communities where people can live, work, play, and move about would mean large-scale private and public expenditures for housing, schools, hospitals, cultural and recreational centers, transportation, shopping centers, and for the plant and equipment needed to assure these areas a sufficient supply of pure water and of power. Obtaining these urban facilities is expected to involve an increase in spending—largely private—of from $64 billion, in 1962, to $130 billion, in 1975 (in 1962 dollars). Constructing these facilities and manufacturing the equipment they utilize could create a substantial increase in employment for craftsmen, for operatives and laborers in the building trades, and for blue-collar and white-collar workers in the durable goods industries. Over 6 million people were directly or indirectly employed in providing urban facilities of all kinds in 1962. To achieve our urban-development goal by 1975 would involve an increase in employment to 10 million. Over 55 per cent of the manpower needs projected for the urban-development goal represent requirements for blue-collar workers.

Estimates for the social-welfare goal are based on a projected increase in private and public expenditures, from $38 billion, in 1962, to $92 billion, in 1975 (in 1962 dollars). These expenditures would provide for adequate income maintenance programs in the event of old age, illness, disability, loss of the family breadwinner, or unemployment. They would also include expansion of the present social insurance programs to cover individuals who are presently excluded, such as farm-workers, plus a family allowance program for families with poverty incomes. However, the bulk of the growth in expenditures, an additional $30 billion, is listed for programs concerned with old age and survivors' benefits.

Increasing social-welfare benefits along these lines would result in a transfer of $90 billion in purchasing power to the individuals receiving the benefits. As the beneficiaries spent these additions to their income for consumer goods and services, production and distribution of these goods and services would directly, or indirectly, require the employment of an estimated 8.5 million people. This represents an increase of 4.5 million over 1962. These expenditures would have their largest employment impact in the white-collar group. There would be a greater demand for the services of doctors, dentists, nurses, and medical and dental technicians. More employees would be required in the sales occupations. The social-welfare expenditures would involve more employment in the service occupations than would be the case for the urban-development goals. However, less employment would be created for blue-collar workers.

MANPOWER PROJECTIONS AND EDUCATIONAL POLICY

The over-all intent of this presentation is to emphasize the broad range of choices likely to be available to Americans in the next decade. Conserving our natural resources, developing an adequate transportation system, or reducing the prevalence of poverty serve social values and they also contribute to economic growth and the demand for labor.

What do these manpower projections mean for educational policy? They suggest that effective educational planning must reckon with the impact of the nation's priorities as one of the important factors influencing manpower needs. The pursuit of programs in research and development, or in health and education, would primarily affect the demand for professional and technical personnel. Assigning a high national priority to rebuilding our cities would create a strong need for blue-collar workers and, especially, for building trades craftsmen.

Preparing young people for the manpower needs of the 1970's is likely to involve two broad groups of measures. One consists of the changes needed to educate and train people for positions at the upper end of the occupational ladder—the positions for which a college education is typically the entrance requirement. The other consists of changes keyed to individuals who lack the education and training necessary to participate in gainful employment. Many of the changes are likely to be directed at young people of school age. New and important programs in adult education can also be anticipated.

Enrollment in institutions of higher education, in the fall of 1963, was about 4.5 million.* An increase of over 100 per cent in this enrollment figure, to 9.5 million, would probably be needed to prepare people for the manpower requirements implied by all our national objectives.

Where could an additional 5 million college students possibly come from? Population growth alone could be expected to increase enrollment in higher education by 2 million in the next decade. Expanding educational opportunities, through greater public and private support for higher education, would be the main source for the others.

Opportunities for higher education have increased on an unprecedented scale in the past generation. However, family income is still an important factor in the decision to attend college. A survey, in the early 1960's, indicated that 13 per cent of the young people who came from families with annual incomes under $4,000

* *Trends,* p. 44.

went on to college, as compared with 47 per cent from families with incomes over $7,500.* Differences in attitude toward higher education, as well as sheer differences in family income, explain some of these differences in college attendance. However, the net result, as summed up by the Senate Subcommittee on Employment and Manpower, is that "the nation . . . is losing, through leakages in the educational system, a substantial portion of its brains and leadership potential."† The Higher Education Act, the assistance available for individuals preparing for health occupations, and the National Science Foundation's fellowship program are significant indicators of our nation's determination to sharply reduce, if not eliminate, the importance of family income as a factor in determining who shall attend college.

It is also reasonable to anticipate that school dropouts, functional illiterates, and people lacking any occupational skills will still be with us in the mid-1970's, although they are likely to constitute a smaller share of the young adult population than they do today. Again, the Senate Subcommittee on Employment and Manpower (the Clark Committee) aptly summarized the problem. Students in the slums, the subcommittee observed, "enter the middle-class oriented school system at the age of five or six with almost insuperable handicaps. The school systems into which they come . . . are those with the lowest budgets, poorest buildings, greatest overcrowding, and the most inexperienced teachers. [Remaining in school until minimum school-leaving age only because of legal compulsion, these students drop out before completing high school] illiterate, untrained, and unmotivated."‡ Meaningful education in the urban slums, as President Johnson pointed out in 1965, "must begin with the very young."§ Yet, in the mid-1960's, almost half the public school districts conducted no kindergartens.

Transforming the young, unskilled, uneducated, and frequently

---

* U.S. Senate, Committee on Labor and Public Welfare, *Report of the Subcommittee on Employment and Manpower* (Washington, D.C.: GPO, 1964), p. 79.

† *Ibid.*

‡ *Ibid.*, p. 80.

§ "Message to Congress on Education," *Congressional Record* (Washington, D.C.: GPO, January 12, 1965), pp. 508–11.

unemployed members of the labor force—the social dynamite of our central cities—into productive wage-earners is likely to involve new types of programs extending considerably beyond the traditional scope of education. These programs would coordinate the community's resources for education, training, and social service so as to reach individuals currently at the margin of society. Some, like Project Head Start, would work with the very young to overcome the initial handicap of cultural deprivation. Others would involve working with young adults, probably in connection with the retraining activities sponsored by the federal government. New attitudes and techniques of teaching would also be needed. Teaching in the urban slums will probably require a new type of teacher—a person who combines the traditional skills of the classroom teacher with the insights of the sociologist or cultural anthropologist, and who understands and can use the techniques that have proven effective in professional social work.

Most of the measures enacted in recent years to expand educational opportunity concentrate on the young—on keeping young people in school, or offering educational and training services to those who have recently left school. Yet, absence of sufficient education is more common among older workers than young adults. For the older worker who was deprived of educational opportunity in his youth, our nation as a whole has no educational program. Of some 15,000 school systems studied by the U.S. Office of Education in the recent past, only 4,800 reported any type of adult-education program.* The literacy education offered along with vocational training, under the auspices of the Manpower Development and Training Act, is an important step toward recognizing that the older worker may be a school dropout and that this will have the same consequences for his employability—and for the nation's job-development needs—as those which have stirred the nation into action for young dropouts.

I have been discussing education from the viewpoint of manpower requirements. But, the basic education that is the prerequisite for a successful vocational adjustment is also the education likely to help individuals to enrich their personal lives and to

* *Congressional Record* (Washington, D.C.: GPO, March 2, 1966), p. 4593.

become effective members of their community. By 1975, weekly hours of work are expected to decline by an average of about 10 per cent, from about forty hours, in the early 1960's, to thirty-seven or thirty-six, in 1975. Annual vacations of approximately one month will probably be standard for most of the labor force in the next decade. Sabbaticals, currently largely confined to civil servants and teachers, will probably become common in many other occupations. They are already enjoyed by steelworkers. Greater leisure, higher family incomes, and a rising level of educational attainment could create a popular basis for revival of the arts, for greatly increased international travel, and for more effective participation in community organizations.

Assuring our nation's future needs for scientists and engineers, social workers and teachers, medical technicians and building trades craftsmen, depends on progress in education. The extent to which we will have the manpower to pursue whatever priorities our nation chooses, in the 1970's, will depend largely on the advance planning done, and the expansion of educational facilities accomplished, in the present decade. Education, from this perspective, is a dimension in all our goals.

CLASSIFICATION OF GOALS AND BASIS FOR STANDARDS*

Consumer Expenditures and Savings

Living standards rise to limit set by savings rate of approximately 8 per cent of disposable personal income. Includes additional increases in consumer expenditures from other goals such as health, education, and transportation, plus family allowance system to increase to $3,300 incomes of families below this level in 1975.

Private Plant and Equipment

Expenditures for plant and equipment needed to produce the level of output anticipated in 1970's plus additional private plant and equipment expenditures projected for specific goals: utilities in urban development, equipment in transportation, private and nonprofit facilities for schools, hospitals, welfare, etc.

Urban Development

Expenditures (generally derived from other goals) attributable to programs for providing adequate transportation, housing, cultural and recreation facilities, schools, hospitals, and industrial, commercial, and governmental buildings for over 75 per cent of the population expected to be living in urban areas in 1975. Also includes expenditures for new mass transit technologies and for control of air and water pollution. Involves over-all increase in spending for urban facilities rising from 11 per cent of GNP in 1962, to 13 per cent in 1975.

Social Welfare

Expenditures from public and private sources for providing typical pension covering cost of "modest but adequate" standard of living for an elderly couple in American cities in early 1960's, plus allowance for increases in earnings levels and standards of living. Also includes provisions for incorporating nationwide protection against income loss from illness as part of OASDI, expansion of unemployment compensation, coverage and benefits similar to proposals of recent administrations, and family allowance system to establish income maintenance floor for families with poverty incomes in the 1970's.

* See Table II and accompanying text.

Health   Stresses programs to enlarge access to modern health technologies by providing families with level of health care equal to that enjoyed currently by families with most comprehensive health insurance, plus expanded provisions for dental and psychiatric care. For persons over 65, includes level of medical care costing 50 per cent more than HEW estimate of cost of adequate medical care for the aged in early 1960's, with two-thirds of costs financed from public funds. Also includes increases in ratio of hospital beds to population, following Hill-Burton Act standards, together with increase in health research expenditures sufficient to support the 77,000 health research professionals NIH estimates will be needed in early 1970's.

Education   Assumes increase in proportion of students from eligible age group receiving high school and higher education, amounting to 50 per cent increase in proportion for college group. Allows for doubling of faculty salaries over decade, increased teacher-supporting staff, expansion of adult education and vocational training role of junior colleges, and increased plant and equipment at all levels of education.

Transportation   Expenditures for transportation equipment and R&D, allowing for projected increase in automobile stock and for changes in transportation resource use along the lines of President Kennedy's 1962 Transportation Message to Congress. Also includes cost of R&D and initial commercial application of technological advances such as nuclear ships, supersonic planes, hydrofoils, gas-turbine engines, etc.

National Defense   Expenditures for an adequate national defense under conditions ranging from partial disarmament to full application of technological advances for maintaining defense capabilities such as antimissile missiles, nuclear aircraft carriers, or space vehicles.

Housing   Includes elimination of all remaining substandard housing between 1966 and 1975, plus increase in number of housing starts from 1.5 million, in 1962, to 2.5 million by 1975, to provide for new family formation, adequate housing for nonwhites, higher income levels, greater emphasis on special housing for the aged, and for vacation "second" housing. Also includes cost of R&D program to develop synthetic building materials, mass production of housing components, and building codes geared to potentialities of modern technology.

Research and Development	Standard stresses increases in "civilian economy" R&D with total R&D expenditures projected to increase from 3 per cent of GNP, in early 1960's, to 4 per cent of $1 trillion GNP in mid-1970's. Includes substantial increases in expenditures for basic research, water desalination and oceanography, health and social science research, R&D information systems, and R&D extension service for the private economy with objectives similar to State Technical Services Act of 1965.
Natural Resources	Cost of programs for increasing and economizing the supply of natural resources required in an urbanized and affluent society. Largest expansion in expenditures projected for water purification and storage with programs derived from studies of Senate Select Committee on Water Resources.
International Aid	Goal includes cost to United States of U.N. Decade of Development target that each industrialized nation contribute 1 per cent of GNP from public and private sources to supply capital to developing nations. Also includes military support to developing nations at early 1960 levels, plus support for international nonfinancial organizations rising to $1.5 billion in 1975, primarily for WHO, UNESCO, FAO, and an expanded U.N. Peace Force.
Space	Expenditures for sustained space research and development program involving manned lunar landing about 1970, followed by exploration of moon, earth orbiting laboratories, and initial steps preparatory to manned landings on other planets, such as Mars, by year 2,000. Also stresses expansion of research in basic space sciences and in applications of space technology in such areas as weather observation satellites and in long distance telecommunications.
Agriculture	Cost of programs to raise income of commercial farm families to a close approximation to income of nonfarm families, plus cost of programs to encourage movement of 150,000 low-income members of the farm labor force into nonfarm employment each year.
Manpower Retraining	Cost of programs for retraining 1 per cent of the labor force a year, following the outlines of the Manpower Development and Training Act.
Area Redevelopment	Cost of expanded programs to create 100,000 jobs a year in accordance with the objectives of the Area Redevelopment Act.

DISCUSSION

DEITCH [presiding]: Let's begin.

CORREA: I would be grateful if you could expand on three points. First, to attain goals in health, for instance, education must do two things. It must provide more doctors, nurses, and qualified personnel in the health service. And it must provide better educated patients. Do you include, in your estimates, these two types of education?

LECHT: Explicitly, we include the first. Implicitly, we include the second, because we assume that the whole educational level of the population will rise. Therefore, it is reasonable to anticipate that we will have better educated patients—though they might be worse patients if they were better educated.

CORREA: The second question is, are you planning to include in your analysis the qualitative aspects of education or only the quantitative aspects?

LECHT: I think it is quite apparent that merely spending more money for education, or transportation, or anything else, doesn't by itself necessarily produce qualitative changes. Frequently, there are a lot of other conditions that would have to change to bring about the qualitative changes. But, we have attempted to do the lesser task, the one which could be done within the constraints of time and of the budget—that is, to concentrate on the cost of the quantitative indicators.

CORREA: Yes, but in the consideration of any one of the manpower classifications—say, engineers—do you consider just the name of the classification with the number of persons? Or do you pay attention to the educational content of that classification, to the curriculum used to form the persons in that classification?

LECHT: Here, again, we try to take qualitative factors into account. With people like engineers, we do so in terms of the ratio of advanced degrees to undergraduate degrees. To say that we have done it more than modestly would be silly. In each one of these areas, there are many qualitative factors that could be a basis for studies lasting several years. We hope we have reflected the major ones. I am sure it is a rough reflection.

CORREA: The last question is, could you present, in more or less general terms, the methodology that has been used in the projections? There is one point in which I am especially interested. Do you have information on the total evolution of the labor force and is this used to project the total size of the labor force in the future?

LECHT: Yes.

CORREA: So, essentially the problem is how to distribute the total labor force in different groups defined by level of educational attainment.

LECHT: Yes.

CORREA: The more common statistical instruments available for making these projections cannot be adapted to this case. Usually, if you make a projection of the different classifications of the labor force, you will find that the total obtained by adding these projections is not equal to the initial information that you had concerning the labor force in the future.

LECHT: In other words, you find that frequently you are adding up small items which, when projected as an aggregate, do not quite equal the sum of all items. The way we handled this was to use the technique economists call input-output analysis. This involves starting out with the total expenditures in these areas, with what is called a bill of goods for each one of these areas for 1975. We had an equivalent bill of goods for 1964 and 1962. We then estimated, from the 1962 and 1964 data, the relationship of output to total employment in each of about twenty-odd industries.

We had this same bill of goods for 1975 and we allowed for changes in productivity. This enabled us to estimate total employment in 1975. Then we went back to the decennial census and we noted how total employment in each industry was distributed by occupation and how the distribution changed between 1950 and 1960. We were able to obtain some unpublished material for 1962 and 1964, prepared by the Department of Labor, which provided a complete occupational breakdown by industry. So we then asked, "Well, how do our 1950 and 1960 occupational distributions check out with the 1962 and 1964 data?" Then, of course, we used our judgment as to productivity changes in the future; this gave us total employment and its distribution according to occupation.

I should add that, no matter how fine the mathematical technique, considerable elements of judgment enter into the estimates; this is true about any projection dealing with the future. But, I suspect that the significance of such projections is not the exact numbers but the directions and the orders of magnitude and the implications they show.

We are making occupational estimates on a limited scale. Some federal government agencies are doing similar work on a more elaborate scale. These efforts involve many judgments concerning what will happen, in the future, to productivity, or to the state of international relations, and other matters. We can make certain assumptions that appear reasonable. We know that most of the people who will be in the labor force in 1975 are in it already. Most of them have an occupation that is not likely to change substantially. Most of them are living in a part of the country in which they are likely to remain. So, on the occupational and labor-force side, much of the data is already there; it is the changes from that base which are the significant items.

CANNON: This is what bothers me about the whole paper. Mine is a conventional question, but I would like to ask it anyway. It can be asked in a variety of ways. One way is to ask: What is the role of active forces—for example, if peace, or some version thereof, breaks out tomorrow? Or, to take a less dramatic instance, let's say federal expenditures in education go from the present $4 billion, in 1967, to $10 billion, in 1969, to $15 billion, in 1972, to $25 billion, in 1975.

LECHT: A standard answer to this kind of question is that we are somewhat like a travel agency. If you want to go to Oshkosh or Timbuktu, you go to a travel agency. They will tell you how to get there and give you an estimate of what your visit will cost. They will not tell you whether it's a good idea to go to Oshkosh or Timbuktu.

Well, we are not telling people either. The goals we discuss are not things we necessarily advocate. But we are saying, "This appears to represent the consensus of American society, as of the early 1960's. If we continue in this direction, this is what it would cost us, in dollars, in the 1970's, and this is an estimate of what it would cost in terms of manpower requirements."

Now, if peace were to break out—let's say defense expenditures fall very sharply—then there would be numerous alternatives that could take up the slack. Rebuilding our cities could go a long way toward taking up any slack in defense expenditure. Similarly, improving our health and education systems or controlling pollution could absorb much of this decline in total demand.

What our country will actually do about these things goes beyond what economics can answer. I think the answers depend on everybody. They depend on the political process and on the decisions of millions of consumers, business firms, and trade unions.

CANNON: What are the kinds of cautions you would advance about your paper, in terms of specific policy-planning, either at the federal level or at the level of the elementary and secondary school systems?

LECHT: I would propose the same kinds of caution one would give to any projection. Projections are hypothetical forecasts that suggest alternatives. They suggest possibilities. They give us some insight into what would happen if we continue going in directions in which we have, in fact, been going for the past ten years. They can also help us to understand the implications of changing our directions.

It is very likely that many of the directions in which our society has been moving, in the past decade, will continue in the next one. But the pace is likely to change, depending on the state of the economy and the political and international situation. If these changes are extreme—say, an atomic war were to break out —then this and all similar papers would lose most of their relevance.

FLANIGAN: I'd like to add to Mr. Correa's comment on educational projections. We don't have basic cost figures, program by program, so we don't know now what it costs to give remedial reading at any grade level. We don't now know most of the costs of vocational programs. Therefore, we cannot do anything but accelerate trend data on a gross basis.

It is very unfortunate that we can't price the educational system we think we need on a more refined basis, program by program. The basic accounting arrangements in the local school systems do not yield this type of data.

McLure: We have made some estimates in that direction. Recently, we estimated that the great cities probably need about one-third more money per pupil than cities of 100,000 to 250,000 populations.

The diversity among individuals is tremendous. But, if we can think of an average and what that means, we figure that the great cities need 30 to 35 per cent more money per pupil to meet their special problems—the problems Fred Strodtbeck has identified as density factors, or human conditions that exist in situations of high density. These conditions include high degrees of retardation and social maladjustment, and excessive concentrations of pupils requiring extra staff members and resources as compared with communities with more normally distributed pupil populations.

But we also have, at the other extreme, the extra costs in rural areas, where population is still declining and per capita costs are rising. There, we find that the cost per pupil runs as high as 35 to 40 per cent more, on the average, than in the medium-size communities.

At the moment, we do not have a structure of costs to reveal the diversity in programs and services that is emerging to take care of individual needs—and of every individual, I might emphasize. However, we are headed in that direction. And, when we get more knowledge, we will have the basis for an accounting system that will be more helpful than the present one for evaluating the costs of education.

Kimball: I wonder if I might add a footnote to what Mr. Mc-Lure is saying. The Benjamin Franklin High School in New York City—a magnificent school, built as LaGuardia's gift to the Italians—now has, by virtue of changing population, a student body that is approximately half Negro and half Puerto Rican. The reading grade level of the students in this high school is the fifth year. The school is a dumping ground for difficult students from other secondary schools in New York City.

New York City doubled the amount of remedial reading available, to help correct the situation. Unfortunately, there was no appreciable increase in the reading levels of the students, because the authorities did not solve the sociological problem of the school, which was more significant than the reading problem. What happened was that these students—who had already rejected the school system, as exhibited in other aspects of their behavior —instead of attending the doubled number of classes, appeared only in the classrooms of teachers they felt were sympathetic to them. One of the great mysteries to the administration (so I am told), is what happens to these hundreds of students who, each day, do not appear in the class but are somewhere in the school building.

This dimension was introduced yesterday by Mr. Strodtbeck, in his discussion of the socializing process in the family. The child reflects, in the outside world, the consequence of his past experience. This problem is not met by additional money, although that is part of it. You need a new definition of the problem. The quantity or quality of the services you offer does not help, unless these services do something else—namely, make the learning situation attractive to students.

McLure: I think we are now on a subject that really would deserve an entire symposium. We have alluded to this educational problem in most of these papers, but I really think these suggestions indicate that education has to undergo change in its basic philosophical assumptions, its aims and objectives, its internal structure, curricula, and supportive services, in the consideration it gives its clientele, and the makeup of its instructional staff.

Lecht: If we look at our national objectives in education, don't we find that a great many of these programs not only call for increases in educational manpower but, perhaps, a different kind of education, a different kind of teacher? I am thinking, for example, of programs in the low-income areas, such as Head Start.

Stoikov: I would like to raise two issues that derive from the paper. You say that joblessness is over five times as great for males with only a grammar school education as it is for those with four years of college or more. I would suggest that this is misleading as it stands, partly because your implication is that all you have to do is somehow go through college. Clearly, the majority of the people with grade school education have a considerably lower ability level than those with a few years of college; no matter what you did, you couldn't get these people through to a college degree and, all of a sudden, reduce their unemployment rate. In other words, the unemployment rate may, to a great extent, be attributable to differences in ability rather than to differences in educational level.

LECHT: I think there is an intermediate term which is probably the critical one, and the intermediate term is occupation. People who go on to college go into occupations that have been virtually unemployment proof, aside from, say, engineers in situations where defense orders have been cut back. Since World War II, the white-collar, and especially the professional, occupations have had very low unemployment rates. I doubt if this differential is related to innate ability, because, in the 1930's, professionals (such as engineers) had high unemployment rates.

The people with little education go into occupations in which there is extensive unemployment; they are primarily operatives, laborers, and, to a considerably lesser extent, service workers and craftsmen.

Now, changing the education of these people would not necessarily change the unemployment rate. There is a far more complex process at work than that. With more education, some of these people, who now go into blue-collar occupations, would go into white-collar occupations, or they would go into crafts, where unemployment is less. If you take the blue-collar workers who are operatives and divide them up by educational level, I believe you will find that those with low degrees of schooling have considerably higher unemployment rates than those with considerable schooling.

The incidence of unemployment, within a broad occupational group, *is* related to education. Employers who have the choice of laying off and hiring create requirements, and these requirements may or may not be functional for the job. But, one of the requirements they frequently create is education. In many situations, this makes it harder for the person with very limited schooling to get a job. He is employed last and, therefore, he has less seniority. This makes it easier for him to lose his job when production falls.

So, it would be a complex process, but I do believe there is a significant relationship between educational attainment and susceptibility to unemployment.

STOIKOV: But, certainly, the implication is that if you gave them more education they would do better. I could take figures on native ability and the unemployment rate and I would get the kind of relationship you have here; then I would infer from it that, if people all had the same kind of native ability, we would do better than we do while it is distributed as it happens to be. I do think that, besides the level of education, native ability is involved here.

LECHT: Sure. I believe you are saying that correlation is not causation. It is true that a lack of educational attainment is associated with high unemployment, but this doesn't necessarily say that lack of education is the cause of high unemployment, because other things are also associated with lack of education. However, the fact is, we can do something about lack of education. We can do little to change innate abilities.

STOIKOV: I am just objecting to the general implication, which comes often and not just here, that only if we manage to educate people through high school can we reduce unemployment to any considerable extent. I do question this.

LECHT: You can push that implication too far. We would very probably change the incidence of unemployment. Unemployment would be more generally distributed. There would be other effects stemming from changes in spending patterns and, probably, in productivity.

Now, we couldn't provide the people who hold jobs as operatives with the same unemployment rate as white-collar workers. However, we could, probably, reduce the blue-collar unemployment rate, with some feedback effects on the over-all unemployment rate. But we need more studies to disentangle these interactions.

STOIKOV: The second point, which is not quite unrelated to this, is one that concerns your question, "Will there be enough growth in blue-collar and service employment to absorb the new entrants with limited schooling into the labor market?" Again, in effect, this assumes that a fixed amount of education is required for certain jobs. Is this reasonable? I am uneasy about the general tendency of manpower experts to forget completely the function of the price system. In effect, the price system is never considered.

DEITCH: It might be helpful, to those among us who aren't economists, if you could explain why those who use input-output analysis might be minimizing the usefulness of the price system.

STOIKOV: I refer to the fact that whether a person is employable or not depends, to some extent, on the kind of wage he requires or the kind of wage that is set. If you set a very high rate by law, you may prevent employers from finding someone employable. At some wage, most people are employable. And this is why, just dealing with categorized requirements on the one hand, and employability on the other, ignores this other kind of relationship where, at some price, any man is employable. In other words, there is a certain amount of flexibility in a system that is not taken into account in most manpower projections—in particular, in input-output analysis and in the kinds of assertions made here.

LECHT: One reason we don't give greater significance to wage rates is that, in terms of policy alternatives, it is reasonable to assume that social legislation—such as minimum wages—is here to stay. It could be argued that, if unemployed, unskilled blue-collar workers were to be employed at $.50 an hour, there would be less mechanization; it would be more worthwhile for employers to hire them. However, insofar as the practical alternatives for policy are concerned, our society made that choice in the 1930's when it enacted minimum wage legislation.

If we were making a study of the impact of minimum wages on unemployment, I would agree that this is a problem worthy of consideration. However, if we look at long-term shifts in employment for different groups, I believe the changes in demand are the strategic variables.

In many of these areas, unions and collective bargaining are also here to stay. Therefore, in terms of what makes sense as policy alternatives, the wage structure—as it has been developing in the past decade—is the most reasonable one for our projections to assume; that is, a wage structure that increases roughly with productivity.

STOIKOV: I am particularly troubled because, from a self-interest point of view, disadvantaged groups have an interest not to increase the minimum wage. I am convinced that raising it is a great mistake, in terms of the welfare of that group. And this is where, again, I am troubled, because we are giving no consideration to the price factor.

LECHT: I can't speak for the groups involved. My hunch is that, if you were to ask them whether they would like to have their wages reduced as a way of increasing their employment, you would receive a negative answer. For simplicity's sake, this isn't a problem we've got to solve for the purposes of our particular projections.

DAVID: I would like to interject a comment on a combination of two points that have been made. In your paper, you pointed out the increase in employment in the educational industry since 1953—an astounding increase. We can anticipate continued increase to meet the goals you have spelled out, and I think this is interesting from two points of view. One is that you have taken a fixed technology as the basis for your manpower projections; I would hope that some productivity studies, some studies of the cost effectiveness of alternative techniques, would lead us away from a fixed teacher-pupil ratio as the kind of thing we have to plan for. The other point is that, undoubtedly, when we get this kind of adjustment in the use of our labor force—where one group is expanding 76 per cent, while the entire labor force is going up only 11 per cent—we can expect some real changes in relative wages, which is Stoikov's point.

LECHT: With regard to this question, I would like to point out that our projections for teachers assume a declining pupil-teacher ratio in the elementary and secondary schools. In higher education, we assume that, because of educational TV, or simply the mushrooming of enrollments, average class size per teacher will increase by about 10 or 15 per cent in the next ten years.

I agree that one of the big questions in any projection, in any attempt to assess the future, is "What about technological change?" This shows up in the kind of productivity increase that is assumed. The Triple Revolution people, the people who argue we are going to have massive unemployment among blue-collar workers, assume very large increases in productivity. We don't. We assume modest increases in productivity, somewhat higher than those of the past decade. Most of the recent studies—such as those of the Bureau of Labor Statistics—that have attempted to measure the influence of productivity changes show moderate changes in productivity.

DAVID: My main point here is, in the educational industry, we haven't really defined our activities and we haven't fully defined our inputs, so we are incapable of making productivity projections.

LECHT: It is also hard to define outputs. What is the output of the educational system?

FOLGER: If you look at the over-all changes in these relationships, they have been very minor, but these are extremely gross figures.

I would like to ask you a question that grows out of your observation that most likely the major shortages will be of highly educated personnel. You projected the need for a college enrollment of approximately 9.5 million by 1975. I would comment that this increase is a very unlikely possibility. It is at least .5 million higher than any of the trend line projections that have been produced—even the most optimistic of them. My question is, what would be the long-run consequences of a forced or draft expansion of higher education? Let's assume that, somehow, you could accomplish this sort of thing. Would you then have expanded the educational system more than would be required by the economy in the long run, in order to try to meet, in a fairly short time, a very ambitious program of national development?

LECHT: Just before coming down here, I was looking at the volume the Health, Education, and Welfare people put out, the *Trends* volume, and their enrollment projection for 1975 is about 1 million less than ours. What we are doing is stating the implications of pursuing national objectives in a variety of areas. The *Trends* figure is a forecast. What we are saying is, if we wish to pursue our programs in health and education, in R&D, and in any number of other areas, this would be the number of college graduates required, and we have broken them down by undergraduates, master's candidates, and Ph.D.'s.

Now, in terms of the question of what it means to the college-age population, it means an increase from about 26 per cent attending college to about 38 or 39 per cent. As we pursue our goals in education, these rising enrollments will have ramifications throughout the economy, whether we pursued them to the extent the goal necessitated or to a lesser extent. Presumably, if we had a much more highly educated work force, this would have a rebound effect on productivity.

Then there is the factor that Mr. Correa pointed out. If we had a more highly educated population, this would show up in many ways. We would have more educated patients. People would go to doctors perhaps more quickly, before they were ill rather than after they were seriously ill; all of these ramifications would certainly have to be considered.

If we concentrated on expanding our educational systems in the next decade far more than we concentrated on other goals, we might have shortages of scientists and engineers or we might have shortages of people working in government, in the performing arts, or as corporate executives. This would probably create a situation where the price mechanism would come into play and, through effects on salaries, would probably change some of these projections.

DANIEL: Mr. McLure mentioned the fact that, in many high schools today, the disadvantaged are very selective. They do some things very willingly under some situations and reject others. It certainly applies to jobs. I don't know whether you are familiar with the work of Arthur Pearl and Frank Riessman. Their book, *New Careers for the Poor,* deserves attention.*

LECHT: I have seen it. It is a very good book.

DANIEL: Some people think that training should be done, not in the schools, but in some kind of job center. I want to know if you have any comment on what is opening in new careers, and if these changes have been considered in your projections.

LECHT: I believe these occupations will probably expand and that training in para-educational institutions will also grow considerably; we already have adult literacy training and job training under the MDTA, which is conducted outside the regular educational system.

You ask: "How much do these affect the over-all occupational projections?" My hunch is, only to a limited extent. These programs will create jobs for some, but I don't think they are likely to move large groups of people out of one occupational stratum and into another. They are likely to be most effective with young

* New York: The Free Press, 1965.

people—those just about to enter the labor market or those who have recently entered—partially, because their flexibility is greater and, partially, because this is where we are concentrating most of our resources.

New occupations are likely to spring up in all categories, and I am sure that what we consider as our present occupations will, in some instances, be outmoded by 1975. There is one big occupation, which is called "office-machine operator" in the Census Bureau occupational statistics, and it has one of the highest projected growth rates. However, there is no occupational definition for "programmer." Many of the people included under the heading of office-machine operator are working in one connection or another with data-processing machinery and are not really office-machine operators. Many are programmers of some kind. So, new occupations will emerge, I am sure.

CORREA: I want to take up the point Mr. Stoikov made, which also seems to be related to what Mr. Daniel just said. The problem was that, in your projection, you assumed that with more education there would be more employment. Mr. Stoikov made the point that perhaps it was not education that contributed to production but the innate capacities of people. I think this is a very real problem. In the end, we are matching personalities with the jobs; or, as Mr. Swanson mentioned in the previous session, the problem is to match the distribution of ability that is supplied with the distribution demanded.

Do you think that the educational system can—or even, should—modify the abilities of the person? Or is its job to make it possible to utilize better the abilities of the person, to help him to adapt better to the job that he is going to fill? Perhaps I can explain myself better. It seems that the economic evolution of society has been demanding higher levels of innate ability from the individual. Perhaps we seek people with more ability, more innate ability, rather than with more education. Now, if we are in this position, it means that the society will develop only up to the point where the abilities are not the scarce resource. Then, an important question is, can the educational system act only to improve the use of the abilities, or can it also improve the innate abilities themselves?

This question is not addressed only to you; I think it is the concern of all educators. Can we expect the educational system to modify the abilities of a population so that this scarce factor doesn't restrict economic development in the future?

LECHT: I don't think we know very much about innate abilities, as they are manifested on the job. They probably are there, but what they are and what the connection is between somebody's genes and chromosomes and how he performs as a secretary, doctor, or machine operator is largely unknown. Furthermore, insofar as abilities are innate, they are not a subject for policy. There is not much we can do about them. Presumably we can't change people's genes and chromosomes.

Insofar as these differences in performance or capacity are institutional, we can do things about them, we can change them. One thing we do know is that employers frequently set entrance requirements for jobs. They say: "You must have an eighth-grade education to work in our factory," or "You must have a high school education," and so on. These are employers' requirements. They may be good requirements; they may not be good, or even wise. But, insofar as these requirements exist, they are factors to be reckoned with, and the person who does not have the entrance-level proficiency will be at a handicap in getting a job. He is likely to have a better chance of being unemployed, especially in a period of substantial unemployment, than somebody who does have the minimum level of education.

In discussing our lack of knowledge of innate factors, I am not casting aspersions on any particular discipline. With regard to occupational requirements and innate abilities, my hunch is that this is a very hard field in which to make many specific statements.

KLEIN: There is a paradox emerging—an inflexible institution attempting to develop flexibility in the product. Dr. Ogorman [Professor of Sociology at Hunter College] has investigated sociological aspects of the professions and his as yet unpublished studies indicate that the professions are the least adaptive in admittance of new members. It appears that, if the demands of society are going to be met, there will have to be dramatic changes in regard to the way individuals can gain acceptance into certain occupations. There is a need for new forms of internship.

DAVID: I can speak on that in two ways. First, what appears to have evolved, in the last generation, is an educational system that is more and more monolithic, with its particular degrees and formal certificates taking on more and more importance as entries into the work force.

This evolution could be countered by providing numerous channels of education, with different types of certificates and different types of training, so that entry could be accomplished in different ways. It seems to me that we need to offer such a differentiated kind of educational system if we are to protect those youths and adults who have made wrong choices at various points in their lifetimes. Otherwise, we will have a closed system, like the English educational system, where failure to pass the school entrance examination at the age of eleven deprives an individual of any higher education.

Second, as more institutions and different channels of education develop, it will be necessary for the employer to evaluate his real needs, rather than some paper certification, and to adopt techniques for finding the most efficient solution to his manpower problems. Thus, multiple channels of education, it seems to me, would avoid the setting up of arbitrary job requirements.

In information-processing electronic computers, it is very important to have redundancies. Different ways of establishing the same kind of information create checks. I think analogous redundancies are required in our educational system so that people who must, for one reason or another, forego one opportunity for a particular type of training, have some access to it at another time or through another channel.

McLure: I think there is more differentiation going on than your statement implies or suggests. For example, the mere fact of holding a doctorate gives very little idea of what the person is competent to do. You have to identify the field of his specialization. I suspect that our knowledge of how both to meet this individual innateness that exists and to design a program to prepare people for something is very limited. I suspect that differentiation is growing at least as fast as our knowledge grows, if not faster. A word of caution against too much fragmentation of programs, against getting too far ahead of our knowledge, might be in order.

Swanson: May I reinforce what Mr. David said? I think his point is something that needs to be re-emphasized. The blue-

collar worker is not really interested in an educational requirement. He is more interested in a series of gatekeepers who stand
outside his door. The school becomes one of the gatekeepers, and
he never makes a judgment about what the educational system
has done to the person. He allows the gatekeeper to make these
choices for him.

I would also like to reinforce what Mr. Correa said. I think
this is an important aspect of policy. The extent to which one can
maximize the quality of the full range of educational equipment
of the population may not be planning policy, but it is certainly
educational policy. I think we have given a good deal of attention
to maximizing the productivity of the upper range of our intellectual stock, but I am not sure we have done so much for the
middle range, and very little, indeed, for the lower range.

DEITCH: We have to think about this gatekeeper function. If
that is one of the very important things that the educational
system is doing, it is a very expensive, and likely not the best, way
of getting that job done. We ought to be able to convince ourselves that education is doing something more.

FOLGER: I would disagree with Mr. McLure in terms of the
thrust of research on selection. If selection is all you are interested
in, you can undoubtedly do the job much less expensively with
tests than you can with an educational program. But I think this
is not primarily why we have the educational programs—although
we are not always very clear about why we do have them.

McLURE: My point was that there are measures other than tests
that give a better indication of what we can do with people. We
have been overlooking people. I would say, for example, that
there are people who never were selected for Ph.D. programs
who are perfectly capable of completing them—and many of them
were rejected by these traditional measures. This is the point I
was making.

KLEIN: You are talking about a very select and small population. The needs of society are great and could be met if the professions would open other ways by which individuals could gain
acceptance to practice. However, current practitioners are reluctant to do this. If you look at the structure of occupations, the
most rigid forms are in your professional occupations. To meet
objectives created by national goals as well as by demand indices,

we will have to use multiple-track systems and other methods of certification to attest to a person's competence to function at professional levels. The single track is not really meeting manpower requirements.

LECHT: It is interesting to notice that one of the few constants we have in the social sciences is the ratio of physicians to the population. This has remained just about the same since about 1920.

CANNON: There has been a change in the past three or four years.

LECHT: The ratio for physicians has changed, in the past few years, primarily because osteopaths are now included among physicians. But what has been happening in health is that the number of doctors has increased very slowly, while the number of other medical people has increased very rapidly. The number of nurses and of medical and dental technicians has increased rapidly; many of the duties the doctor performed twenty and thirty years ago are now performed by the nurse or by the medical technician. As the pressure for more and better medical care comes about, because of the influence of programs such as Medicare, the increase in the number of nondoctors in the health occupations—say, five or ten years from now—will be considerably greater than the increase in the number of doctors. This is partially because of the gatekeeping requirements, mentioned earlier, and partially because it takes a long time to train a doctor.

KLEIN: There is an interesting experiment that has gone on for many years in New Zealand. Women are trained in two years to repair cavities and do cleaning operations under the supervision of a dentist. Representatives of the American Dental Society have gone there and have come back impressed.

KIMBALL: One of the things we have been giving emphasis to is the skilled individual and how his skill is related to his ability and his training. But, no matter how well you train a person, if you put him into an organizational environment in which he cannot adequately utilize his skills, you still don't get the productivity from him that he has been prepared to give. The people who have been doing work in industrial relations have case after case in which the evidence is clear that bad organization, which goes beyond mere personality differences, leads to bad productivity.

One such study, done in a General Motors plant in New Jersey, made it very clear that, when certain kinds of changes took place in the nature of the arrangements by which people related to each other, there were extensive changes in the nature of the morale of the people, as well as in the productivity level. I want to add this point to the discussion and ask Mr. Lecht to what extent he considered this? I would argue that the organizational environment is significant in the training process and in what happens to the individual afterward.

LECHT: I am sure that is true. Frequently, things like social attitudes, the influence of the work group, or the extent to which employees have absorbed the "culture of work" can affect productivity.

Some of the studies of the unskilled unemployed mentioned in earlier discussions indicated that their difficulties, at times, stem from the fact that they don't know how to go about applying for jobs and that they are unaccustomed to factory discipline or the work situation. Part of the training that has been important in helping them to obtain employment, and to keep it, has been a kind of acculturation that gets them used to the work situation.

KLEIN: The policy, under the terms of the Economic Opportunity Act, should be broadened so that there could be paid work experiences in private enterprise.

CORREA: In the case put by Mr. Kimball, I would like to ask him this: You are considering two social systems; that is, the educational system and the firms in which people are working. The educational system is not producing the people required by the firms. Do you suggest the educational system should change, or the firms should change? And, more generally, how do we choose which of two sectors of society should change when, for one reason or another, they don't fit together?

KIMBALL: There is a study, relevant to the question you just asked, that was done by Simon Marcson, of the RCA Laboratories in New Jersey.* These laboratories employed people with

* *Scientist in American Industry* (New York: Harper & Row, 1960).

high scientific and engineering skills who had acquired a style of working with others during their educational training.

In the laboratories, they were subjected to bureaucratic procedures, which Marcson called "executive authority." They found it difficult to adjust to these because of the earlier pattern of work, which Marcson called "colleague authority." Hence, there were tensions that grew up between the bureaucratic organization, with its goals, and those with technical and scientific skills.

In reply to the problem you raised, I would comment, first, that a diploma that gets you past the gatekeeper may or may not represent a quality of high skill. A diploma is a diploma, but behind the diploma is a person. And even where the educational system has been successful in transmitting prized skills of one kind or another, if the environment into which the individual goes is not conducive to the use of these skills, then it is not the failure of the educational system; it is the failure of the system of organization.

CORREA: Consider the case of the productive system receiving somebody from the educational system that it cannot use. If we see this case from the point of view of the productive system, we will conclude that the educational system is bad. However, the conclusion will be against the productive system if we see the case from the point of view of the educational system. How can we decide which point of view is the correct one?

KIMBALL: This is a rough one that Mr. Lecht should answer. This has to do with projections and the nature of the evolution of our type of society.

LECHT: Aside from the projections, one thing that occurs to me is that at one time it was very difficult for handicapped people—say the blind, or those who had lost limbs—to get employment. So long as the work situation was not organized to use their skills, they were, in fact, unemployable in most cases. However, once many employers changed the work situation, these people could get jobs where their skills could be used and many of them did, in fact, become employable. So, I think the answer to each of these special problems depends on the specific difficulty involved.

Obviously, there will be many changes in our educational system. One of the changes that was mentioned earlier was, for example, the development of two-year post-high school technical training institutions. This is in response to an area of the economic system that is creating substantial demands, and is likely to create greater demands, for medical and dental technicians, electronic technicians, and related specialists. The changes in educational institutions have only partially caught up with the economic changes.

DAVID: There is another aspect to this, which ties in with Mr. Kimball's paper yesterday. With the tremendous growth in the education industry that we anticipate, we must recruit a great many young people into teaching as soon as they graduate from the educational system. In other words, the educational system is building itself up by taking its own product. This is good, so long as it is the educational system that is going to create new kinds of jobs, new technologies, new skills that have a pay-off in terms of consumer goods and the national product. But it is not so good if the educational system needs a feedback—some direct experience of what is going on in the organization of industry, for example—in order to improve its teaching methods and its analysis. This problem leads me to ask, has the educational system ever had a feedback, from your point of view?

KIMBALL: Yes, it has. The one instance that comes to mind is a survey that MIT made, some thirty years ago, of the corporations that employed its engineers. What they discovered was that the average life of a practicing MIT graduate engineer was four years. These employers were saying, in effect, that they could find plenty of engineers, but that they were interested in individuals who could move up to administrative and managerial activities within their companies. One consequence of this study was to introduce change in the MIT training program. Among other things, greater emphasis was given to humanities and applied social science. At about this same time, greater emphasis was placed on mathematics and theory, rather than on practical mechanics. One reason for this latter change was that no institution could provide the new industrial machinery for training purposes because of its rapid obsolescence and high cost. Specific training became an on the job experience.

The inbreeding to which you refer is a very serious matter in the public schools. The student comes out of the public school system into a teacher-training institution, and back into the public school system. During this process, he has had practically no contact with new educational procedures. This ensures a circular perpetuation of teaching skills, from one generation to another.

FLANIGAN: That is not quite true, because not all of the new supply of teachers comes from the immediate graduating class.

KIMBALL: Well, I would modify my own point about inbreeding by adding that, in New York City, people who could have certificates beat the system by not taking a certificate. This is because, if you take a certificate, you are subject to school assignment by the bureaucracy. If you do not take a certificate, you can serve as a substitute, and the rules governing substitutes give you latitude in the choice of a school. Hence, many of those who teach in New York do not take certificates—are not quite so tied to the old techniques.

FLANIGAN: Freshness also comes from the fact that a high proportion of the staff turns over each year. The Office of Education estimates that over 100,000 teachers leave every year and are replaced. This is in addition to teachers taken on because of enrollment increases and expanding programs.*

* The following table indicates the extent of these changes:

ESTIMATED TOTAL DEMAND FOR CLASSROOM TEACHERS IN U.S. PUBLIC
ELEMENTARY AND SECONDARY SCHOOLS

Year (fall)	Total teacher demand	Demand for additional certificated teachers			
		For enrollment increase	For replacement of substandard teachers	For teacher turnover	Total
(1)	(2)	(3)	(4)	(5)	(6)
1960	1,408,093	—	—	—	—
1961	1,461,055	52,962	654	112,647	166,263
1962	1,507,552	46,497	8,988	116,884	172,369
1963	1,577,777	70,225	—545	120,604	190,284
1964	1,648,184	70,407	500	126,222	197,129
1965	1,716,285	68,101	952	131,855	200,908
1961–65		308,192	10,549	608,212	926,953

SOURCE: U.S. Office of Education, *Projections of Educational Statistics to 1975–76* (Washington, D.C.: GPO, 1966), Table 24, p. 45.

DEITCH: I think that is gross, rather than net, turnover.

FLANIGAN: Net turnover is conservatively estimated at about 8.5 per cent.

TAYLOR: There are examples of exposure to the world of work outside the school system. We know there is a high proportion of teachers who moonlight or engage in an economic activity during the summer months. Women teachers who re-enter the profession after careers as mothers also bring fresh exposure and insights.

FLANIGAN: But the system probably doesn't provide the necessary outside contacts with the world of work that may be needed in some areas of the curriculum.

SWANSON: This is my point. How valid are the experiences professors get from the so-called outside world? Where do they obtain these experiences?

CORREA: I don't know if personal contact with the outside world is essential for professors, but, in some way, the educational system has to adapt itself to what is going on in the outside world. I think, for instance, the content of the curriculum should be modified in order to satisfy the needs of society. If the educational system has a life all by itself, it simply is not fulfilling its function.

SWANSON: I certainly agree with this point. I am also impressed with the extent to which those people in higher education who have been very influential in affecting curriculum at the secondary level, in areas such as social studies, languages, mathematics, and physics, have not been nearly as instrumental in affecting curriculum in the higher educational institutions in which they are located. If you examine physics, modern languages, or social studies at the higher educational level, what changes have occurred?

BURNETT: Many times, changes on the college level have come because of pressure from high schools whose programs have changed more rapidly than those within the universities, at the undergraduate level. The colleges have had to change their entrance requirements and redesign certain courses because they are dealing with a much more sophisticated high school graduate.

SWANSON: This is true. The outside world, for the university, has been the secondary school. I think it has had a greater influence on college entrance requirements than any other element of pressure from the outside world.

FOLGER: I think the shifting structure of knowledge and the redefinition of problems have had major impact upon the curriculum in a large number of areas in the universities. Medical school curriculum has been substantially revised in the postwar period, as have those of business, engineering, and other schools. In many specific subject areas, such as foreign languages, there have been substantial changes. I think this is, to a considerable extent, a result of federal interest in improved language training.

But, we are being too pessimistic about the kinds of change and interaction. We have a university system that is certainly far from ideal, but it surely interacts with the society in many ways.

KLEIN: Viewing the institutions of education as a unified education industry, what types of questions should the educator begin to ask himself if future economic measures are to reduce the error factor in planning?

LECHT: One of the important questions, in this area, is timing. We hear a lot of discussion about the number of physicians the country will need five or ten years from now. Increasing the number of physicians—or simply keeping the same ratio of physicians to population—by 1970, would involve building many medical schools now. For a medical school, it takes from five to ten years to get from the planning stage to the operational stage. Much of the advance planning to meet manpower needs in the next decade must be done in the 1960's. I think this is one of the problem areas of educational planning.

Another problem area is the development of educational institutions to meet the new and growing demand for technicians. Junior colleges have frequently moved into this area, especially on the West Coast, but I believe the whole problem of education for technicians is still an open one.

At the other end of the spectrum, we must ask what kind of teacher is needed in the new programs concerned with children in urban slums. The kind of education needed for this teacher is, also, very much an open question.

KIMBALL: May I add that it is not only a new kind of teacher for the urban slums that is needed but also a new organizational structure for the schools.

BEASLEY: I think an important point was brought up earlier by Mr. Swanson. Many externally produced innovations have been brought into the educational system. If the external forces are removed, will innovation continue? Will this become an ingrained part of the system? I suspect that innovation will continue in many areas that have shown deficiencies. Some innovations may be rather faddish and, once the fad moves on, they will be dropped or become vestigial.

BURNETT: Again, I think you have to look at the school as an operating system. Innovation depends on the accommodation of that system to what has been initiated. If the system is going to take financing from sources other than those regularly available at the local or state level—that is, from the federal government —then innovation may cease once this financial aid ceases. Furthermore, if you haven't developed, within the system, the personnel organization that can continue to support it, it is unlikely that innovation will continue.

KIMBALL: I would like to raise another question. I am very much interested that what Mr. Lecht presented here is, naturally, cast in the American style of looking at problems. I recently heard Harold Noah describe the process of planning in the Soviet Union, and it is considerably different from our approach. Once the Russians have decided upon the nature of a manpower need in the light of national goals, they do whatever is necessary to make certain that it is realized. I gather, from Mr. Lecht's presentation, that this is the direction in which we are moving, but, it seems to me, there is a difference in the manner in which the American looks at this type of problem.

LECHT: I think the term planning, in the United States, implies a context very different from the Russian use of the term. In Russia, the items in the plans are not just targets or projections. They are a kind of law. They are an imperative, which somebody who is an employee of the state is to carry out. Planning, in the United States, is much harder to put your finger on. It is much harder to identify with a particular institution, because many institutions, formally or informally, public and private, participate in formulating and pursuing our society's objectives. The planning organizations operate, largely, as centers of information, as formulations of projections; this is the sense in which we think of over-all economy planning. We also plan for specific objectives —for example, federal government spending heavily influences hospital and medical school construction.

In terms of the federal government, planning consists, to a large extent, of setting up a fiscal and monetary framework to influence over-all growth and the level of activity of the economy. Then there is a whole range of group planning, from formal groups—such as the U.S. Office of Education—to professional organizations, or civil rights groups. These groups influence our nation's programs and objectives. From this perspective, we think of planning as defining the directions in which we, as a country, are moving, or want to move, rather than as an integrated set of objectives, inputs, and outputs that some agency has drawn up for us to follow.

CANNON: I would disagree with that, basically, because I think your model is awfully static and conservative.

LECHT: I think it is a reflection of our current socio-economic organization and our aspirations.

CANNON: Your type of planning doesn't recognize what has happened under the Elementary and Secondary Education Act. We have taken on a problem of teaching poor kids. There is a goal, a program, and an objective—and a measurable one, a very active one. It is not just general fiscal and monetary policy. There is a target here. There are 8 million or more poor kids. You can estimate the inputs and measure the outputs.

STRODTBECK: One of the products of planning is the capacity for change. For example, the University of Illinois, already having a medical school in the Chicago area, could create another one on campus, in a very short period of time, by the reallocation of its resources. This institution has the capacity to stretch itself, at any given point in time, to respond to an urgent need.

McLURE: The distinguishing feature that you are talking about is the capacity to expand with additional resources, but not to reallocate committed resources. You cannot reallocate committed resources for this type of change.

5

Measuring Education's Contribution to Economic Growth *

HECTOR CORREA

Since economics began to be a science, economists have been concerned with economic development and its relationship to education. The modern emphasis, in economics, is on measurement; this approach is especially interesting because it provides —or seems to provide—a more solid basis for decision-making. However, if we restrict ourselves only to measuring the contribution of education to development, we will be ignoring important aspects. On the other hand, an attempt to go beyond measurement and study all the contributions of education to economic development seems hopeless. Without exaggeration, it can be said that education contributes to every human activity, and every human activity contributes to economic development.

Using the economist's narrow view of economic development, this paper will present the most important contributions of education. The aspects of the contribution of education that have already been measured will fit this general framework, along with those aspects on which our knowledge is more limited. My hope is that this approach will provide a basis for a systematic effort to measure all contributions of education to economic development.

* I wish to thank Dr. Alphonse G. Holtman, of Wayne State University, who read a first draft of this paper and made many valuable suggestions. All personal opinions and errors are, of course, my own.

THE ECONOMIC FRAMEWORK

Concept and Measurement of Economic Development

If there is one sure way to start a heated discussion among economists, it is to propose a definition of economic development. For some economists, economic development would imply simply an increase in total production. For others, not the total but the per capita level or its distribution, or both, would be central. Still others would add not only the income received by each person but also the way it is used; they would want to consider the progress made in health, education, housing, and so on. As is the case with any definition, each of these is both good and bad: good if used for scientific analysis, and bad if used to describe what economic development is.

In this discussion, I will base most of my analysis on the first definition—that economic development is an increase in total production. Consistent with this definition, the expressions "level of economic development" and "volume of total production" will be used interchangeably. The same is true for the expressions "economic development" and "increases in total production."

One of the reasons for adopting this definition is that there are methods for measuring total production. This may be done with national accounts, a fairly well-developed branch of economics. Since national accounts play an essential role in the analysis that follows, I should point out their limitations. First, national accounts do not measure total production, but only the part of it that is bought and sold in a market. Some segments of total production—for instance, that of housewives—are left out. Another aspect not included in national accounts is that of improvements in the quality of goods. It is likely that education makes important contributions to these excluded aspects. Finally, the value of total production is, and has to be, expressed in monetary terms. As a result, in intertemporal comparisons, it is impossible to distinguish, with precision, between changes in the quantity of the goods produced (that is, economic growth) and changes in their prices (that is, inflation). The index numbers used for this purpose are a very poor instrument.

Factors of Production

The next question that must be answered is: What determines the volume of production and its growth? From the simplest point of view, there are three main factors of production: entrepreneurs, capital, and labor. From a wider point of view, but still on strictly economic grounds, demand is another determinant. Finally, political stability, social conditions, and so forth also influence economic development.

It should be observed that education has not been mentioned among the determinants of production. The reason for this is that education, as such, does not influence production; its influence is embodied in the factors already noted. This makes our task more complicated: First, the total contribution of the factors of production has to be evaluated and, second, from these totals, the part corresponding to the education embodied in them has to be found.

Measuring the Contribution of a Factor to
Economic Development

One is inclined to think that the contribution of a factor to production is the part of the total product that is created by that factor. Unfortunately, it is impossible, in most cases, to break down accurately total production, because the product can be made only by using the combined contributions of all the factors. A simple example will illustrate this point. Suppose a society were composed of three people: a worker, a capitalist, and an entrepreneur. The worker, using his bare hands, can dig X cubic feet of coal per unit of time. The entrepreneur puts the capitalist's shovel into the hands of the worker; now the worker can dig Y cubic feet of coal per unit of time. The problem is to determine what part of Y was dug by the worker, what part by the shovel, and what part by the entrepreneur. From the worker's point of view, the total amount Y belongs to him, because the shovel could hardly be expected to dig anything by itself. However, the capitalist and the entrepreneur will insist that, at the least, Y minus X belongs to each of them, because this is the increase in production made possible by the contribution of the equipment they put into the hands of the worker. I cannot think of any logical or mathematical basis for dividing Y, or Y minus X, among these three, and the same is true for any other production process.

It is conventionally accepted, in economics, that the contribution of one unit of a factor to production is the increase in production observed when one such unit is added to the production process. This increase in production is known as the marginal product of the factor. For instance, suppose 1,000 workers, using $3 million of capital, dig 1,000 tons of coal per day. If an additional worker is taken on, and if production increases to 1,001 tons per day, the additional ton is conventionally considered to be the contribution to production of the additional worker. However, this is only an assumption, as can be seen by going back to the example of the worker, the capitalist, and the entrepreneur. It is impossible to determine, without some conventional basis, whether the worker is the marginal addition to the shovel, with Y the marginal product of the worker, or whether the shovel is the marginal addition to the worker, and Y minus X is the marginal product.

In this paper, I will follow the conventional method of *assigning* to a factor its marginal contribution to production. However, this does not solve all problems, because it is necessary to obtain actual evaluations of these marginal contributions. Conceptually, this could be done by means of experiments—say, in one firm. Unfortunately, since these conceptual experiments cannot be carried on in every firm in a country, another method of estimation must be found in order to obtain estimates for the economy as a whole.

In economics, an effort has been made to develop methods for solving this problem, taking into consideration the fact that, in practice, the value of a product is distributed among the factors that participate in its production. This distribution of the value of the product is made by means of the amounts paid to the factors. It is important to observe that the amounts paid to the factors of production are determined, essentially, on an institutional basis. If favorable conditions are created in a society, demand and supply will determine the amounts paid to the factors in the market. In societies having different economic systems, the mechanisms for distribution will also be different.

The most commonly used method—at least, in our part of the world—of relating the marginal contribution of a factor to production with the amount paid for the services of the factor is based on the assumption of perfect competition. Under this assumption, supply, demand, and market have special characteristics, unlikely to be found in reality, but simplifying the abstract analysis. In any case, the assumption of perfect competition limits the validity of the analysis to societies that, at least in theory, adhere to the principles of individualism, and this is a very important limitation. Using the assumption of perfect competition as a starting point, it is possible to prove that, in conditions of equilibrium, the amount paid for a factor is equal to its marginal contribution to production. In all the estimations of the contribution of education to economic development that have been made thus far, this method has been used.

FIRST STAGE: ECONOMIC GROWTH AND THE EDUCATION EMBODIED IN THE FACTORS OF PRODUCTION

Production and the Quantity of the Factors

As already stated, I will consider three factors of production: entrepreneurs, capital, and labor. Since there is no way to measure entrepreneurship, I will, in some cases, speak only of capital and labor. Wherever it is required, the role of the entrepreneur will, if at all possible, be introduced into the analysis.

The first explanation offered for increments in production is to attribute them to increments in the production factors. However, it is easy to determine that this is not the case. Included in my book, *The Economics of Human Resources,* is a breakdown, for the United States, of the increments of private, nonfarm GNP during the period 1909-49.* For this period, increments in the GNP due to increments in labor amounted to 14.1 per cent; those due to increments in capital amounted to 16.9 per cent. Increments in productivity accounted for the remainder, 69 per cent of the increments of the GNP. Hence, the principal conclusion I arrived at was that 69 per cent of the increases in production during this period could not be attributed to increases in the

* Hector Correa, *The Economics of Human Resources* (Amsterdam: North Holland Publishing Co., 1963); see, especially, Table XI-1-2.

production factors—that is, to increases in the quantity of capital and labor. Rather, these were due to increments in the productivity of the factors of production.

Production, Productivity, and the Quality of the Factors of Production

In the preceding section, I made the point that a large part of economic growth is due to increments in the *productivity* of the factors of production. The next problem is to explain the reasons for this increase. This I will do now, paying special attention to the role of education.

Economies of scale could be one reason for increases in productivity. This means simply that, due to the characteristics of the production process, when the factors are combined in larger quantities they have higher productivity; among other reasons, this is sometimes due to a better division of labor. Here, I will assume, without presenting any empirical evidence, that the influence of economies of scale is negligible.

Only the following three ways to increase productivity will be considered here: (1) Better entrepreneurs make more effective combinations of labor and capital, without altering the quality of either; that is, they change capital per worker; (2) entrepreneurs of unchanged quality combine unchanged amounts of labor and capital, but this labor and capital are of better quality; (3) more effective combinations of higher quality labor and capital are made. Hence, the *quality* of one or more factors of production plays a role in each of these three ways to increase productivity. This fact distinguishes these ways from economies of scale that could increase productivity without any change in the quality of the factors.

The three ways to bring about increments in the productivity of the factors will be classified into two groups: first, the increments in productivity that can be considered as by-products of the production process itself; and, second, the changes in productivity that are determined by factors outside the production process. This classification is not intended to be very precise, but I think it is worth using.

If a strictly scientific position is adopted, there is no basis for assuming that the observed increments in productivity are due to one or another of these three ways to increase productivity, or for deciding whether these ways are a consequence of the production process itself or are determined by outside factors. Neither is there any basis for the assumption that increases in the quality of the production factors that are due to the production process itself and increases due to influences outside the production process are independent of each other. Whatever the position adopted, it requires empirical verification. Unfortunately, at the present time, the availability of statistical information and the methodology in use make it impossible to carry out such analyses.

In this analysis, it will be assumed—without empirical basis for the assumption—that both the increases in the quality of the factors due to the production process itself and the increases brought from outside the process are determinants of the increases of productivity. An additional assumption is that these two reasons can be studied separately.

Experience as a determinant of increases in productivity. The first type of determinant of increments in productivity—the one that can be considered as a by-product of the process itself—is experience. The essential point is that experience is completely endogenous to the production process. If production increases, experience does likewise and permits a reinitiation of the process of production-experience. The only limitation is human capacity.

When the level of production of a firm, or of an economic sector, is considered, the importance of experience in increasing productivity seems clear. Rapping, in his study of shipbuilding during World War II, concluded that, due to experience, firms increased production at a rate of about 30 per cent per year.*

Despite the considerable importance of experience in providing increments in productivity at the level of the firm, its contribution to the economic growth of a country as a whole is not likely to be very large. To see this, you have only to observe that experience depends, mainly, on the time a worker spends with the same equipment. If the average age of the worker and of the equipment remain constant, despite the fact that young workers

* Leonard Rapping, "Learning and World War II Production Functions," *The Review of Economics and Statistics,* LXVII, No. 1 (February, 1965).

and new machines replace retiring workers and obsolete machines, the total experience in the labor force remains constant. During the period studied by Rapping (World War II), it can be said that the age structure of the labor force and equipment in the United States remained more or less constant; so, our conclusion follows.

It is important to observe that the above analysis provides the basis for the assumption that increases in the productivity of the production factors are determined by factors outside the production process itself. However, this analysis is valid only in part. Later in this paper, I will indicate other ways in which experience influences production and, hence, comes to be of major importance, after all. Nevertheless, there are reasons for believing that we should look outside the production process for the determinants of increases in the quality of the factors of production.

Education and improvements in the quality of the factors of production determined from outside the production process. The results of the previous section suggest that something outside the production process itself causes changes in the quality of the factors that bring about increases in productivity. However, these results do not tell which is the factor, or factors, having a larger productivity. Moreover, even if the productivity of entrepreneurs and workers has increased, there is no basis for relating such change to more or better education.

These observations show the need for methods to verify that, whatever the reasons for the increments in productivity, education of entrepreneurs and workers plays an important role. The problem can be stated in a different way. We do not know whether increments in productivity are brought about by better entrepreneurs, better capital, or better labor; neither do we know whether more or better education can be considered as one of the reasons for better entrepreneurs, capital, or labor.

At this point, it should be observed that no problem of verifying the importance of education in economic growth arises if it is assumed that conditions of perfect competition exist. This is because, in conditions of perfect competition, more educated entrepreneurs would have higher incomes and more educated workers would receive higher salaries only if their marginal productivity were higher—that is, only if their contribution to production were higher and only if this higher contribution were due to their education. However, in this paper, I reject the assumption of perfect competition.

Entrepreneurs, education, and economic growth. Unfortunately, no quantitative information is available for determining the contribution to economic growth of entrepreneurship. Somewhat better information exists with regard to the educational background of entrepreneurs and the relation of their education to economic growth. In this respect, the statistical information prepared by Newcomer is illuminating.* Newcomer studied 253 executives classified into two groups. In the first group were the executives of fast-growing companies; the values of the assets of these companies increased at least five times between 1924 and 1949. In the second group were the executives of companies whose assets did not at least double in the same period.

Newcomer found a much *smaller* proportion of executives having some graduate training—usually in engineering or law—in the fast-growing companies. Of those executives who actually held degrees in engineering or law, by far the greater proportion were to be found in the slow-growing companies. Interestingly enough, Newcomer's results also showed that the education of executives increased with the size of the corporation.† From these results, it can be said, provisionally, that the education of executives somewhat reduces their ability to contribute to economic growth.

Education of the labor force and increases in productivity. I have used the fact that capital-intensive techniques are needed for higher productivity to test whether more highly educated workers are required to attain higher levels of productivity. In my study, I used data of capital per worker and level of education of the labor force in 144 manufactures in the United States, in 1947.‡ Analysis of this data provided the basis for my conclusion that an increase in the volume, or the intensity, of capital requires an increase in the educational level of the labor force.

---

* Mabel Newcomer, *The Big Business Executive* (New York: Columbia University Press, 1955); see, in particular, Table 33.

† *Ibid.*, Table 26.

‡ Correa, *op. cit.*, pp. 179–84.

This means that, whatever the reasons for increments in the productivity of labor and capital, a precondition is a higher level of education of the labor force.

Measuring the contribution of education to economic development. Up to this point, I have argued that: Economic development is, to a large extent, due to increments in productivity; the reasons for these increments do not include education; whatever the reason for these increments, the educational level of the workers plays an important, though as yet undetermined, role; the case for education does not appear equally clear with respect to entrepreneurs.

The next problem is to measure the contribution of education to development. In the case of the education of entrepreneurs, no measurement is possible, because not even the contribution of the entrepreneurs themselves can be measured.

The situation is less complicated in the case of the contribution of the education of the labor force. A method to evaluate this contribution has been presented by both Denison* and by me.† Using Denison data, I find that 14.6 per cent of the economic growth between 1909 and 1949 can be attributed to the education of the labor force.‡

The estimation presented here has several limitations that stem from the fact that all people engaged in economic activity are included, as well as all their income. As a result, the contribution of the education of entrepreneurs is lumped together with the contribution of the education of workers. Moreover, the fact that all income (corrected for the part attributable to innate abilities) of those engaged in economic activity is considered together causes several distortions. For one thing, income depends upon experience, but, in these estimations, the increase due to experience is attributed, instead, to education. This error is especially important because, despite the contribution of experience to in-

---

* For his statement of approach, see Edward F. Denison, *The Sources of Economic Growth in the U.S.A.* (New York: CED, 1962). For the data referred to in my evaluation, see his article "Measuring the Contribution of Education to Economic Growth," in the OECD publication *The Residual Factor and Economic Growth* (Paris: OECD, 1964).

† Correa, *loc. cit.*

‡ Support for this figure can be found in Gary S. Becker, *Human Capital* (New York: Columbia University Press, 1964).

come, its contribution to growth may be minimal. These figures provide no clues to the answer to this question.

Other reasons for increments in productivity. It should be observed that, in the foregoing analysis, not all increases in the productivity of the production factors have been explained. This means that the education embodied in the workers is not the cause of all these increments. No explicit attention will be given to other reasons that explain these increments or to the factors in which they are embodied. Other reasons for the increments in productivity could also be embodied in the labor force—better nutrition and better health, for example. Better quality of capital goods could also be a reason for the increments in productivity. Since a detailed analysis of this aspect is not needed for the present topic, it will not be considered in this paper.

SECOND STAGE: HIGHER-ORDER DETERMINANTS OF THE INCREMENTS IN PRODUCTIVITY

Concept of Higher-Order Determinants

In the method of analysis adopted here, I have been moving, in time, away from the actual production process. First, looking at the production process with a short time horizon, I observed that entrepreneurs, capital, and labor were the determinants of the volume of production. Next, one step further away, I considered the determinants of the increments of productivity embodied in the factors of production. In particular, I estimated the contribution to economic growth made by the education of workers. Now, I will adopt a new point of view, going one step farther from production, to consider second-order determinants.

Among these second-order determinants, I will consider the education of the scientists who contribute to the development of better capital goods, and the factors that contribute to the increments of the quantity and quality of the education of the labor force.

The analysis of second-order effects is important because it illustrates the following point: The measurement of the contribution of education to economic development is somewhat arbitrary. It is closely related to the number of steps away from production that we want to take or, in other words, it is closely related to the number of higher-order effects that we are willing to include. It might even be true that all production could be attributed to education if an infinitely large number of higher-order effects were considered.

On the other hand, there is no logical reason to stop our analysis of the contribution of education at one level of determinants instead of another. The only justification for such a cut-off can be found on practical grounds—that is, on the use that will be made of the information. This question leads to the analysis of the integration of economic and educational planning, a topic that will be dealt with in the next section.

Education and Increments in the Quality of Capital Goods

Better quality capital goods can be considered one of the determinants of the increments of productivity, and new knowledge could be one of the factors that determine these increments in quality. Viewed this way, a second-order determinant of the increment of productivity will be the education required to produce the knowledge that brings about better capital goods.

The information on this point is very scarce. Research by Schmookler, into the educational background of inventors, produced data that is far from conclusive.* Without referring to the capabilities of the inventors or to their experience in the production process, Schmookler's data does give some idea of the educational characteristics of a sample of inventors. (In his sample, one-third of the patents granted in October and November, 1953, were studied.)

It can be estimated, on the basis of Schmookler's data, that the average number of years of study spent by the inventors in his sample was 14.33; this is considerably higher than the average, about 9 years, of the labor force as a whole at the time. Schmookler found that 56 per cent of the inventors he investigated had university degrees or had done postgraduate study. The majority of these were technologists, rather than executives. This is particularly interesting because Schmookler also found that technologists have a lower average age than executives.

Although his data favors the hypothesis that the higher educa-

* Jacob Schmookler, "Inventors Past and Present," *Review of Economics and Statistics,* August, 1957, pp. 221–33.

tion of personnel occupied in the production end of science increases the product, it cannot be considered to prove it. Since it is a fair assumption that the innate capabilities of personnel having a university education are greater than those of the rest of the population, the higher productivity of science could be a consequence of the higher level of innate capabilities, rather than of the higher educational level.

Another tentative hypothesis suggested by his data is that education and experience may work interchangeably. That is, the greater level of experience—extrapolated from the fact of higher average age—of the executives may balance out the higher level of education, but lower average age, of the technologists. This is one of the reasons why experience might play an important role in economic growth, despite the observations made earlier in this paper.

Determinants of the Quality and Quantity of the Education Received by the Labor Force

The first determinant of the educational level of the labor force is the educational system. It is tempting to an economist to use the techniques applied to the analysis of other input-output systems for the study of education, but this would carry me outside the main topic of this paper.

The educational system, however, is not the only determinant of the quality and quantity of the education of the labor force. Two additional influences require consideration: the intergenerational effects of education and the socio-economic determinants of the characteristics of the educational system.

It is an established fact that the educational level of the parent is one determinant of the level that will be attained by the child. This is what is meant by the intergenerational effect of education. A direct consequence of this effect is that part of the income received by an individual during his active life pays for the education he received as a consequence of the educational level of his parents. Swift and Weisbrod* measured this payment, as well as the cost of the parents' education, which caused it to be made.

---

* William Swift and Burton A. Weisbrod, "On the Monetary Value of Education's Intergeneration Effects," *The Journal of Political Economy*, December, 1965, pp. 643–49.

One conclusion that has been drawn is that these payments, up to high school, are greater than the cost of the parents' education. The opposite is true for higher levels.

A higher level of socio-economic development also influences the quantity and quality of education; through improved education, future levels of development are determined. The level of socio-economic development may affect education in two ways. First, higher levels of socio-economic development mean greater availability of resources. This permits greater expenditures for education in the form of better buildings, libraries, laboratories, teachers' salaries, and of more personnel for administrative purposes. These facts suggest the hypothesis that the level of socio-economic development influences the quality of education.

To test this hypothesis, I ranked groups of nationals of different Latin and Central American countries according to their grades on tests given, simultaneously, to all of them.* These rankings were then matched with rankings according to the level of per capita income in each country. I found that the rank correlation between the two sets of figures was 0.617, significant at a 5 per cent confidence level.

The second way the level of socio-economic development influences education is through its impact on the demand for enrollment—that is, the increase in the public demand for education —and on the acceptance and, indeed, the demand that young people remain in the educational system. From my own study, I was able to conclude that, wherever conditions permit, an increment of $100 per capita will bring about a 3 per cent increase in enrollments.†

INTEGRATION OF ECONOMIC AND EDUCATIONAL PLANNING

There are two main points to be considered with respect to the integration of economic and educational planning. The first is the adaptation of the educational system to economic growth. The second, the inverse of the first, is the adaptation of the economy to educational growth. Both aspects follow naturally from

---

* Hector Correa, "Quality of Education and Socio-Economic Development," *Comparative Education Review*, June, 1964, pp. 11–16.
† *Ibid.*

the analysis thus far presented and both are needed for successful planning.

It should be observed that, if planning is considered as a whole, there is no way to determine theoretically whether economic targets should be fixed and the educational system adapted to them, or whether educational targets should be fixed and the economy adapted to them. Actually, a discussion of this question has very little practical value; due to the interdependence of the two systems, economic targets set without taking into consideration those of education cannot be achieved, and vice versa.

The Adaptation of Education to Economic Growth

The first problem, in economic planning, is to decide how much to save and invest for future growth and how much to consume in the present. Since investment is the main force in economic growth, this decision also determines the future growth rate of total income.

Once the amount of resources to be invested is known, it must be allocated among the different sources of growth; education should be considered one of these sources. The first problem of the integration of economic and educational planning is the determination of how much is to be allocated to education.

There are two main ways to make this decision. The first is based on the estimated returns on educational investments; the second is the manpower approach. These two ways complement each other and should be used together in actual planning.

When the rate of return approach is used, returns on different alternative investments are compared. Resources are allocated to the source of growth with higher rates of return. According to the law of diminishing returns, successive increments of resources allocated to any one factor will diminish the returns of these increments, making investments in other sources more attractive.

What has been said in the previous paragraphs in respect to total investments in education could also be said of investments in the parts—that is, in elementary, high school, and college education. There is no reason, at least in theory, why investment in education should be considered aggregated in one monolithic block. Any appropriate subdivision could be considered. It is not enough to know the total amount of resources needed. We must also know how to distribute them among the different types of education and, in each type, among the teachers, libraries, buildings, and so on. This cannot be done, at this time, using the rate of return approach, mainly because we lack the statistical information.

In order to link the rate of return approach with the manpower approach, it should be observed that the counterpart of the decision to increase or decrease investments in education, relative to investments in other capital goods, is the fact that the relative scarcity of qualified manpower will be decreased or increased. In the manpower approach, an attempt is made to estimate how many people with different levels of education will be required to attain the levels of production set as targets in the plan.

Once the number of workers with different levels of education is known, the first stage in the manpower approach to educational planning is completed. The second problem is to find out how many people the educational system should produce. This number is equal to the total number of workers required, less the number of workers surviving from previous periods. Once the output for the educational system is known, it is possible to estimate the student flows required, as well as the number of teachers and physical facilities needed. Using these results, along with information about educational costs, the amounts of resources that should be allocated to education can be determined. That is, the last step in the manpower approach gives the required investment, which was the first result of the rate of return approach.

From a technical point of view, an ideal situation would be to use both approaches simultaneously. Thus far, lack of data has been the main obstacle to doing so.

Adaptation of the Economy to Educational Development

Earlier, I noted that one of the determinants of the quality and quantity of education is the level of socio-economic development. This means that, to attain a level of educational development considered as a target, a necessary precondition is to reach a level of socio-economic development. This presents the planner of educational development with the problem of determining the level that the economy must achieve in order to reach the educational targets. This is exactly the inverse problem of that of the economy-planner.

To solve this problem, a method similar to the one used in the case of the adaptation of education to economic development can be used. The method is as follows: Once the educational targets, usually in terms of enrollment, are fixed, their implications—in terms of per capita income and in terms of quality and quantity of teachers, buildings, and so forth—have to be estimated. Per capita income is introduced here because the demand for enrollment depends on the level of per capita income. So, a first target, induced by the impact of educational requirements on the economy, is found.

The next stage is to estimate what is needed to obtain the resources to pay for the required teachers and implements. These needs are additional induced targets that the economy must satisfy if the educational targets are to be reached. As a conclusion, if the economy is not geared to the educational system, the educational targets will not be attained.

CONCLUSION

In this paper, an attempt has been made to study the contribution of education to economic development and to present some policy implications of the results. Despite the fact that the point of view adopted has been somewhat broader than that generally used by economists, it excludes some important questions. To mention just one, the influence of education on the rate of population growth and, as a consequence, on per capita income, has not been raised. I would point out that, in the long run, this might be the most important influence of education on economic welfare.

One of the main reasons why it is impossible to deal with such problems is the lack of data. Actually, in the limited analysis carried on here, strain has been put on the statistical information available. I have been forced to present a patchwork of data collected for other purposes and adapted, by force, to my objectives.

I hope that, following the lines of this study—or other lines, if they are more convenient—a systematic study of the contribution of education to economic development will be attempted.

DISCUSSION

BEASLEY [presiding]: This session is open for discussion.

DEITCH: Could you explain the connection between the theoretical models you used and the conclusions you reached? How did you get around to competitive models?

CORREA: I begin with a consideration of two factors in production, capital and labor. Mathematically, production can be expressed in terms of salaries and the return per unit of capital. Production, in each moment of time, is distributed between labor and capital. If we increase the marginal amount of either labor or capital, the mathematical analysis usually is based on the differential.

We can estimate the differential mathematically. If increments of labor and capital (X and Y) are small, the increment of production (Z) likewise will be small. If we reduce the increment of X and the increment of Y, the increment of Z will approach zero.

DEITCH: And Z is measured in dollars and is, in fact, the GNP.

CORREA: Yes. All I am saying here, with this mathematical equation, is that the volume of production depends on the volume of labor and the volume of capital. The total value of production will be distributed between labor and capital. This is a statistical fact. Our problem is to estimate how production will change if one worker (or one unit of capital) is added to the labor force. Simply, I consider that this change in production will be approximately equal to the salary paid to the worker (or the return of one unit of capital). This conclusion is usually obtained, in economics, with the assumption of perfect competition. In my paper, I have tried to avoid this assumption.

In nontechnical terms, the basis for my conclusion can be explained as follows: The assumption of perfect competition permits us to use one mathematical technique (the differential) to obtain an approximation of the value of the increment in production brought by the additional worker. I think that other mathematical techniques, not based in that assumption, permit us to obtain other approximations. Now, why should we use the technique based on a dubious assumption?

STOIKOV: Rather than start with production and substitute for those marginal products the particular wages that are returns to capital, which would be a substitute only under perfect competition, you are trying to escape this kind of assumption, and are starting simply with an identity?

CORREA: Yes.

BROWN: I don't really understand how this enables you to avoid assuming a competitive economy.

LLOYD: You are objecting, I think, to too much reliance on the marginal productivity theory of wages.

BROWN: Yes. I don't see how you use marginal productivity analysis without the assumption of a more or less perfectly competitive economy.

DAVID: One justification, perhaps, for Mr. Correa's procedure is the assumption that, whatever the increase in economic output, the market structure is unaffected; so we have the same balance of monopolistic and oligopolistic elements. This is a rather strong hypothesis, but it is one that might conceivably support some approximation.

CORREA: Another way to justify my conclusion is that deviations from conditions of perfect competition will not greatly modify the estimate of increase in production brought by one additional worker.

DAVID: I would like to make three observations. One is that, in very recent times, contrary to the evidence in your paper, there apparently has been a decline in the average life of equipment, so that we can expect the experience factor that you mention to be going in the opposite direction from increasing productivity. This is reflected in the fact that business and the U.S. Treasury have agreed that the depreciable life of assets will be shortened and that we will have a shorter write-off period for our capital investments.

Second, it seems to me that, beyond what you say, we have had substantial changes in the organization of the production process. You attribute the changes either to entrepreneurs or to management, but it isn't clear to me that you can validly make the assumption that excludes reasons not "within the production process." For example, we have linear programming techniques for minimizing inventories, for improving personnel assignment, for solving the problem of transporting goods from one place to another. All of these techniques are vastly improving the efficiency of our organization on a given set of physical facts.

Last, it seems to me that, although Newcomer's work shows an interesting fact, it doesn't demonstrate anything about the effect of education on our national product. Suppose the executives of the slow-growing companies had the same low level of education as executives of the fast-growing companies. Is it necessarily the case that we would then have had an improved national product? I think not, because it is in the nature of things that a corporation the size of General Motors has more limited possibilities for growth on its size base than the XYZ Laundry Company down the street.

CORREA: With respect to your first statement, there may be some change in the average age of equipment, but its impact on the average experience of workers will be small. It seems to me that these changes cannot substantially modify the magnitudes involved. In any case, only additional research can provide a definite answer.

With respect to the second point, I believe that I have not been very clear about what I mean by changes brought to the production process from outside. I agree that there are new techniques that management is now using, but the introduction of these is due, let's say, to the education of the managers; so I can say that they were brought from outside.

DAVID: Not necessarily by a process of formal educational attainments.

CORREA: Not necessarily formal education. I didn't want to go into the question of what formal education is. In any case, the new techniques in management cannot be considered a result of the production process, in the sense used in my paper. The meaning, in my paper, is taken from the learning curves used by the psychologists. These curves show that if a person works with a machine, production will, in time, increase, just as a consequence of the interaction of machine and man, and nothing else.

As to your third point, I agree with you that Newcomer's results do not prove that the education of entrepreneurs is disadvantageous for economic growth. I don't think any statistical analysis proves anything. But, in any case, the data gives a hint that education might not be an important factor in the capacities of entrepreneurs. As I said, I think the only thing that can be done is to conduct more research on this question.

STOIKOV: On that same point, if you standardize for each kind of industry, you might get exactly the opposite result from Newcomer's. A fast-growing company might be, for example, a laundry; slow-growing companies might be in chemicals. In some industries, management has to know something about the production process; so, in effect, if you studied them by industry, you might get just the opposite result from the one you have here.

CORREA: I think that, even if explicitly you are not accepting my conclusions, you are suggesting a different way to test them, and that is all that can be done with this evidence.

FOLGER: Your main thesis is that a portion of residual economic growth should be assigned to education and you have estimated how much ought to be so assigned. There have been a number of studies that show a very low relationship between educational performance and subsequent career performance. Don't these findings raise some questions about this sort of assignment of the aggregate to the educational effect?

STOIKOV: Your example is based on people who have finished a particular educational level. You are asking them how they perform at that particular level in relation to their income performance afterward. The question is, what do different levels of education contribute toward income?

FOLGER: We know there has been a great deal of analysis showing that people who have different levels of education have different levels of earnings. Even when you control for occupation, there is still a difference remaining—although most of the difference would be attributed to the occupation.

STOIKOV: Yes, but that is not relevant. The only way you enter the occupation is through education. That is what an education leads you to and that's why it doesn't make sense to standardize for the occupation.

FOLGER: That's really the sort of thing I am reporting on. It is not a very precise standardization, but, in effect, you are asking, "In this occupation, what is the man's educational performance?"

DAVID: In 1959, we conducted a national survey in which we related the average weekly earnings of heads of households and of wives to a wide variety of factors, including education, an approximate measure of achievement orientation (the need achievement that Mr. Strodtbeck mentioned in his paper), physical handicaps, geographic location, occupation, and so on.* Differentials in income were observed between high school and college graduates and, also, high school dropouts. Each age cohort was assigned different income effects according to its educational attainment. I think, by examining the limited younger age group, we avoided confounding the effect of level of education with the different qualities of education received by people who got their education at vastly different times. The income differentials within the cross section reflected the current earning power of these different educational age cohorts. When they were capitalized, I believe they implied something like a net difference, in present values, on the order of $10,000 for advancing from a completed high school diploma to a completed college diploma, if you discount the expected lifetime earnings at a 4 per cent rate.

This is a somewhat different value of education than is found in Becker or some other sources. But, it is an attempt to clear away some of the other influences and look at the net effect, after other relevant influences are accounted for.

There is more of this kind of sophisticated work being done now. A group of us, at Wisconsin, are now looking at a time stream of income and observing the interaction between people of a given age and their operation in the economy over time. That is, we are studying the actual lifetime earnings pattern of an in-

---

* These results are published in J. N. Morgan, M. David, *et al., Income and Welfare in the U.S.* (New York: McGraw-Hill, 1962); see also their article "Education and Income," *Quarterly Journal of Economics,* LXXVII (August, 1963), pp. 423–37.

dividual, in the context of historical increases in productivity and changes in the economy. The kinds of data I have just reported tell us only differences between individuals at a given point in time. And those individuals may have rather different life histories.

LLOYD: Is this the same type of thing Herman Miller did in his study, reported last fall in the *American Economic Review?**

DAVID: Miller has done some very interesting work, particularly on the white-nonwhite earnings differential.† He did not make as great an effort as we did to determine the influence of these other factors, such as geographical location, motivation, and so on.

LECHT: Have any of these studies taken into account the social status of the families from which people come?

DAVID: Our study experimented with the effect of the father's education on the child's educational attainment. That attainment is correlated with current earnings. The father's education did contribute to the average educational attainment of the child and was, by far, the most important factor included in that analysis.

STOIKOV: Mr. Correa's paper is an outline of how one might proceed to determine the effect of education on development. Some very important things were not taken into consideration. Particularly, I thought you could have mentioned on the job training, which, in fact, is education that contributes to production. Some people have estimated it to be of a size almost as large as formal schooling. Where would you fit it into your scheme of attacking the whole problem? Clearly, you would have to include this kind of education.

CORREA: Well, when one studies the effect of education on the economy, the influence of formal training and on the job training should be taken into account. The problem is, we cannot separate the two effects, because there is no information about on the job training.

DAVID: You cited Denison's work at length in your paper. Actually, the development of a set of models for measuring the contribution of a factor to the production process has gone substan-

---

* "Lifetime Income and Economic Growth," *The American Economic Review*, Vol. LV, No. 4 (September, 1965).

† See his *Rich Man, Poor Man* (New York: Thomas Y. Crowell, 1964).

tially beyond the work of both Denison and Solow.* Solow set out to determine, in an aggregate production function, how much of the increase in product could be attributed to an increase in measured amounts of labor and capital. In doing that, he discovered a rather small part was attributable to actual changes in the inputs—something Mr. Correa's work substantiates.

There have been various theories to deal with the remaining change in productivity. Benton Masell has developed an index of technological change. This is the notion that the remainder is something that comes out of a knowledge sector of the economy and goes into the production function and simply lifts it up every year. With the passage of time, in this model, increases in technology occur automatically. That is sort of a direct input.

The economists weren't satisfied with this. Phelps, Solow, and several others experimented with what they called models of embodied technological change. Instead of just having the passage of time and the diffusion of information change the production process, the notion was that you had to put a machine in place. The embodied-change hypothesis implies that a graduate of an institution, in 1965, must be added to the industrial process in order to introduce certain kinds of problem-solving into the system. Just as an automated cylinder borer had to be placed in the automobile plant before the technological improvement could be realized.

This has been applied to the capital side; presumably, the same sort of thing could be applied to the educational side. I would like to see work on the logic of such a model. Then, it would be appropriate to ask how we estimate such a model.

There is still a third model of the effect of education on productivity that seems relevant to me. We can affect the effectiveness of our labor or management components by various kinds of training and retraining—inputs that are not embodied but require additional investment in existing factors. So we have three possibilities: first, direct diffusion of change, which is just a matter of information becoming available so that it is free to be used; sec-

* Robert Solow, "Investors Past and Present," *Review of Economics and Statistics*, No. 39, August, 1957.

ond, embodied change, which requires a new generation of people or machines; and third, modifying our factors by in-service training. I think we need this kind of model to settle the question on the contribution of education to development.

CORREA: I think the most recent work on the problem of embodied capital, education, and economic development was done by Nelson.* The problem with technological change embodied in capital is that we don't have, as in the case of changes in quantity embodied in the labor force, an index. In the case of the education embodied in the labor force, we have an independent index. In the case of the quality of capital embodied in capital, we don't have that index. And what Solow† and, again, Nelson did was to develop a statistical method to study the changes in quality embodied in the capital goods, needed because there is not an independent index. So, if I had discussed, in more detail, the embodied changes in the quality of capital, I would have had to use one of the methods just mentioned, because there is no independent index.

DAVID: I think you underrate these models. In fact, we know that the increasing education that is being applied has higher qualities to it. On the other hand, we know it is being applied more generally because people in society have a higher average educational attainment now than they did fifty years ago. I am not so sure that a given number of years of education in 1910 and in 1950, or 1960, mean the same thing.

CORREA: They don't mean the same thing, and that is why I use the numbers of days per school year as a correction factor—that is, I use comparable years of education. I know that, in addition, there are some other qualitative aspects, but, in any case, the difficulty that we had with capital exists less in the case of labor. In the case of labor, we have an independent index—good or bad, we have one—of qualitative changes. This is not available in the case of capital. The models for the study of technological

* Richard P. Nelson, "Aggregate Production Functions and Medium Growth Projection," *American Economic Review*, Vol. LIV, No. 4 (September, 1964), pp. 575–606.

† Robert Solow, "Technical Change and the Aggregate Production Function," *Review of Economics and Statistics*, No. 39, August, 1957, pp. 312–20.

change embodied in labor are different because of this basic difference in the data available.

DAVID: Not only for that reason—for theoretical reasons as well.

CORREA: Well, if you had an independent index of capital, you could apply to capital the same procedure we are applying here to human capital.

ARNESEN: There are two questions I would like to ask: Does the matter of consumption of goods and services have any relationship to economic growth? If it does have some relationship, then does education have anything to do with the consumption of goods and services and, thereby, have an effect on economic growth?

CORREA: I tried to dispose of the question of consumption when I defined growth as increments in the capacity to produce. In a more general approach, I will agree with you that supply and demand should be considered in the study of economic growth. It would be interesting to study the effect of education on consuming and, through this, its influence on economic factors and on economic growth.

FOLGER: Let me shift the discussion and ask you about the use of this model, either in its present form or in a more elaborate form, for planning decisions in education. Most educational planning in this country proceeds from the question of what the student demands for education are, without relation to careful estimates of demand for workers with various levels and types of education.

If you examine educational plans, you will see a rather limited reference to the demands for graduates. I am not trying to depreciate this approach, because I think it is very important for us to know what level of investment in education might contribute to future economic growth, but, on a more specific level of state planning, do you see this as having any application?

CORREA: I would like to consider your question from different points of view. I am not proposing, here, that this model should be used directly as an instrument for planning. I think, even when we are only considering the technical aspect of planning, of how to make a plan, a more detailed analysis will be required. The model here could be used only in the initial steps to make some global allocations and then to proceed to a more detailed analysis.

As I mentioned in my paper, I think demand for education should be taken into consideration in the preparation of a manpower plan. If we make a manpower plan and find that the requirements are too different from the growth trend in the demand for education, we won't be able to implement the plan.

It seems to me that a rational policy should consider not only what people want to do, in terms of vocation, but also some long-term yield. Actually, I think this is done, in any case, implicitly or explicitly, because education is considered as an investment. So, what we are doing with this type of model is explicitly rationalizing the procedure.

I am not acquainted with the statements made by policy-makers in the United States but, for instance, in Ecuador, since our independence, we have been saying that education is basic for the development of the country. What we are trying to do is to give more concrete form to this statement.

STOIKOV: I am wondering if Mr. Folger is complaining that states plan simply according to the demand for entrance into college?

FOLGER: I said that was the major factor and I think, if you examine state plans that have been prepared in the last decade, the thing they are concerned with is how many students are going to want to enroll at the various levels of education.

STOIKOV: What puzzles me about this kind of approach, if it is accepted, is that the demand will depend on the pricing policies adopted. If the state, at the same time, also controls the pricing policy, it can set the demand, itself, at any particular level. That is, the kinds of fees it is going to charge at state universities, and the kinds of scholarship programs it adopts, and so on, will influence demand; so you are saying that the state determines the demand and that the demand determines the state's educational investment.

FOLGER: No. I don't think they start out that way at all. I think they start with the notion that everyone ought to have an opportunity for all the education that he is able to profit from.

STOIKOV: But some price is always put on it.

LLOYD: It's about the same price, though, isn't it, for students in all fields?

STOIKOV: You can set the same price across the board, for all occupational fields. But, also, you can set the price much lower for all, in which case you will have more students coming in. In other words, the student demand is affected by the price. The question is, where do you set the particular price level?

LLOYD: It is very arbitrary.

STOIKOV: This is what puzzles me—if this is, in fact, what the state is doing. In fact, the state is setting the demand for education; then, supposedly, from that it can decide how much education to offer.

DEITCH: I think price mechanisms regulate the demand somewhat, particularly for out-of-state students.

FOLGER: What is the contribution of economic growth to social development? Are there not three factors—educational, economic, and social—to be considered?

CORREA: The main trouble I have with that is defining social development.

LLOYD: Isn't this what Harbison and Myers have discussed, in terms of strategies that include political and social considerations?*

CORREA: I have said this so many times to Harbison that it won't hurt to say it once more: The main problem, in their work, is that their statements are too vague and too imprecise to permit any measurement. Some workers in sociology have tried to be more precise in their concept of what society is, and, from such work, we can define and plan social development. Part of social development will be economic and educational development. If we start with these sociological analyses, we will find that, besides the economic and the educational systems, there is a political system, and there we have another type of problem.

LECHT: Along these same lines, it seems to me that one area of your paper raises grave problems for this kind of analysis, and that is the area of second-order effects. The significance of much

* Frederick H. Harbison and Charles A. Myers, *Education, Manpower, and Economic Growth* (New York: McGraw-Hill, 1964).

of education, in terms of its effect on economic development, arises from these second-order effects. An increase in education, for example, would affect output—only in part because of its effect on research and development. It would probably affect output because of its effect on health. It would probably affect output because of its effect on people's habits and on how they fit into the work culture once they can, say, read directions. I suspect that excluding the second-order effects keeps out so much that is significant that, in terms of planning, the analysis loses much of its relevance as a tool for policy.

CORREA: I think that social scientists have not obtained enough scientific results to permit them to replace politicians. Politicians still have a feeling for the social realities that we cannot replace with our scientific analysis. The scientific analysis that we make now can help them to see some aspects more clearly, but not all; for instance, I don't think that what I am saying here, about the interaction between economics and education, should be the only basis for planning. If a plan is made, in addition to what I've mentioned, all the rest of social activity should be considered. Unfortunately, the moment that we define some aspects of social development in more precise terms, these aspects tend to have more weight than those that cannot be expressed in this way.

DAVID: I would like to comment on that. This notion of second-order effects is a very important one. Although I don't know what kind of data we really have on this, the thing that comes to mind is that we have second-order effects in the field of consumption. About thirty years ago, some economists started to worry about these second-order effects in the consumption function and they came up with a theory of full-employment adjustment, which is the Keynesian theory. They worked out the logic of the interrelationship of the various parts of the system. It seems to me that is precisely what you are calling for when you say we need to analyze the interdependence of education and the economic system. It would be a great mistake to neglect an explicit logical analysis of the second-order effects, where they enter the system.

CORREA: What we can do, now, is to study certain interrelationships between the educational system and the economic system. I am not qualified to study the interrelationships between the educational system and the political system, or between education and culture. But these should be included in any social plan and in any political decision. However, I don't know if it is possible to present, with the same precision that I have presented some of the relations between economics and education, relations in the other categories.

BEASLEY: You are saying that economics is one aspect of the total matrix that should be constructed for social planning. But you are also saying that, because your findings will come out in precise terms, they may be given more weight than some other aspect. I wonder if this is true. I wonder if politicians may give more weight to something that is a little nebulous than to a precise figure or percentage.

FLANIGAN: In your analysis, if you found, let's say, that a high percentage of engineers were unemployed and that income from engineering was below the average income of workers with a college education, would that have any implications for this model you are proposing?

CORREA: The implication and the policy of education would be that the number of engineers should be reduced.

FLANIGAN: Then, would you cut off the training of engineers?

CORREA: To answer that, I am going to give you a particular example. Educational planners, on economic grounds, are advising just such a cut-off in the training of lawyers in underdeveloped countries. However, there is evidence that the legal profession is the main source of policy-makers in underdeveloped countries; so, maybe fewer lawyers would mean a drop in leadership in those countries.

LECHT: This reminds me of an article I read criticizing the classical oligopoly theory. The author's opinion of the theory was summed up as, "It is better to be vaguely right than precisely wrong." Similarly, in many of these areas, we may not know, with great precision, what the factors are, or we may not be able to fit them into our models. However, it may often make a great deal of sense just to define the problem in broad terms first, to enumerate the key variables, and get the feel of what is significant. I think, once we have this feel of what is significant, we are in a much better position, either to gather data or, perhaps, to go on to more formal methods.

But, I find it difficult, in this type of presentation, to get a feel of what the problem is. What is its significance in terms of policy? What is it that is not significant?

KLEIN: I think Mr. David has a key here, in that the theoretical model needs development; until there is an investment in the construction and application of this model, the vagueness will continue to exist.

FLANIGAN: Isn't some of this dilemma rooted in the failure to have a plan, in our society, similar to the kind of thing you find in the society that must plan its manpower allocation?

CORREA: What dilemma, exactly?

FLANIGAN: Once an economic determination is made, there are social—and other—considerations. Even though as you indicated, it might be true that we should stop training lawyers, if sufficient faith existed in lawyers to make us want to go on training them, we would. So, I see some dilemma in comparing different systems, in regard to planning. There is a difference between a system that is in short supply and must allocate its training, and our system, which, despite its many problems, seems to feel prosperous enough to oversupply and to take a chance on an oversupply.

CORREA: I don't think one of these models should be used in policy-making. You need models that are more detailed than this. Also, some model, implicit or explicit, is always used for policy-making. Models inform the policy-maker of some of the results, some of the implications, of his acts. I don't think all the complexities of a society could be caught, could be understood, by a person without some explicit frame of analysis, and this frame is a model. It is true that the available models do not cover all the complexities of social life. However, if they cover just a few of them, they reduce both the burden policy-makers carry and the possibility that they will make mistakes.

The setting of goals depends, mainly, on the system of values used by policy-makers, and this is influenced by the society in which they are acting. But, going specifically to your point, if the policy-maker believes that lawyers are very valuable, despite the fact that they don't produce a high economic return, he has a specific set of values and the planners have to accept them and say, "We are going to produce lawyers, in spite of the fact that they don't have enough economic value."

FLANIGAN: But, we do some planning that is not always integrated into our total system, not even for the lower categories, especially the technicians. In the military, if a person going into the service is eligible for the training and wants to take data-processing, he might be told data-processing is closed, but that he could take electronics. So, in the area of training technicians, I think it is important that we do operate with some sort of plan, whether it is an economic plan or a military plan.

CORREA: I think one of the problems here is that we understand the term "planning" in different ways. I don't think taking a plan and saying "you should use this plan" is a workable approach.

FLANIGAN: I still feel planning is very necessary and I am trying to get at a statement of the reasons why, particularly why educational planning is necessary now.

DEITCH: What sort of countries are you referring to?

FLANIGAN: The United States. I think that educational planning is a check, at least an intellectual check, and a source of investigation, and knowledge. To some people who have access to policy-planning, this is extremely important.

COLM: If I understand the question, it is: What is the use of a theoretical model for a practical plan? In Washington, a very lively debate has been going on. The President has instructed all departments and agencies to adopt what is called Planning-Programing-Budgeting. This is a method worked out by The RAND Corporation; they call it cost-effectiveness analysis. It was first applied in the Defense Department. Now, all the agencies are busy trying to adopt it. Many have established special offices concerned with this aspect of planning their program, establishing goals, and weighing alternative means most suitable for reaching those goals with minimum costs. This is meant to provide at least a measure of the effectiveness of various programs.

There is much skepticism among administrators, who say, "We know how decisions are made in Congress. All this is nonsense. The President wants to cut our program; that's all it amounts to." I feel that there is, certainly, a gap between, on the one hand, the highly sophisticated models proposed here and the models worked out by The RAND Corporation, and, on the other, what the agencies are supposed to do, in practical politics. I think the new approach has two purposes: first, to justify the costs the agencies are recommending for the next five years, and, second, to re-examine, in extreme cases, programs that are only carried forward because of some tradition.

In our kind of society, we shouldn't have great illusions about planning. We know how decisions are made in a realistic world. If we don't know, we should know, and it is important to study decision-making. But, the planning and analysis, which might appear abstract, has a value: It makes it difficult to defend highly irrational action or omission. And it sometimes helps a program that is highly desirable but has not been successful in gaining the full support it needs. So, the fact that the practical people, in Washington, are right in being skeptical and that they know decisions are not made according to a rational model should not discourage us. I do think planning has some effect in cutting out extremely irrational programs that just can't be defended and in giving support to other programs that otherwise, perhaps, would not have been adopted.

I think there must be some reconciliation between presenting a rational program and being realistic about policy-making. It seemed to me that Mr. Correa based his paper on the assumption that our decisions are made in a highly rational way. That may be a useful first assumption. We know, however, that it isn't the case, in reality. But, still, we shouldn't throw out the assumption. We simply should not get too disillusioned when decisions are made differently.

BEASLEY: Our time is about up. I think we will give Mr. Correa a chance to make a parting statement.

CORREA: With respect to planning, I think some rationality always enters policy decisions. The only thing we are trying to do, now, is to expand it with planning. The human mind is not able to consider all the variables that the policy-makers should consider in making decisions. We are trying to help them, showing them the effects, the indirect effects, of their decisions.

6

Educational Policy and National Goals

GERHARD COLM

I am very happy to participate in a symposium concerned with education in a world of change. When I went to high school—a classical school in Germany, quite a few years ago—I was frustrated by the fact that there was no relation between our world of study and the world we read about in the newspapers. I had to satisfy my desire to understand the world into which I was growing by efforts outside the school. Today, we simply cannot escape looking at education in the context of the rapid economic and social changes we are experiencing. The rapid increases in total production, income, and tax receipts make it possible to finance very large increases in educational programs, for which advanced planning is necessary. These same economic and social changes require, in turn, new educational achievements in quantity and quality. Without adjustments in our educational programs, the potential increases in production and incomes may not come about, or economic advances may be thwarted by social conflict.

These economic and social changes, too, should not be seen in a vacuum. They reflect international, technological, and attitudinal developments of epochal significance. I will concentrate, in this paper, on the technological aspects, but we cannot evaluate economic developments and their impact on education without referring, also, to developments on the international scene and in the minds of men. To these I can refer only briefly.

The Upheaval in the World Order

Under the impact of two world wars, the almost 500-year-old world order of colonialism has broken down. At the end of World War I and, again, at the end of World War II, we had hoped for the creation of a new order under a world-wide organization—the League of Nations and the United Nations, respectively. The League, partly because of American failure to participate, could not prevent the conditions that made possible the rise of Hitler and resulted in World War II. The U.N., even with American participation, has not been able to solve the conflict of the Cold War, nor has it, as yet, filled the vacuum created by the liquidation of world colonialism. This vacuum has been filled by many conflicting forces, with three—possibly four—giants emerging: the United States, Soviet Russia, Communist China, and, possibly, an integrated Western Europe. In addition, the many new nations are resurrecting almost obsolete nationalism in their struggle to find a place in between the big powers. The result is a delicate balance of tension that is maintained by the fear of mutual annihilation, by actual conflict in several parts of the globe, and by the great political uncertainties under which the majority of mankind lives today. These uncertainties aggravate the severe maladjustments in international economic relations with which international organizations like the World Bank and the Monetary Fund try to deal. But the maladjustments persist and, in turn, have repercussions on the domestic economic conditions in virtually all countries. Technological innovations and our increasing ability to guide economic developments are giving mankind a glimpse of a truly humanitarian epoch, but the sunny outlook of advancing human welfare is marred by ominous shadows from a cloud of international uncertainties and grievous conflicts.

The Technological Revolution

We have been living in a period of rapid advances in science and technology, a period that stretches over the past 250 years. However, the pace of scientific discoveries has quickened in recent decades. Not only have great and startling scientific discoveries been made but, also, the period between basic scientific discovery and introduction of the innovation as a commercial product or process has been shortened. In the early twentieth century, this development period was about thirty-seven years; it dropped to twenty-four years during the interwar period; and, since World War II, it has fallen to fourteen years—considerably less than half of what it had been at the turn of the century. Scientific and technological progress has been truly spectacular.

That many scientific inventions have resulted in early technological applications should not make us overlook the fact that a large part of scientific effort is still related to basic research for which no practical application is in sight—for example, high energy physics. This may appear astonishing to those who believe in the alleged predominance of a utilitarian attitude in America. Besides the urge to know for knowledge's sake, there is a strong element of international competition in science, which I regard as one of the lesser evils of competitive nationalism. However, in this paper, I limit myself to those scientific developments already being reflected in technological achievements.

What we are experiencing every day would have been regarded as the product of the fertile but somewhat feverish mind of the science fiction writer a few decades ago. Let me classify some of these technological advances in a manner that permits the subsequent evaluation of their economic impact.

Perhaps most spectacular advances have come in weapons technology. The nuclear bomb is the most dramatic, but not the only, example of a development that has brought mankind to the brink of annihilation. But, because of the suicidal character of total war, the existence of these weapons may have prevented, and may continue to prevent, a third world war. In any case, they have changed military strategy and have had a deep impact on world politics.

A whole category of scientific advances has led to new ventures, particularly in outer and inner space: exploration of the moon and the planets and, perhaps in the future, exploration beyond our immediate cosmic neighborhood; exploration of the depths of the oceans and the interior of the earth. We do not yet know the practical consequences of our space ventures, but we do know that the ocean has the potential to provide us with food, minerals, and power for centuries to come.

Synthetic work materials, in use for decades, are being produced in great diversity. Plastics have already become conventional materials, in competition with natural materials like wood and metals. Entirely new perspectives for creating materials to meet exacting specifications are opened up by the possibility of molecular rearrangement under the impact of gamma radiation.

New methods—or rather dimensions—of production have been advanced by weapons and space requirements. They include automation, miniaturization, and systems engineering; they permit counting on a degree of reliability unheard of even a few decades ago. These innovations in industrial processes justify speaking of a new "technological revolution."

Recently developed products for personal use are revolutionizing everyday living—for example, television, air conditioning, and many other kinds of modern household equipment.

Another category of technological development relates to modification of our natural environment. Outstanding is the advance in our understanding of weather, which probably will lead to influencing or controlling weather within a foreseeable period of time. Recognition of the degree of pollution of air, water, and soil is also a new—even though not very pleasant—achievement. This knowledge is essential if we are to devise methods of pollution control.

Finally, we have the spectacular advances in medicine and biology. Most dramatic are the advances in birth control and in the conquest of disease. Of still unknown consequence is the advance in deciphering the human heredity code, with the possibility—or should I say threat—of the ability to influence heredity.

This list, sketchy and incomplete as it is, demonstrates the justification for speaking of a new technological revolution, which must have a profound influence on attitudes and economics in our age.

CHANGES IN ATTITUDE AND EXPECTATIONS

One of the important changes in Americans, and in people everywhere in the last few decades, is that they have become goals conscious. In the past, we took it for granted that when someone served his personal interest, whether in business or private life, he also served the general interest. *Laissez-faire* was the general attitude, even of people who had never read a word written by Adam Smith. The only exceptions were emergency situations of international political conflict. Where the individual could not achieve what he needed, it was taken for granted that he would obtain help from his neighbors and help them in return. Government was regarded, more or less, as a necessary evil, or as something to be exploited by those who knew how.

The trauma of the Great Depression changed that drastically. It was generally recognized, for the first time, that government was responsible for assisting the unemployed, the home or farm owner in danger of foreclosure, the businessman or banker under threat of bankruptcy for failures resulting from factors beyond individual control. The war demonstrated the ability of government to exert great influence on economic conditions, even in the private sector. Government responsibility for preventing mass unemployment and promoting conditions of economic growth, reasonable price stability, and balance in international economic relations was built into the Employment Act of 1946. But, there, the concern was primarily with maintaining a high level of economic activity and preventing both wasteful recessions and excessive booms and inflations. This concern with economic performance was based on the tacit assumption that, once economic activities were running at a high level and rising steadily, we could safely leave it to the market and conventional political methods to decide how resources should be used, in either the private or the public sector of the economy. National goals, in that phase, could be called *performance goals,* because they were mainly concerned with performance of the economy.

In recent years, there has been a growing concern with another question: High activity for what? This concern with *achievement goals* arose with inescapable urgency during World War II, in the form of the "guns or butter" question. But, with the end of the war, the question receded from general public concern. However, another traumatic experience during the period of "competitive coexistence" has made the American people realize that they must be concerned not only with performance of the economy *per se* but, also, with what is being achieved through public and private activities. This traumatic experience came as a result of Russia's successful orbiting of an earth satellite some time before America was able to do so. Now, we have become increasingly concerned with deficiencies in education and in our urban living, and with the fact that we have glaring poverty in a nation of high affluence. Of course, the American people have been concerned all through their history with certain deficiencies—for example, in education and health—and they are acquainted with the misuse of economic power. But, for the first time, the various national goals, in such areas as education, research, and cultural development in general, are seen in their interrelationship with each other and with economic growth.

The goals consciousness of Americans is expressed not only in their determination to avoid depressions and inflation but, increasingly, also in their concern with achievements in crucial national and social objectives. This does not mean that individual decision-making and the market process are being replaced by collective action. On the contrary, the spectacle of life in totalitarian regimes has made us (and many people living under totalitarian regimes) aware of the benefits of a market system that is not centrally directed. However, the absence of central direction does not mean the absence of policies that influence private decisions, policies that take account of the general interest. Nobody can say, with certainty, what organizational forms will emerge in this process of blending private and public interests. What concerns us here is that our experience with war and competitive coexistence has created a climate that calls for a concerted public and private effort.

Until a few years ago, the notion that a democracy could pursue national goals of sustained economic growth still met with skepticism from most political leaders: It was regarded, at best, as an interesting but untested economic theory. But, the experiment with the massive tax reduction of 1962–65 had approximately the result predicted by theoreticians. This has caused something of a break-through in public opinion. It adds to the attention now given to the same economic theoreticians when they recommend tax increases to meet changed circumstances.

The growing consciousness of goals and the growing confidence in our capability to influence economic development are closely related to the fact that people in distress have become impatient. In our increasingly affluent society, people suffering deprivation are no longer satisfied with a slow evolutionary development toward the standard of living in which they sooner—or, more likely, later—will participate. They expect that their living conditions and the opportunities for their children will be improved *now*.

The time is past when questions of technology and economics were subjects on which only a small elite with graduate degrees dared to have an opinion. Whether we welcome it or regret it, these have become issues on which election campaigns are fought and which are debated both on and off the campus. That is one reason these developments are of the utmost importance for education.

ECONOMIC SIGNIFICANCE OF CHANGES IN TECHNOLOGY AND ATTITUDES

Different Evaluations of the Impact of Technological Advances

Some economists believe that the truly revolutionary developments in science and technology and in public attitudes must be matched by an equally revolutionary development in economics. They believe that, in the age of automation, the sky is no longer the limit of our productive capacity and that the age of scarcity and the economics of scarcity belong to the past. For the future, we need economics that are suitable to the age of affluence. In this age of affluence, only a small proportion of the adult population—so it is argued—will be needed to run the machines that will produce all necessary goods and services. This means an end to the economics, and the ethics, that hold we must work in order to live. The concern of these economists (Robert Theobald and other advocates of the Triple Revolution) is no longer with adequate production but with the question of how people, without working, can conduct meaningful lives and obtain the purchasing power with which to buy the end products of our machine-run economy. Other economists—and I believe they are the majority —do not share this view. They see the technological revolution resulting only in gradually increasing productivity; gradually rising incomes of managers, workers, and investors; and rising tax revenues. With rising income, it becomes possible to do many things, in public and private life, which could not have been done in the past and which urgently need to be done. This latter view (shared by the National Commission on Technology, Automation, and Economic Progress) leads to the conclusion that a growing labor force with improved productivity can still be busy for many decades to come. There will be a further shortening of hours, more paid vacations, and possibly longer periods for study and training. But, in a well-managed society, rising productive capacity will be matched by rising demand. However, the technological revolution does result in a substantial change in the *kind* of labor that is required, and very substantial changes in education and training will be needed.

How, then, do we explain why explosive advances in technology will result only in a gradual increase in productivity? First, we have to remember that many of the most spectacular technological advances have had no impact on labor productivity. The walk in space is such a case. Actually, the space accomplishments may explain some of the errors in economic evaluation. The layman is impressed by the demonstration of what human beings *can* do. If we can walk in space, why can't we automate the factory, using only a few human beings, to man the control switches? True enough, such factories could be built and have been built, but there is still a great difference between what we can do technologically and what we can do economically. Factories are still operated by a considerable work force, though admittedly a work force of different character from that of the past, and such factories are still commercially superior to the fully automated factory.

We must also consider that new developments in technology produce their own countervailing forces. Society would not tolerate wholesale dismissal of workers supplanted by machinery, unless some provision were made for retraining them and caring for their families. Thus, there are arrangements for severance pay or, in some industries, for profits from automation to be used, in part, to retrain and relocate displaced workers, and so on. This increases the costs of labor-saving processes, which slows down the automation process.

It is not only that provision must be made for displaced labor.

Large capital investments in the existing machinery mean that the decision to install the most modern equipment must include allowance for the depreciation write-off on the existing machinery.

Another factor is that existing institutions, particularly when supported by vested interests, may be slow in adapting to technological advances. For example, local building codes, often influenced by labor unions, make it practically impossible to erect mass-produced prefabricated houses in metropolitan areas. On a broader scale, political fragmentation in metropolitan areas is a severe obstacle to planning and coordinating urban redevelopment and mass-transportation systems.

We also have to count on certain consumer reactions. Despite a plentiful supply of huge, efficient supermarkets, we see, springing up in many cities, hundreds of little stores for people who just prefer to shop where the manager or clerk knows their tastes and can pass the time of day. I believe that it is not merely a matter of chance that, at present, when consumer staple products are becoming more and more standardized, department stores all over the country are beginning to feature handicraft products. Some consumers yearn for an individualized product. The rising income and standard of living that is made possible, in part, through the technological advances also promotes a demand for highly labor-intensive products and services and thereby limits the average rise in productivity and provides outlets for labor replaced by technology. But, let me emphasize again, these new labor demands very often require new and different skills.

There are many more factors that explain why I believe, as probably most economists do, that even a dramatic technological development will result only in a gradual increase in productivity. I must limit myself to the examples I have given.

Gradual rather than explosive productivity advance is only one of the reasons why I think technological unemployment need not be the problem some observers fear. The other, and possibly more important, factor is that rising productivity and income make it possible to do many things in our society that, for lack of resources, we could not do adequately in the past. Dr. Lecht has already referred, in his paper, to what we call the aspiration goals in American society. I will emphasize only a few of these.

The largest item is to raise the level of expenditure—for all consumers, generally, and, particularly, for the one-fifth or one-third of the nation living now in poverty or deprivation. If this were generally understood, the war against poverty could probably be conducted with a high degree of consensus, not only because it appeals to our social and humanitarian motivations but because it is clearly good business to tap this largest of the potential markets in a period of rising productivity.

The next biggest item is probably the need to rebuild large parts of our metropolitan areas and the transportation systems that serve them. Then come goals in education, research, public health, and all the others mentioned in Dr. Lecht's paper. Considering our society's deficiencies and our desire to correct them as soon as possible, I am inclined to say that our problem for some time to come is more likely to be scarcity than a redundancy of productive resources. Therefore, I do not believe we are actually nearing that paradise where work, the curse of mankind, will be abolished.

The Need for Planning in a Private Enterprise Economy

In part, the areas of increased potential demand are of a character that requires the cooperative effort of government and the private sector of the economy. The broad potential market—of people now living in poverty and deprivation—will not be opened up unless the economy is experiencing a healthy rate of growth and unless special provisions are made to fight the underlying causes of poverty, which very often are inadequate education and training and poor health. There are other causes, like the breakup of the family, which cannot be cured by any program, but whose consequences can be mitigated if sufficient provision is made for the remaining members of the family. Also, many new technological developments, like those in outer and inner space, depend to a large extent on cooperation between government and business. Still, it is expected that most of the expansion in economic activities will be carried forward by the response of private enterprise to market opportunities. That is, the government-business cooperation we are observing does not replace, but rather supplements, the market forces.

Business enterprises themselves are making increasing use of planning techniques, even though their plans are constantly checked by current market indicators and, if necessary, revised accordingly.

Under the Employment Act, the government's responsibility for promoting "maximum employment, production, and purchasing power" implies the need to develop long-range policies in which technological developments are of paramount importance. There is an urgent need to promote technological advances, not only because they add to satisfaction of consumer demand and create better working conditions but, also, because they have an impact on international economic relations. A high-wage economy cannot compete except by high and rising productivity. A policy in support of long-term technological advances must, however, also face up to the requirements in education and training, and to the social problems of dislocation, of adjustment of smaller firms to technological requirements, and of the temporary unemployment that may be a consequence of technological advances. These tasks require long-range government planning, to include not only fiscal policy but, also, educational and training programs and programs designed to aid regions hit by dislocations in the course of technological advances.

It is interesting to observe, in Communist countries, the attempt to build some market mechanism into central-planning systems. Reformers in these countries are saying, I believe rightly, that some use of the market system does not necessarily change the basic character and purposes of a socialist system. Similarly, the capitalistic countries are building some elements of planning into their market systems. I think here, too, we can rightly say that this is not necessarily incompatible with a private-enterprise economy and not inconsistent with the historical development of our Western societies. We have no good name for the systems of modified capitalism which are emerging in the Western world. But we can say with assurance that they are equally different from centrally directed socialism and *laissez-faire* capitalism, if such systems ever really existed outside of textbooks.

The Effect of Rising Income

Though, in the foreseeable future, we should not expect to change from an economy of scarcity to an economy of abundance and redundancy of labor, still, with rising income, consumer preferences will change and deeply affect the demand for goods and services and for leisure time. We are, right now, observing one such change with the adoption of Medicare, which will have a tremendous impact on the demand for nursing homes, hospital beds, and all kinds of medical services. We are badly prepared to meet this demand, which was not foreseen early enough in the planning of medical education and construction. Severe scarcities will result in this field.

With rising incomes, particularly of people in the lower- and middle-income brackets, we observe a change in the possibilities for, and the use of, leisure time. Here, too, we see a rather dramatic development. In the past, recreational and tourist facilities were, to a large extent, tailored to the needs of a well-to-do upper class. Today motels, cabins, and camping spaces are expanding fast to accommodate the needs of the many millions of workers and their families who, for the first time, are enjoying both a paid vacation and the means to travel.

EDUCATION AND TECHNOLOGICAL CHANGE

The Impact of Economic Growth and Technology on Education

Economic growth means a rising tax revenue without equally rising tax rates. This is most obviously true of federal income taxes, which are highly responsive to economic development. However, with some time lag, it applies also to property taxes, which are still the main financial resource for primary and secondary education. It is by no means utopian to estimate that, within a ten-year period, we may almost double expenditures for education, assuming reasonable price stability. This necessitates a great deal of planning for educational facilities, teacher-training, and so on. Otherwise, it may be that educational possibilities will fail to materialize, not because of lack of money but because of inadequate quantity and quality of teachers. Such planning should also include experimentation with the use of new technological tools, such as closed-circuit television and programed learning. I am skeptical when these devices are regarded as substitutes for good teachers; I doubt that there is a substitute for the personality of a teacher. But the devices may basically change the functions and interrelationships of the teacher, the classroom, and homework. Educational technology may not solve the problem of scarcity of teachers, but it could help lift education to a higher level.

The Impact of Education on Economic Growth

While economic growth and the accompanying tax revenues are essential for educational progress, the converse is also true. Without educational achievements, the potential economic growth may not materialize. Particularly, the new technology requires training for special skills and new directions in education. I want to give only a few examples.

We have an increasing need for the training of technicians, particularly training that goes beyond current emphasis on the purely occupational, but stops short of that given engineers, scientists, or other professionals. In a number of states, institutions have been created for this purpose; in some states, junior colleges have been converted. I believe, however, that the demand for such technicians is still very much in excess of the supply.

Modern technology requires not so much specialized skills as a great adaptability and alertness. This, again, will have a substantial impact on the curriculum and kinds of training to be provided in elementary and high schools.

In the past, education ended for most people at age fifteen or sixteen, when they entered the labor force. Today, we need life-time education. Working periods will have to be interrupted by periods of retraining, so that we can keep up with changing technology and prevent rapid obsolescence of skills. In this connection, a beginning has been made in a collective agreement for steelworkers. They have obtained the right to several months' vacation with pay after several years' work. Such a sabbatical period may be spent in additional training, retraining, or for any change in activities which may enrich the individual's life and, in the long run, add to his productivity.

The Wider Horizon

I emphasized, earlier, that in modern life every voter—really every individual—is called upon to form some opinion about policy issues that deeply involve economic, social, and often technological and scientific problems. Not everybody can be educated to be an economist, social scientist, physicist, or engineer. However, everybody in our society should know enough about these problems to be able to form a reasonable opinion of the views advanced, to be able to distinguish the demagogue or quack from the man with a valid proposal. I know I am touching on a very difficult problem. Before we can talk about educating all individuals in the elements of these fields, we have to answer a preliminary question: Do we have the teachers to teach these subjects?

Related to this wider involvement in public issues is the fact that our globe is shrinking, due to transportation and communication technology. We are deeply involved in the problems of other countries and other cultures. Educational "isolationism" is coming to an end, for we need an ever greater understanding of various cultures and economic systems.

This wider horizon pertains to the creative use of leisure, as well. I noted earlier that we have not yet entered an age of abundance in which machines abolish the need for most work. Nevertheless, I have also emphasized that, gradually, there will be increasing time for nonremunerative activities and leisure. How well does education prepare for creative use of leisure time? To some extent this function is recognized even in elementary and high schools, in the opinion of some people, too much so, for they see it coming at the expense of more traditional disciplines.

Throughout life, education is needed to help individuals develop creative activities. I do not mean only hobbies but preparation for an active voluntary role in civic affairs, in education, in the guidance of adults or adolescents who are in trouble, in nursing, in the arts. Some of that preparation may come to full fruition only after retirement.

New Orientation of Universities

Universities, which have always had three characteristic functions, are now changing their role dramatically. Previously, they provided scientific research, instruction, and advice and counseling to government and private organizations. Now, these functions are confounded and their importance is altered. It is claimed, for example, that research and advisory functions, particularly under government contract, are pre-empting so much faculty time that the function of instruction is neglected. Proposals have been made, and to some extent adopted, that the advisory function, particularly under contract, be fulfilled by research institutes, which may or may not be affiliated with universities, so that teaching staffs can, again, be primarily engaged in teaching and untied research. That may be a partial solution, but I do not think it is the whole solution. Here, I am raising a question to which I do not know the answer.

Discussing the dramatic technological advances of our time and their present and future impact on our economic and social life, I cannot help but think of the old fable of Prometheus, who provided mankind with the first great technological advance. He stole from the gods the ability to make fire and was cruelly punished for it. I think there is deep wisdom in this fable. We want advances, but we have to pay a price for them. Technology promises us a better life, but it also threatens our civilization with suicidal war. Overpopulation resulting from medical advances is a worldwide threat; unless we make proper adjustments we may experience economic failure. Increasing leisure, if it does not have a creative outlet, may lead to a mental crisis of boredom and meaninglessness. This is an age of the greatest opportunities, but also of the greatest dangers for the human race. Prometheus could only be freed after a godlike creature decided to become human. It was Chiron who consented to this sacrifice in the fable. In our age, it is the educator who may determine whether mankind will be a victim of the curse connected with technological achievement or will reap the full benefits of its blessing. And so it is fitting, perhaps, to close with this question: Who will educate the educators to live up to this task? I hope somebody knows the answer.

DISCUSSION

SWANSON [presiding]: The meeting is open for discussion.

CORREA: Besides the aspects mentioned by Mr. Colm, I should add the change in the attitude of the developing countries. I think the influence of these attitudes on America is very large and will increase in the future. I would be very grateful if Mr. Colm would elaborate on this point.

COLM: I talked briefly about the change in attitudes, mainly in the United States and only from one particular aspect, namely, of goals consciousness. The same development is probably much more pronounced in the so-called developing countries, which we used to call, in a more impolite but clearer way, the underdeveloped countries. By more pronounced, I refer to the quality of impatience. And I say that without any criticism, because it is a very understandable attitude.

It is also an attitude of ambiguity, which consists of, first, looking up to the developed countries—which they regard as a model of what they want to achieve (higher income, industrialization, and so on); and, second, a desire for independence, which often shades over into hostility.

My main point was that we have not yet found any world-wide organization that gives us some degree of stability. We still have a world political situation of extreme instability resting on mutual fears, without any assurance that a new world order is really in the making. It is this situation of extreme uncertainty that, I think, hangs like a cloud over the outlook of every country, developed or developing.

CORREA: You have pointed very clearly to the situation. I would say that education should prepare the American public to respond to this new world situation. Perhaps, in the long run, more important than the analysis of the needs of the American economy will be the analysis of the political needs of the American society in a position of world leadership.

COLM: I think what Mr. Correa says is quite correct. It is an education for responsibilities of world leadership. But it is also a recognition of the other forces in the world. For instance, the 1964 U.N. Conference on Trade and Development showed, for the first time, the voting power of the developing countries *vis-à-vis* the developed countries. The developing countries were able to gain a new agency in the United Nations, despite the opposition of the developed countries. Raoul Prebish, of Argentina, is the director of this agency and the intellectual leader of this world bloc of developing countries.

This creates a new and uncertain situation, with which the American public is not really acquainted. We don't know what the situation of the United States is in the world. I think what we have here is a function of education on every level—from the elementary school to adult education, through all the media—to make us more aware of the changes occurring in the outside world. Two figures demonstrate, in a way, the ambiguity of the U.S. position in the United Nations. We have 35 per cent of world production, but we have only 6 per cent of the world's population. I think the great educational task we face is to make people aware of what is implied in these figures, in terms of the power of this nation, on the one hand, and its minority status in the United Nations, under present voting procedure, on the other.

FOLGER: Let me ask you another question about the increased goals consciousness of the American people. Doesn't this develop certain problems of national expectations, of the sort that you referred to when you spoke of Medicare and our unpreparedness —in terms of personnel and facilities—for that program? Don't we have some problems with the rate at which we bring about educational change, and the rate at which people do educational research, as these rates relate to the expectations of the American people? And do you see any way in which we can deal with this problem of the difference in the time perspective of the politician, on the one hand, and the educator and researcher, on the other?

COLM: I saw this conflict very clearly when the Budget Bureau, on the request of President Kennedy, prepared five-year budget estimates. (The first such effort by the Budget Bureau had been made under President Eisenhower.) When President Kennedy saw the five-year estimates, he is reported to have said, "This is very interesting, but stamp 'Top Secret' on it."

I understand that, when President Johnson announced the Great Society program, his cabinet officers were frequently asked at Congressional hearings, "What will this program cost when it is in full swing?" There was a strange similarity in the responses of the various cabinet officers involved in the program. In effect, the answer was "We have not had time to figure that out." This, despite the federal statute requiring that requests for program authorization be accompanied by estimates of the costs, and not merely in the initial years.

There is, however, one hopeful sign. President Johnson has initiated a program called "Planning-Programing-Budgeting," which has to be adhered to by all departments and agencies. This system requires that all agencies make five-year forecasts for alternate programs. He has acknowledged that program budgeting just one year ahead doesn't make sense.

It is recognized that, in this age of change, we have to look at next year's development from a long-range perspective. But the long-term projection conflicts with the political hesitation to make commitments. You never can predict quite what the shock will be if people know what is involved in successive steps. So, it is safer, politically, to talk about only the first step. But, how do you know that your first step is in the right direction if you don't know where you really want to go? This is the conflict we face.

You ask what the solution of that conflict might be. I think we will overcome the political hesitancy. I think it is recognized that we have to look further ahead. We have had some statements from the last three Presidents—Eisenhower, Kennedy, and Johnson—that such planning is necessary. Each one of the three backed away from the projections when it came to implementing the goals, but I think the logic is so strong that I firmly believe we will have to look further ahead. I think the public has to be educated to look into the future.

The doctrine of decision-making under conditions of uncertainty is such that it is important to recognize that the decision has to be made in the perspective of the most likely development. At the same time, the decision-making process must incorporate provisions for constantly checking up on developments and possible change. These provisions have to be built into the system. In these terms, I deplore the "apology" given by the Administration when it asked Congress to rescind some of the tax reductions enacted in the previous year. People must recognize that conditions change and that new conditions require elasticity and flexibility.

FOLGER: Let me push this just one point further. My own experience at the state and institutional level has been similar to the experience you recount at the federal level. So, I should like to ask if, from your experience, the people at the local institutional and state level are as sensitive to this need for long-range planning as are the people at the national level?

COLM: I can't answer with respect to the state and local level. That is outside my experience. But I would like to say that, in general, I think we need exactly the same kind of long-range planning at the state and local level as we need at the federal level. It seems to me that, for most policies, the degree of flexibility is less at the state and local level than at the federal level. I am talking, in particular, about fiscal policy. Decision-makers at the local level may have to recognize that, because of the war in Vietnam, some programs will advance more slowly than otherwise would be desirable. But it would be a mistake if local programs, for example in education, would actually be reduced. I think we need a long-range program in which—unless there is a basic national contingency like a world war—flexibility is provided at the federal level. The federal government should be a shock absorber for the nation as a whole, a balance wheel, so that state and local governments can go ahead on a steady course, leaving the greatest flexibility at the federal level.

KLEIN: You mentioned federal assistance. Should this assistance be earmarked assistance, or should it be returned to the states on some formula basis?

COLM: We are getting into a big problem here. In recent years, we have become aware of the fact that, in a growing economy, tax revenue at the federal level increases faster than tax revenue at the state and local level. The federal government makes much use of the progressive income tax, which is most responsive to economic development. But the real estate taxes and the sales taxes, which form the basis of state revenue, are somewhat less responsive—at least, they always have a time lag.

We realize that rising taxes at the federal level may create a drag on economic development; if they lead to budget surpluses —depending on the monetary policy adopted at the same time— they may have a deflationary effect. It was primarily this theory of the fiscal drag, developed by the Council of Economic Advisers under Walter Heller, that formed the background for the proposed tax reduction in 1964 and 1965.

Heller was concerned with the possibility that we may face such a situation every few years. What would that mean? While the federal government could reduce its income taxes repeatedly, the state and local governments—which carry the greatest burden, because of the fast rise in expenditures for education, police, and so on—might be forced to increase their tax rate, especially for real estate and sales taxes. As a result, we are getting, for the nation as a whole, a less and less progressive tax system—progressive income taxes are constantly reduced and the taxes on which state and local governments depend, which are not progressive, are constantly increased.

Heller proposed, therefore, that the federal government, instead of reducing tax rates, make some of that money available to state and local governments. This would relieve them of the need to increase their property and sales taxes. In short, two purposes would be accomplished. The fiscal drag at the federal level would be avoided, and the tendency toward less and less progressivity in the tax system of the nation as a whole would be halted.

Quite a number of people were in favor of the proposal—particularly state governors, who would like to get that money and determine how it should be used. To make the proposal politically feasible, Heller recommended that this money be turned over to the states without any strings attached. They would be able to use it in lieu of an increase in their own tax sources or for increasing their program expenditures, or for channeling it to local governments.

However, the plan conflicted with another development that has been going on, namely, the constant increase in specific grants-

in-aid to state and especially to local governments. The force behind that development was twofold. First, the different financial
ability of states to do things that needed to be done; some states
were very able and others not. In the grant-in-aid system, there is
the greater possibility of manipulating the formula for distribution in such a way that states with greater need get more. The
second force was a recognition that there are matters of national
concern; grant-in-aid money could be used as leverage for promoting certain national standards, standards of performance, for all
parts of the nation. These were the arguments of those who
favored expansion of functional grants-in-aid.

In the last fifteen years, while these specific grants-in-aid were
increasing four or five times in amount, they were also proliferat-
ing in kind, so that we now have, I think, something like 400
different grant-in-aid items. We have a complexity which is close
to anarchy. Nobody finds his way out, and very often the same
program gets various grants-in-aid according to various criteria
of distribution. So, there is a general feeling that something needs
to be done.

The Heller proposal has been set aside because of the Vietnam
war—suddenly, it was realized that there was nothing to distribute
and that this would likely be true for a number of years to come.
When Heller made the proposal, it appeared that, for the first
few years, there might be a $6 billion surplus each year available
for distribution and, later, even larger amounts. With the expansion of the war, however, the federal government has found itself
in a situation in which tax increases are more likely than budget
surpluses. Assuming the Vietnam war is settled, one way or another, the long-term problem will, however, reappear. I venture
the opinion that what probably will happen is not an adoption
of the Heller proposal, which just gives the money away, but
rather a rationalization of the grant-in-aid system into a smaller
number of programs of block grants-in-aid. Standards would still
be attached, but with a much greater freedom for the states to use
funds according to their needs. Consolidation of grant-in-aid
programs into blocks—one for education, one for road construction, one for public health, pollution control, and so on—on a
program-wide, rather than project, basis, is, in my opinion, more

likely than adoption of entirely "untied" revenue-sharing plans.

SWANSON: When you mentioned education, in your paper, you said that expenditures would likely double within ten years. Earlier, Mr. Cannon—from the Bureau of the Budget—said that they may increase fourfold.

COLM: He talked about federal money. I talked about federal, state, local, and private—including parochial school—expenditures.

SWANSON: You have raised questions about the educational system's capacity to expand, to train enough teachers and technicians, and to prepare for lifelong education. If, indeed, there is a restriction on its capacity to absorb, to expand, what are the essential elements of the planning function?

COLM: I must say, quite frankly, that I cannot answer that. I can only draw a parallel with the experience in Medicare, where we are adopting what I regard as a very good program. But, we are not prepared to meet the demand, which is an outgrowth of this program, for training facilities for doctors and for nursing homes and hospitals.

DAVID: It strikes me that we are calling upon education to teach analysis and problem-solving in order to make people more aware of, and more receptive to, various kinds of information. One thing the economists need to contribute to this is a better understanding of the economic impact of information and how the organization of information assists us both in the organization of production and in some of these other nonconsumptive activities to which you allude. Do you have any comments on this?

COLM: Well, I have two comments. I agree and I disagree. I agree that we need to know more. But I see the need for action and I say: "Forget about all the refinements. Let's act with the little knowledge we have until we have developed this additional information, which would be useful for more perfect educational planning." I think we have to go ahead with the knowledge we have.

We do know a few things. We have the demographic picture. We know where the big impact will be. It hit first at the elementary school level; I think that first wave (at the elementary level) is behind us. The high birth rate of 1945–47 has been absorbed by the school system and we are now getting the second wave—the children of those born to that generation. We know pretty well what has to be expected, quantitatively.

Qualitatively, also, we know a few things. I am still very much concerned with the question of educational planning, raised earlier, to which I really don't know the answer. In this field, we have a political fragmentation and we want to have decentralization. We want *local* schools. We don't want to have a centralized school system. We see value in the political fragmentation. But how do we get national standards and long-range planning for what the standards should be ten years from now? We should have started long ago; as it is, we haven't the educators in these fields.

FLANIGAN: There is the frustration: An instant program requires instant action; it skips the process of data collection, planning, experimentation, and evaluation. This is, potentially, a very discouraging situation in education, because, having been given few guidelines for appropriate programs, we now hear that classroom teachers can't do the job. For example, there is no supply of classroom teachers experienced in the area of teaching the disadvantaged. If the central authority in Washington were to decide to stimulate a variety of new programs, then preplanning would be required.

FOLGER: I would like to ask whether the attachment of preplanning requirements to grant-in-aid programs would really be a positive approach? Would people respond favorably to this? In the mental health field, for example—where more federal support has been going for a longer period of time than in education—after several years, federal authorities suddenly decided that every state must have comprehensive plans. I was really on the outskirts of this program, but I heard much grumbling.

SWANSON: I can't answer your question, but I can say that there are several programs that require planning, in which planning is an essential element. Title III of P.L. 89-10, for example, invites planning grants. The Regional Laboratory development requires planning periods with planning grants available for this purpose.

FOLGER: But we would hardly think these are ideal.

SWANSON: We are talking about planning for specific purposes, not for the general purposes of education. I don't know how one would answer the question about planning for the general purposes, for the input into education as a whole over the next decade or two.

KLEIN: Why not through the system Mr. Colm suggested, the modification of the Heller plan? That is, returning funds to the states for use in programs, as opposed to specific projects. There is need for direction, but considerably more flexibility is needed in regard to how these funds are to be applied. Mr. Colm may have stated the solution.

ARNESEN: I am sure that there has been a tremendous amount of good accomplished by the application of federal funds to the purpose set by the federal statutes under Title I of the Elementary and Secondary Education Act of 1965. At the same time, however, there is frustration for the local school authority trying to administer a total program of education for a particular community.

By way of example, in the school system with which I am associated, we have forty-one elementary schools, twelve junior high schools, and four senior high schools. Only nineteen of the forty-one elementary schools, four of the twelve junior high schools, and two of the four senior high schools can qualify for these funds. As a result, we are presently creating some tremendous imbalances in the kinds of educational programs that are being offered the children of our community. For thirty-two of our schools, we lack local resources to match the services federally provided to the twenty-five schools in the so-called disadvantaged areas.

When this kind of categorical aid is thrust upon a school system, it creates a certain amount of frustration.

FLANIGAN: I would add that, in that case, there was no discussion of the egalitarian concept versus the need special children have for additional programs. The community was not philosophically prepared to accept such differential treatment of children in the schools.

DANIEL: What we are talking about now should not be addressed to the economists but to the politicians. The problem that I see, since I live in Washington, is the way the Congress acts, or doesn't act, and this is determined by the fact that somebody or some group is pressing for some special program.

MCLURE: I think the conflict here is between the politician's approach, which singles out children from families of a given income level to serve as a criterion of educational need, and the educator's approach, which deals with children in relation to their family situations. The educator would not classify them for educational purposes according to the politician's approach. Here is, I think, a basic conflict. The politician is saying, in effect, "Your principles of classifying and identifying individual needs are not right. Here is a way of doing it." And I think there is a fundamental conflict between the politically expedient method of distributing funds and sounder principles that have been developed from years of experience in financing education.

KLEIN: I think the Title I approach is good. You may have to create shock at times, even though you may not want to. A bomb may be necessary. The question is, having dropped the bomb, what are your responsibilities? I think it is the responsibility of the federal government to consider what they have released as a result of their programs. At times, it is hard to believe a great deal of planning takes place before decisions are made.

Washington has helped to create a new profession. The profession's function is to disseminate information for fund-seekers concerning what monies are available. They translate requests into the myriad of forms and take their just commission. It has been reported that, even within Washington circles, the maze has reached such a point that one agency put together a directory showing interrelationships.

STOIKOV: We heard from Mr. Lecht about implications and goals to be set on behalf of the demand for manpower. I think this convincingly deflates the kinds of worries that have been circulating about triple revolutionists. If that is not convincing enough, one should consider that the time will come when, if we are to protect our civilization here, we may be required to furnish a massive foreign aid program to the underdeveloped countries. This would have further implications for manpower needs.

Have you ever, in the same sense in which you considered some of these other goals, considered what might be required, in terms of skills and talent, for a massive foreign aid program?

COLM: Yes, we did. Over the years we have worked on this particular problem under contract with both the predecessor of AID and the Senate Foreign Relations Committee. Foreign aid is also one of the goals for which dollar and manpower requirements are calculated in the studies on which Dr. Lecht has reported. This goal assumes implementation of the U.N. Decade of Development target, which proposed that each developed nation allocate 1 per cent of its national income for private and public capital flow to developing nations.

STOIKOV: Just out of curiosity, does this imply a need for more skilled people?

COLM: No, not more than for meeting domestic demand. In a study my organization made, we found that foreign aid wouldn't make a big impact on the distribution of skills. Actually, the technological development has a much bigger impact on the distribution of skills than foreign aid, because foreign aid goes pretty much down the line from agricultural products to manufactured products, and much less into services. Nationwide, we have: agricultural employment going down; mining employment going down, in spite of rising production; manufacturing increasing production something like 50 per cent over a decade; and manpower requirements increasing by just above 5 per cent; so, there is a near stagnation in manpower requirements with a very dynamic development of production. There is a whole expansion of employment in the field of trade (retail trade particularly), in financial and professional services, and in government—where, again, the biggest increase is in education.

The foreign aid, we have felt, in a way helps mitigate the shift, because it puts more emphasis on agriculture and manufacturing products.

McLURE: Are you suggesting that, if education really has the capability we ascribe to it for affecting economic growth, maybe we have neglected the production of a surplus of human talent for export as a form of aid to developing nations? We have been operating on a principle of scarcity. We have been afraid of oversupply of educated persons in all fields. We are not afraid, any more, of oversupply of corn and other agricultural products—at least at the moment. Might we consider helping other nations by developing an oversupply of educated people so as to exchange more human talent in addition to physical products?

COLM: I think this is an excellent question. As you know, in foreign aid we meet with a new frustration every few years and some innovation is attempted; now, emphasis on aid to education in foreign countries is being tried. Whether we can get more enthusiasm, in and out of Congress, for that sort of approach I don't know.

I think the situation is similar to the case in health, where we certainly have no surplus of medical personnel. Nevertheless, we feel giving public health aid is a first requirement. I think we should not look at foreign aid to education as a way to get rid of some surplus educators. We give this aid even though we know it creates scarcities here. It must be a high priority from a political or humanitarian point of view. You may know a few educators you wouldn't mind sending out to Africa, but that wouldn't do the Africans any good and I don't think it is a good plan for surplus disposal. So I think the justification has to be entirely on its merits, and we should give high quality educational aid even though it creates temporary scarcities here. In the long run, this may be also to our own advantage.

In that respect, the Peace Corps has been a very productive undertaking. Certainly, some of the best young people went abroad. In the short run, it creates shortages of talent here. In the long run, these people come back with broad experience; I think they will make better educators here with the experience of perhaps two years in a foreign country. In the longer run, there may be some mutual advantage in it.

FOLGER: You know, corn is a fairly homogeneous commodity, although I am sure the farmer can distinguish differences. But the manpower problems that seem to me most urgent are the problems of distribution rather than of oversupply. If you just take elementary and secondary teaching, for example, it is quite clear that the requirements in the last half of this decade, taken as a proportion of the total number of college graduates, are going to be much less than they were in the first half of this decade. But this by no means indicates that we will not have problems of distributing the right kind of people to the right kinds of jobs.

McLURE: I was searching for a positive principle, because I really think that our oversupplies are a result of a lack of worldwide mechanisms to meet needs. We haven't really found a positive principle for distributing corn, for example, and that is why we have it stored up, at times beyond normal reserves. It isn't because the excess isn't needed somewhere.

LLOYD: The analogy can be carried much too far for our purpose as educators. You say corn is homogeneous. I say it is not, based on the DeKalb Agricultural Association's successful hybridizations. Corn has been developed that can creep, that can climb, that can grow 10 feet tall or 6 inches high. I think there was, in Mr. Colm's paper, a reference to the dangers in our increasing knowledge that might affect the transmission of inherited traits among individuals.

FOLGER: I think there is another danger here, an assumption we tend to accept, perhaps because it is consistent with our values. It is that the free, individual choices of our young people will produce an occupation distribution that is, in the end, optimum for our economy. I think there is no real evidence that this is likely to occur in the future.

KLEIN: We have seen shortages in certain occupations, due both to low wages and to the lack of attractiveness of the occupation in terms of the social evaluation that is given to it. How are these occupations to be made more attractive, and what does this mean for our policies of immigration, which, historically, helped us fill these occupations?

COLM: I think here you are touching on a very broad problem. Earlier somebody asked me a similar question: How do you implement this tendency of our modern economy to require more alertness and versatility, rather than the specialized training of a craft? And I think that mobility, including immigration and internal migration from one kind of work requirement to another, is extremely important.

Probably, we should do the best possible job of providing the fundamentals, and this means more than adding tool shops and all kinds of specialized training to the curriculum. We should do this in the form of a training in general abilities to handle a job, rather than our present method of providing particular vocational training for a mechanic who is then unprepared to do anything else. A very good general school training is what I think is behind the economic development of Japan in the last twenty years.

I was greatly impressed during the Korean War as I watched some Korean farm boys who had come down from the North. They had no formal schooling. They stole parts from automobile junk yards and put them together into cars. They stole some gasoline and then ran around the country endangering everybody. While the Military Police didn't like it, something in it drew my admiration, because it showed what skillful people can do even without specialized training.

BEASLEY: You state that the education of an individual requires not so much specialized skills as a great adaptability and alertness. Is there an attitude toward adaptability that should be taught or instilled?

COLM: I think so, but I am sure everybody here in the room knows more about it than I do.

DAVID: One aspect of this puzzles me. One of the ways we invest in training, with very little financial pay-off, is by preparing people to pass various kinds of occupational licensing examinations. In my own university, the law school professors complain that the law school is not seen as one of the leading institutions. That is, students don't see it as one of the leading institutions for training for an occupation. Yet, probably the most creative review of the institutions governing our society comes from lawyers. It appears difficult to train for adaptability. You don't do it by putting your students in a role where they are going to have to pass a certification exam, do you?

BEASLEY: I am talking about students at the primary and secondary level. What should we do in our educational process, from the moment we first get the child until he terminates his compulsory education, that will help train in adaptability, or instill adaptability?

COLM: I have one negative proposal. I would forbid, by constitutional amendment if possible, any occupational ability test, which I think is one of the most vicious things ever invented by mankind. After some manipulative tests, a person is told, "You are able to do this, so that's your job for a lifetime."

I am not condemning all testing, but only the highly specialized testing that purports to find out what a youngster's particular ability is. In contrast, I am all for the testing of general ability by the so-called projective methods.

FOLGER: Would you give us an example of what you consider to be a particularly nefarious type of test?

COLM: No. I don't want to get in trouble with anybody.

FLANIGAN: Are you speaking about the vocational identification tests or about the vocational licensing tests of the kind a barber must take before he may practice?

COLM: Don't take me too seriously on that. I think you got the general idea.

McLURE: Certification is based on the principle of a minimum standard to protect the public against charlatans and incompetents. The minimum-level concept is really set too low, in practice, to meet the problem effectively.

DAVID: Except that, when you enact certain requirements that may be quite unnecessary, you limit the available supply of teachers.

FLANIGAN: Not really. I think about 10 per cent of the teaching staff is functioning with less than the state requirements. Within the certification requirements, there is also provided a way that you may enter if needed and if you are minimally qualified on another lower standard.

DAVID: All I know is that I hear of numerous cases. The most recent involved a friend of mine who has been teaching social studies in a junior high school for a number of years. The administrative board that makes appropriate judgments recently determined that she hadn't had enough training in social studies; they recommended, instead, that she teach a foreign language, because that's what showed up on her college certificate, obtained some ten years ago.

FLANIGAN: I would be doubtful of having someone teach social studies who hadn't had sufficient background in this field. I think a lot of our trouble is that we certify a teacher in social studies and from then on she teaches mathematics. The fact that she has taught mathematics for ten years doesn't mean that she has been exposed to sufficient theory to adapt to a change in the curriculum.

KLEIN: If you look at certification as a minimum standard for entrance into an occupation, what equivalencies might be substituted?

DEITCH: This question is particularly relevant when we think of returning Peace Corps volunteers. I have heard that many of these young people have had a difficult time getting hired as teachers because, even though they have had considerable practical experience, they do not meet the formal requirements for certification established by many local districts.

FLANIGAN: There was a very interesting dialogue that went on when the Peace Corps people first came home. The U.S. Employment Service said that Peace Corps volunteers could return to teach in the public schools. The National Education Association's Commission on Teacher Education and Professional Standards said that it was happy to have Peace Corps volunteers, providing they met minimum qualifications or would become qualified. And there it ended. Since then, there has been no friction, and a number of Peace Corps returnees are in the public schools as teachers or are affiliated with other programs where certification is not required.

SWANSON: It seems to me that there has been a lively and, certainly, a wide range of discussion this morning, starting out with the topic of the paper, and winding up with the rigidities of licensing procedures for various professions. I would like to say that I think the paper this morning, and the discussion that followed, were a good climax to the entire symposium. I think it appropriate to ask Mr. Colm if he would like to make a summary comment.

COLM: I am greatly impressed by this whole enterprise. The fact is, we don't know the answers to the basic questions of educational planning and we have not provided the answers here. But, prior to finding an answer must come an awareness of the problems, and I think the problems have been pointed out and highlighted in this discussion.

We cannot plan without a planning agency and we cannot plan if the planning agency lacks necessary information and the means for making decisions. In this connection, one thought occurs to me. At the moment, virtually every large American corporation has a planning group. They plan their investment program five or ten years in advance, trying to foresee future markets. They are to a very large extent guided by projections coming out of Washington—some out of the federal government, such as, in the demographic field, that supplied by the Census Bureau. Our own organization and other organizations serving similar purposes supply economic projections. Nobody compels them to use the information. But they are using data simply because they gain by being guided by the best estimates that they can get. Since all major corporations are guided by some similar estimates about future events, we get a certain coordination into our free market system without any centralized planning. All are guided by some similar anticipations. We are getting some substitutes for central planning entirely compatible with the self-responsibility of these organizations.

I wonder whether, in the educational field, something comparable is not possible. It means setting up some organization to struggle with these problems, to develop standards, to develop knowledge of what the future task might be and what the best implementation methods might be. Nobody would be compelled to follow these suggestions. The state and local organizations would be left to implement these ideas, using knowledge as a guide for federal programs, but not in any way as a means of strict enforcement.

I think one of the great tasks of our civilization is to meet the requirements of technological change without deadly centralization and without getting into an authoritarian state. If there is any overwhelming need for development of social techniques for marrying centralized guidance and decentralized responsibility for actions taken, then I think this is the task ahead of us. I wouldn't know any field where it is more important than in education.

SWANSON: Thank you, Mr. Colm.

7

Social Change and Educational Planning: A Selective Summary

JOHN K. FOLGER

This symposium had as its theme "the educational requirements of the next decade in the light of economic, political, technological, and social developments." To develop this broad and ambitious theme, papers were presented by four economists, a cultural anthropologist, and a social psychologist. As might be expected from the backgrounds of the major speakers and other seminar participants, although the discussions ranged over a wide variety of topics, economic changes and their influence on education were given more emphasis than social changes, and political changes were hardly discussed at all.

The task of preparing a summary of the preceding papers and discussions has been difficult for two reasons. First, I wanted to organize the paper around one or two major ideas or themes. This proved difficult because the six papers and subsequent discussions ranged widely and, while they were related to each other, they lacked a central focus. It was more a seminar of discovery than of conquest; the participants were introduced to a variety of topics, but they did not linger over any part of the terrain. Second, I wanted to discuss the implications of the symposium's contributions for educational planning and policy-making rather than simply to provide a digest of presentations and discussions. Implementing this idea also proved to be difficult because the topic of educational planning is itself very complex and would form an appropriate topic for a separate seminar.

This paper is best described as a selective summary of the symposium's proceedings, and will focus on two questions. First, what ideas from sociology, anthropology, and economics were presented to the symposium, and what do these indicate about the societal forces that will affect education in the next decade? Second, how can these ideas be used to plan needed changes in education?

Of necessity, some of the ideas and insights of the participants will be omitted and others will be treated inadequately. Apology is made to the participants for any violence done their ideas, and the reader is warned to consult the actual texts and transcripts, which appear in this volume.

Of great pertinence for education are the ideas presented by Mr. Kimball. In his paper on educational congruency, he has shown how increasing urbanization, secularization, and work specialization have affected individual values and culture in American mass society and, at the same time, have increased the importance of education's function as the bridge between the private world of the family and the mass society of work and politics. Despite this increasingly important function the schools perform, they have largely remained community oriented and locally controlled. As yet, they have not changed their organizational structure sufficiently to make them properly responsive to changing conditions in the larger society. This lack of adaptiveness can be seen most clearly in the organizational structure of schools in the large cities, but it exists, in less obvious ways, in small towns and rural areas as well.

A changed and more flexible organizational structure will not, by itself, provide the necessary improvements in education. Fundamental changes in the curriculum and in teaching methods are also needed. To this end, Mr. Kimball pointed out that educating for today's—and tomorrow's—world means emphasizing cognitive development. This ability to recognize and solve problems is, at present, not the focus of education in our schools.

Mr. Kimball has suggested that organization of the public schools should be similar to the corporate pattern of the university, which has more flexibility and can adapt to rapid change more readily than the hierarchical organizational form now used by most school systems. At this point, the discussion came to one of the areas in the social sciences that may make a major contribution to education in the future. A substantial body of new ideas and concepts relating to the management of complex organizations has been developed. This new field is sometimes called administrative science, but it also includes ideas from organizational sociology and techniques from systems analysis. Research in this field is concerned with the ways in which large-scale organizations function, how they establish their goals, evaluate progress, and provide for communication. This research emphasizes the systematic relation of one aspect of the organization to others; for example, the progress of curriculum improvement may depend on the type of interpersonal relations existing between teachers and pupils, which, in turn, is linked to the patterns of supervisory authority used by principals, superintendents, and the school board. The discussants have not dwelt on these new social science concepts of organization and management, but they have made it clear that the traditional community-centered simple organization of the schools is inadequate for our large and medium-sized urban areas, and that those organizational adaptations the school systems have made and are making are often equally inadequate.

During the next decade, nearly all school systems will have to develop new organizational forms to deal with the new programs being thrust upon them by a society that is both changing rapidly and expecting more of the schools. This is manifest most clearly in the increasing number of federal programs that call on the schools for new and different kinds of education. However, federal programs are merely symptoms of the general changes in society outlined by Mr. Kimball. Knowledge about new concepts of organization and management can be very useful to the schools as they respond to these pressures for change.

Mr. Strodtbeck's paper, dealing with the problems of inadequate social interaction by dependent members of the lower class, provides specific illustrations of the problems that face the schools and other social institutions in their attempt to educate children from inadequate family backgrounds so that they can participate effectively in a more specialized and complex urban world. The inadequacies of schools in slum areas have received a great deal of public attention in the last few years. While Mr. Strodtbeck may appear to be dealing with nonschool problems when he describes the fragmentation of family kinship ties, the inadequacies of social interaction, and the general sense of threat that pervades the lives of the dependent poor who live in the slums of our large cities, he is describing a set of basic conditions that explain a substantial part of the school's failures in attempting to educate the children from these backgrounds.

The fragmented, threatened, and impoverished families described by Mr. Strodtbeck present special problems; most school programs are based on a set of assumptions about pupils that do not fit the children from these families. The ensuing discussion concerned the ways in which the schools could reach these children and with the kind of adaptiveness the schools need if they are to establish contacts with these children, with dropouts, and with their parents. A large number of school-related programs have been launched, in the last three or four years, to help the urban poor and the culturally deprived. Research has been launched, too, and it is aimed at providing more guidance for the future design of similar programs.

The symposium has not attempted a detailed discussion of recent research on the education of the culturally deprived, nor has it suggested specific approaches to new educational programs for these children. It has made clear what is probably obvious to most readers: A great deal of the educator's attention in the next decade will be concentrated on the problems of educating those groups who have had least access to, and benefit from, education as it has operated in the past. Social science research will be helpful, both in suggesting the necessary conditions for more effective educational programs for the disadvantaged and in evaluating programs already established. The research of Mr. Strodtbeck and other social scientists has a great deal of potential value for educators who are going to be developing programs for the culturally deprived.

The economists, in their discussion of the effects of technological change on the economy and society, have presented another useful group of ideas. Mr. Ross pointed out that economic planning by the government to promote full employment and economic growth is now widely accepted in America. He and Mr. Colm noted that recent successes in stimulating economic growth by tax cuts and by manipulation of interest rates have led to even greater acceptance of the desirability and necessity of certain kinds of government intervention in economic affairs.

At the same time, economists have become aware of the importance of education to economic growth. Classical economic theory held that land, labor, and capital were the three components of production and would determine the level of economic output. Mr. Correa, who presented a paper on the economic value of education, is one of a number of economists who have shown there has been a great deal of economic growth that cannot be explained by changes in the three basic factors of production. This additional economic growth may be caused by a number of influences, including technologically useful discoveries, a higher level of skill and education in the labor force, organizational efficiencies, and so on. A number of economists have emphasized education as one of the important explanations of this extra economic growth.* The logical extension of this new view of education as a vital factor in economic growth is the inclusion of education as one aspect of economic planning. The federal government, in the past, engaged in only a limited amount of educational planning. Most such planning has been done at the state and local levels and has been concerned with planning for more pupils, rather than with planning the kind of education needed to achieve greater economic growth. In recent years, and primarily at the federal level, educational planning has focused more on economic and social problems.

Mr. Ross's discussion of the history of the government's commitment to ensure a full-employment economy provides a good example of the new view of the government role in the economy.

---

* For a good review of the new way in which education is viewed by economists, see Mary Jean Bowman, "The Human Investment Revolution in Economic Thought," *Sociology of Education*, XXXIX (Spring 1966), 111–37.

It also shows how educational programs have become part of government efforts to decrease unemployment. Most of the recent debate about the government's role in promoting employment has been concerned more with defining that role than with questioning its validity.

Mr. Ross's analysis of the two main approaches to dealing with problems of unemployment—the structuralist and the aggregative —is of particular interest. The structuralists concentrate attention on making the labor market operate more effectively by improving information services, job-retraining programs, education in basic skills for the underemployed, and similar approaches to the problem. The aggregate demand theorists believe that the major way to prevent unemployment is to increase the level of economic activity. Arguing from the fact that, in time of war, unemployment drops to very low levels and even people with marginal skills enter the labor market, they conclude that the government ought to promote a high level of employment by controlling taxes and interest rates, even allowing a small amount of inflation, which may be necessary to keep the economy moving. Mr. Ross pointed out that these two strategies were not inconsistent. The government has actually supported worker-training programs, job-market information services, and other activities designed to make the labor market function better, while, at the same time, it has decreased taxes, made capital investment more attractive, and used fiscal and tax policy to stimulate the economy.

Even when unemployment drops below 4 per cent, as at present, there are important groups in the population that have much higher rates of unemployment—Negroes, teenagers, and people with little formal education are examples of this. Mr. Ross pointed out that many other countries did not have the teenage unemployment problem that exists in the United States. The discontinuity between school and work in this country probably reflects the primary concern of our secondary schools with college preparation. For the student not headed for college, the secondary schools do much less than they could to relate school to work. Combination work and study programs, which have had a limited development in our secondary schools and colleges, may offer a much better way of smoothing the transition from school to work, thereby reducing teenage unemployment and delinquency.

As the federal government increases its contribution to, and concern with, education, the problems of planning and coordinating the various sources of support for education will become more complex. Because education is so often viewed as a "solution" to economic and social problems like delinquency and teenage unemployment, the public and the legislators may expect results at a more rapid rate than is realistically possible. A bigger investment in more sophisticated planning, along with a bigger investment in educational research, will be needed if our educational institutions are to deliver on the new expectations that are being generated by economic and social planning.

The central theme of Mr. Colm's paper is the impact of technological change on the economy and, particularly, its impact on the demand for educated workers. New technology, Mr. Colm argued, is likely to produce evolutionary, rather than revolutionary, changes in the economic structure. Over the next twenty years, we can expect to see a gradual increase in the number of occupations requiring advanced levels of education as a condition of employment and a concomitant decrease in the availability of jobs for those with less than a high school degree. Since these changes in educational requirements are continuations of trends that have existed for some time, it is reasonable to believe that economic projections indicating future levels of employment and economic costs could be developed on the basis of past trends in the economy and society. Mr. Colm's colleague, Mr. Lecht, has been preparing a set of economic and manpower projections which, in addition to taking account of past trends, relate projections of the future economy to national goals. These goals, in education, transportation, slum clearance, and about a dozen other areas of national life, were recommended by a committee of distinguished citizens appointed by President Eisenhower.

Mr. Lecht has been translating these goals into dollar costs and, then, into manpower requirements. His study provides a very comprehensive and general estimate of what will be needed by educational institutions—in terms of dollars and personnel—in the next decade and, even more important, what society is likely to request, by way of educated manpower, from the schools and colleges of the nation.

The estimated costs of achieving the national goals seem likely to be 10–15 per cent more than the economic growth, based on the assumption of a full-employment economy, projected for 1975. Therefore, choices will have to be made about which goals to emphasize. Even if economic growth were sufficient to permit the achievement of all goals, manpower shortages might arise and these would prevent full goal achievement. For example, the number of doctors who will be trained between now and 1975 will probably be inadequate to meet the health goals, regardless of the number of dollars expended. A big increase in higher education will be required to meet the manpower requirements implicit in these national goals. Working from the number of graduates needed to achieve these goals, we can predict the need for a college enrollment of 9.5 million by 1975; this is about 800,000 more than the most recent projections of the Office of Education and about 400,000 more than the highest projections of the Census Bureau. If enrollment falls below the 9.5 million level, the output of graduates probably will be inadequate to achieve all the goals by 1975. Hence, shortages of educated manpower will necessitate choice among goals, although Mr. Lecht's figures suggest that the educational system will come closer to providing the educated manpower to achieve the goals than the economy will come to providing the necessary dollars. Nevertheless, for some goals— health, for example—manpower shortages may be the principal limitation to achieving the goal.

The type of study being made by Mr. Lecht provides a very broad and general indication of educational requirements that arise from the needs of the economy. As is the case with all such projections, they are potential needs; they may or may not be translated into actual demand for graduates in future years. As the occupational needs of a future full-employment economy are projected in greater detail, they will provide a range of demand estimates. These should give us the information we must have if we are to plan the expansion of education so as to provide the needed number and kind of graduates.

The analysis of the economy made by Mr. Lecht indicates the correlation between the demand for educated workers and an evolving economy. As such, it provides valuable background information for educators. However, much greater specificity than was possible in a study of this type is needed to guide the planning of individual schools and colleges. Which types of educational expansion should have the greatest priority? Are there likely to be surpluses in some fields, despite shortages in others? Can anticipated national needs and supplies be used by local groups to plan institutional expansion? How can educators best deal with the margin of uncertainty in all projections? These are some of the questions that must be answered as educators try to decide how they can use the results of studies like the interesting and important work of Mr. Lecht and the National Planning Association.

Mr. Lecht's paper is not the only one to deal with national problems and trends and implicitly to raise questions about the relation of this information to local schools. Most of the presentations have focused on general trends and problems, which may seem remote from local school problems and issues. How can we generate concerted local action, in hundreds of separate communities, to deal with national problems? Should we create more national educational policies to guide local action, or will our historic dependence on local action without federal initiative be adequate to deal with these complex national economic and social problems? The symposium has not tried to resolve this question of a greater federal role in the formulation of national educational policies. It is, however, a question that takes on great importance when you begin to think about the way in which education can contribute to problems of economic growth, full employment, and the achievement of national goals.

To many, a greater federal role in planning educational policy is still repugnant. There is, however, an analogy in the economic sphere. Today, thousands of private corporations and businesses, responsible for their own affairs, are in some way regulated by the government. Certainly, they are influenced by government fiscal and tax policies. As several of the symposium participants have indicated, we now accept a more active federal role in formulating policies to assure full employment and economic growth. While these policies in some ways limit the freedom of private companies, if successful, they will create the kind of economic growth that will make private enterprise flourish.

Although the situation is changing, national educational policies are less developed than national economic policies. Yet, it is unlikely that thousands of local school systems can act together, in the absence of federal policies, to deal with economic growth, teenage unemployment, and other problems where an educational contribution is needed. It is virtually certain that more national educational policies will be developed to assure that education makes a contribution to economic and social problems. In their absence, local action is likely to be fragmentary and often ineffectual. The consequences of our strong belief in the power of education to solve national problems, and the continuing public concern with economic and social issues, make it virtually certain that the federal government will develop more national educational policies.

What form will federal educational policies take? Will they stimulate local initiative and local planning to deal with educational issues? Or, will the initiative for implementing policies be retained at the federal level, with local schools and colleges responding to federal initiative? There is a strong and widespread belief in the value of local initiative in education, and it seems likely that the implementation of federal policies will place heavy reliance on local initiative as long as that approach works. In situations where it doesn't work, the federal government is likely to assume more of the responsibility for policy implementation. School desegregation is an example. When local initiative produced little progress in desegregation, the federal government assumed a more active role. It seems likely that this pattern will be repeated in the future; if schools do not initiate more effective programs for culturally deprived children, they may find the federal government turning to industry and other groups for help and developing more specific program requirements to assure that the funds distributed to local schools are used effectively.

In a recent speech, Lyle Spencer, president of Science Research Associates, stated: "I have observed that new approaches to education for a changing world do not come easily to the mammoth establishment of our middle-class dominated educational world. The pressure for change usually comes from somewhere out in left field, and the location of left field keeps changing. Right now, left field is the war on poverty. The so-called culturally deprived child sits in the eye of a hurricane that is shaking the foundations of education."*

The kind of national programs that will be developed probably depends, to a large degree, on the adaptiveness of local schools and their readiness to accept the initiative for planning and developing new programs to implement national policy objectives. For most school systems, this will mean a greater sensitivity to social and economic issues than they have had in the past and a greater capacity for self-examination and self-improvement.

The improvement of the quality of education is likely to emerge as one of the key issues in maximizing the contribution of education to economic growth. The argument is that, for maximum economic growth, we must have maximum development of our human resources, and the schools must improve their programs to bring this about. National policies to promote improved quality of education are likely to become a key issue in the next decade. Difficult questions are sure to be raised. What are valid measures of educational quality? Who should assess quality? What should be done about low quality schools? In the attempt to resolve these questions, relations between federal government and local communities are likely to become strained.

The symposium participants have touched on these issues a number of times. The future course of federal-local relations in education is a complex matter, which cannot be predicted very accurately. We can predict, however, that these relations will have a great deal to do with shaping the schools' responses to social and economic changes.

Only a few of the social and economic changes described in the papers and discussions have been included in this summary. The symposium presentations underline the fact that change in the society will have a major influence on the future of education in

* Reprinted in the American Council on Education newsletter, *Higher Education and National Affairs*, XV, No. 24 (July 21, 1966).

the United States. One way that educators can prepare to deal with these influences is to inform themselves about current trends and problems. Hopefully, the symposium has made some contribution to this increased understanding. Nevertheless, although a general knowledge and awareness of socio-economic problems and issues is important, it is not enough. It is quite clear that the pace of change in our society is so rapid that educational institutions, school systems, and state and regional educational agencies must be prepared to respond more rapidly and must use a much wider range of information in program-planning than ever before.

Economic planning is based on an elaborate set of statistical indicators. For government economic planning and intervention to succeed, basic technical information must exist. As compared with the value of economic statistics for economic planning, the educational statistics and information now available provide a much less detailed and useful information base for educational planning. Educators have also made much less progress than businessmen or economists in applying the information they do have to the planning and management of schools and colleges.

It is not a question of whether education is going to be run as a business; education is not a business, and one major difference is that the teaching and learning process is far more complex than the processes with which most businesses must deal. The real issue is whether educators can develop and adopt new planning and management systems that are adequate for the complex tasks that face education.

At the present time, most colleges and school systems are not well organized to apply new ideas and concepts from educational research, economic research, or social-psychology research. Concern about the slow rate at which new ideas are adopted in education has been expressed by the federal government, which is providing funds to establish a network of regional educational laboratories. A major function of the laboratories will be the dissemination of new educational ideas, which includes providing support for their introduction into the educational system. It is too early to tell how well these new organizations will work, but if they are to be of maximum utility, changes in the way that many school systems plan and operate will be necessary.

For example, the development of a successful new work-study program to reduce teen-age unemployment, which is one of the underlying causes of delinquency, presents a big challenge to the planning capabilities of many school systems. Though there are successful models of such programs in various parts of the country, the application of the idea may be difficult in some local settings. A school system may lack adequate information on the kinds of work programs that will fit the local and regional job market; it might not appreciate the kinds of resentment—and resistance—students and teachers may harbor toward such innovations. How do you convince the student who needs such a program to enter it? Which teachers will be most effective with this type program? How much will it cost, and are there substantial hidden costs? Complex management decisions are necessary, and even where findings from previous research and facts about various aspects of the new program are available (and they often are missing), they may not be used very effectively. In general, educational institutions are undermanaged and underplanned, and until some change in this basic condition occurs, regional laboratories or other new types of organization are not likely to have their maximum impact.

The symposium presentations make it very clear that social change in America is accelerating and that the schools have an important part in maintaining a strong economy and in helping to deal with a wide variety of social problems. Ideas and concepts from the social sciences will be increasingly important for educators in tomorrow's schools; the effective administrator must understand at least some economics, sociology, political science, anthropology, and psychology, in addition to educational philosophy, curriculum development, and the politics of his school board members. It will not be enough for the educational administrator to have a general knowledge of the social sciences; he must be a part of a planning and management process that is prepared to apply ideas and complex techniques from the social sciences to practical problems.

Many educators would prefer the good old days when educational problems were simple, localized, and could be solved by face to face conversations among a few people. But the symposium papers illustrate the complexities of the modern world and the need for new methods of educational planning. Some educators will feel that new management procedures threaten their independence and will visualize the computer replacing the principal or superintendent. However, these new approaches, when properly used, will increase the educational administrator's scope of action and control over educational processes. In their absence, the educational administrator may soon find that he is like the farmer without a tractor: He's still in control of his mule, but he may have lost control of his farm.

Hopefully, this symposium has provided some useful clues to the direction and magnitude of the changes ahead. If so, it may also have served to stimulate thinking about improved educational planning and management, as well as to provoke a further examination of relationships between local schools and the federal government in the development of national educational policies to deal with the changes that will come.

Contributors

GERHARD COLM, Chief Economist of the National Planning Association, is the author of *Essays in Public Finance and Fiscal Policy* and the co-author of *Economy of the American People* and *Federal Budget Projections*. Dr. Colm has served as Senior Economist to the Council of Economic Advisers and as fiscal analyst in the Bureau of the Budget where, from 1940–46, he was Assistant Chief of the Fiscal Division. In addition to an active career in government, Dr. Colm taught for many years. Before going to Washington, he was Professor of Economics and Dean of the Graduate Faculty at the New School for Social Research in New York; later, he held the position of Professorial Lecturer at George Washington University. Dr. Colm has had many special assignments with international organizations, including the United Nations and the Organization of American States, and he has been a consultant to the Joint Economic Committee of the U.S. Congress, the National Science Foundation Advisory Committee for Economic and Manpower Studies, and the U.S. Treasury Department. In 1966, he was president of the Association for Comparative Economics.

HECTOR CORREA is a frequent contributor to scholarly journals and the author of *Economics of Human Resources* and the forthcoming *Educational Planning: Its Quantitative Aspects, Its Integration With Economic Planning*. Dr. Correa has taught at the Universidad Central del Ecuador, the Universidad Cátolica de Ecuador, and the Centro Interamericano de Estadística in Santiago, Chile. Currently, he is an Associate Professor of Economics at Wayne State University. In addition to considerable experience as an economic adviser and administrator in Ecuador, Dr. Correa has served as a consultant to the Organization for Economic Cooperation and Development, the Agency for International Development, the U.N. Department of Economic and Social Affairs, and Puerto Rico's Department of Education, and as a staff member of the International Institute for Educational Planning and of the Netherlands Economics Institute. As the Ford Foundation's expert on human resources, he participated in the National Planning Office's Educational Planning Seminar, held in Caracas in 1964. He is widely known for his contributions to international conferences and seminars.

STANLEY ELAM is Editor of Phi Delta Kappa Publications and a frequent contributor to journals and periodicals. He is the author of *Public Relations: An Experimental Evaluation of Student Recruitment in a Teachers College* and a contributor to *School Executive's Guide.* He has edited or coedited over fifty books but considers editorship of the *Phi Delta Kappan,* an influential professional journal in education, as his primary work. In 1964–65, Dr. Elam was a regional director of the Educational Press Association of America and is now vice-president and president-elect of that organization. Before joining the Phi Delta Kappa staff he was a teacher and administrator in Illinois public schools and Director of Public Relations at Eastern Illinois University. He is the recipient of the first Distinguished Alumnus Award (1966) given by the School of Education of the University of Illinois.

JOHN K. FOLGER, currently on leave from Florida State University where he is Dean of the Graduate School and Professor of Sociology, is Director of the Commission on Human Resources and Advanced Education of the Conference Board of Associated Research Councils. Dr. Folger has served as the Associate Director for Research and Programs of the Southern Regional Education Board and as Chief of the Technical Services Division, Human Research Resources Institute, of the U.S. Air Force. A contributor to numerous publications, Dr. Folger is the co-author of the forthcoming *Education of the American Population,* a contributor to *Nuclear Energy in the South* and *History of the Southern Regional Education Board,* and the author of *Future School and College Enrollment in the Southern Region.* Dr. Folger is a member of the Executive Committee of the Council of Graduate Schools and of the Technical Advisory Committee to the Census Bureau on the 1960 and 1970 Censuses of Population.

SOLON T. KIMBALL is Graduate Research Professor in the Department of Anthropology at the University of Florida. Prior to assuming this position, he was a Professor of Anthropology and Education at Columbia University's Teachers College and he has been a visiting professor at the University of Chicago, the University of Puerto Rico, the University of California, and Princeton Theological Seminary. Dr. Kimball has made major contributions to journals of anthropology, sociology, and education and is the co-author of *Family and Community in Ireland; The Talladega Story; Education and the New America;* and *Culture and Community.* In addition to extensive field work in New England, Ireland, the Navajo Reservation, Michigan, Alabama, and Brazil, Dr. Kimball served in the departments of Agriculture and the Interior, and with the War Relocation Authority. He was a UNESCO consultant on research in community and education at the Brazilian Center for Educational Research in the Brazilian Ministry of Education and has served as campus coordinator for an AID project with the Peruvian Ministry of Education (1963–64). He is past president of the Society for Applied Anthropology and has been a Faculty Research Fellow (Social Science Research Council), and a Guggenheim Fellow.

LEONARD A. LECHT is Director of the Center for Priority Analysis of the National Planning Association. Prior to assuming that post in 1967, he had served as Director of the NPA's Goals Project. Dr. Lecht has taught at Columbia University, the University of Texas, Carleton College, and Long Island University where, from 1956 to 1963, he was Professor and Chairman of the Department of Economics and Sociology. Currently, he is Adjunct Professor in the Department of Economics at Temple University. In addition to numerous articles in professional journals, Dr. Lecht is co-author of *Toward Better Utilization of Scientific and Engineering Manpower* and the author of *Goals, Priorities, and Dollars —The Next Decade; The Dollar Cost of Our National Goals;* and *Experience Under Railroad Labor Legislation.* He is currently completing a study for the U.S. Department of Labor, which will translate dollar costs into manpower requirements by occupation. He has served as a consultant to several government agencies, including NASA and the President's Science Advisory Committee,

and he directed the pilot study of scientific and engineering manpower requirements for the 1970's for the Killian Committee.

WILLIAM P. McLURE is the Director of the Bureau of Educational Research and Professor of Educational Administration
at the College of Education of the University of Illinois, and
Chairman of the Phi Delta Kappa Commission on Education,
Manpower, and Economic Growth. Dr. McLure has had wide
experience as a teacher and administrator in the Alabama school
system and, before going to the University of Illinois in 1948, he
was an Associate Professor and Director of the Bureau of Educational Research at the University of Mississippi. He has also
served as a consultant to numerous state and urban school systems
and he is a member of the Executive Advisory Committee of the
Rural Education Department and Area Superintendents of the
National Education Association. His many monographs include
*Fiscal Policies of the Great City School Systems, The Structure
of Educational Costs, Financing Public Schools in Illinois,* and
The Intermediate School District in the United States. Dr. Mc-
Lure has contributed to several studies, including *Vocational
Technical Education in Illinois* and *A Study of the Public Schools
of Illinois.*

ARTHUR M. ROSS is Professor of Industrial Relations at the
University of California at Berkeley where, from 1954 to 1963, he
was Director of the Institute of Industrial Relations. Concurrently, he is Commissioner of Labor Statistics in the U.S. Depart-
ment of Labor. Dr. Ross is co-author of *Industrial Conflict* and
Changing Patterns of Industrial Conflict; editor of, and contributor to, *Unemployment and the American Economy, Employment
Policy and the Labor Market* and *Industrial Relations and
Economic Development;* joint editor of *Employment, Race, and
Poverty;* author of *Trade Union Wage Policy;* and contributor to
numerous periodicals and books, including *Grammar of American
Politics, The Law and Labor-Management Relations,* and *New
Concepts in Wage Determination.* In addition to private arbitra-
tion work, Dr. Ross has served on many government boards and
committees, most recently, the National Manpower Task Force,

the California Governor's Commission on Employment and Retirement Problems of Older Workers (of which he was Chairman), and the Secretary of Labor's California Farm Labor Panel. A Guggenheim Fellow, Dr. Ross has served as vice-president of the National Academy of Arbitrators and as a member of the Executive Board of the Industrial Relations Research Association. He is a frequent participant in international conferences and seminars.

FRED L. STRODTBECK is Associate Professor of Social Psychology, Training Director of the Social Psychology Training Program, and Director of the Social Psychology Laboratory at the University of Chicago. Prior to coming to the University of Chicago in 1953, he was Associate Professor of Sociology at Yale and, later, a Fellow of the Center for Advanced Study in the Behavioral Sciences at Palo Alto. Dr. Strodtbeck is a consultant to the Veterans Administration, the Institute for Juvenile Research, and the Nurse Scientist Graduate Training Committee of the National Institutes of Health. A frequent contributor to the *American Sociological Review, Sociometry,* the *American Journal of Sociology* (he is a member of its Editorial Board), and other professional journals, Dr. Strodtbeck is the co-author of *Talent and Society* and *Variations in Value Orientations.* He has contributed material to numerous books, including *Sociology in Perspective, 1950– 1960; The Character and Scope of Social Psychology; Interaction Process Analysis; The Language of Social Research; Law and Sociology: Exploratory Essays;* and *Urban Education and Cultural Deprivation.*

Panel Participants

ARTHUR E. ARNESEN, President, Phi Delta Kappa, and Assistant Superintendent, Salt Lake City Schools, Utah

KENNETH L. BEASLEY, Associate Professor of Education and Director of Graduate Study in History and Comparative Education, Northern Illinois University

MAYNARD BEMIS, Executive Secretary, Phi Delta Kappa, Bloomington, Indiana.

ANN MAYHEW BROWN, Assistant Professor of Education and Economics, College of Education, University of Illinois

JAQUETTA BURNETT, Assistant Professor of Education, University of Illinois

DAVID S. BUSHNELL, Director, Adult and Vocational Research, Department of Health, Education, & Welfare, Office of Education

WILLIAM B. CANNON, Chief, Education, Manpower and Science Division, Executive Office of the President, Bureau of the Budget

WALTER G. DANIEL, Professor of Education and Director of Educational Research, Howard University

MARTIN DAVID, Associate Professor of Economics and Director of the Center for Household and Labor Market Research, Social Systems Research Institute, University of Wisconsin

KENNETH M. DEITCH, Instructor in Economics, Harvard University

JEAN FLANIGAN, Assistant Director, Division of Research, and Staff Contact for the Committee on Educational Finance, National Educational Association

IRIS GARFIELD, Executive Director, National Committee for Support of the Public Schools

RAYMOND S. KLEIN, Educational Consultant for Training and Research, State of New York, Department of Labor, Division of Manpower

JOHN W. LLOYD, Professor of Economics, Northern Illinois University

AMOS J. SNIDER, Assistant Dean, University of Missouri

VLADIMIR STOIKOV, Associate Professor of Labor and Industrial Relations, University of Illinois

GORDON I. SWANSON, Professor of Education and Coordinator of International Projects, University of Minnesota

ROBERT E. TAYLOR, Director, Center for Vocational and Technical Education, Ohio State University